Narrative Landmines

NEW DIRECTIONS IN INTERNATIONAL STUDIES

PATRICE PETRO, SERIES EDITOR

The New Directions in International Studies series focuses on transculturalism, technology, media, and representation, and features the innovative work of scholars who explore various components and consequences of globalization, such as the increasing flow of peoples, ideas, images, information, and capital across borders. Under the direction of Patrice Petro, the series is sponsored by the Center for International Education at the University of Wisconsin–Milwaukee. The Center seeks to foster interdisciplinary and collaborative research that probes the political, economic, artistic, and social processes and practices of our time.

A. ANEESH, LANE HALL, AND PATRICE PETRO, eds.
Beyond Globalization: Making New Worlds in Media, Art, and Social Practices

DANIEL LEONARD BERNARDI, PAULINE HOPE CHEONG, CHRIS LUNDRY, AND SCOTT W. RUSTON
Narrative Landmines: Rumors, Islamist Extremism, and the Struggle for Strategic Influence

MARK PHILIP BRADLEY AND PATRICE PETRO, eds.
Truth Claims: Representation and Human Rights

MELISSA A. FITCH
Side Dishes: Latin/o American Women, Sex, and Cultural Production

ELIZABETH SWANSON GOLDBERG
Beyond Terror: Gender, Narrative, Human Rights

LINDA KRAUSE AND PATRICE PETRO, eds.
Global Cities: Cinema, Architecture, and Urbanism in a Digital Age

ANDREW MARTIN AND PATRICE PETRO, eds.
Rethinking Global Security: Media, Popular Culture, and the "War on Terror"

TASHA G. OREN AND PATRICE PETRO, eds.
Global Currents: Media and Technology Now

PETER PAIK AND MARCUS BULLOCK, eds.
Aftermaths: Exile, Migration, and Diaspora Reconsidered

FREYA SCHIWY
Indianizing Film: Decolonization, the Andes, and the Question of Technology

CRISTINA VENEGAS
Digital Dilemmas: The State, the Individual, and Digital Media in Cuba

Narrative Landmines

Rumors, Islamist Extremism, and the Struggle for Strategic Influence

Daniel Leonard Bernardi
Pauline Hope Cheong
Chris Lundry
Scott W. Ruston

Rutgers University Press
New Brunswick, New Jersey, and London

Library of Congress Cataloging-in-Publication Data

Narrative landmines : rumors, Islamist extremism, and the struggle for strategic influence / Daniel L. Bernardi . . . [et al.].
p. cm. — (New directions in international studies)
Includes bibliographical references and index.
ISBN 978-0-8135-5250-7 (hardcover : alk. paper)
ISBN 978-0-8135-5251-4 (pbk. : alk. paper)
ISBN 978-0-8135-5322-1 (e-book)
1. Rumor in mass media. 2. Rumor—Political aspects. 3. Rumor—Social aspects. 4. Islamic fundamentalism. 5. Terrorism—Religious aspects—Islam. 6. Terrorism and mass media. 7. Mass media—Influence. I. Bernardi, Daniel, 1964–
P96.R86N37 2012
303.6'25014—dc23

2011023508

A British Cataloging-in-Publication record for this book is available from the British Library.

Visit our Web site: http://rutgerspress.rutgers.edu

Manufactured in the United States of America

For Our Students . . .

CONTENTS

ACKNOWLEDGMENTS

Much like the rich and multidimensional nature of narratives, this book represents a partnership spanning academic disciplines, national histories, and personal experiences. We would like to thank the following groups and individuals for their invaluable assistance.

We acknowledge our kind and supportive colleagues at Arizona State University, particularly those at the Center of Strategic Communication (CSC), including Steve Corman, Angela Trethewey, Jeffry Halverson, and Bud Goodall, as well as Bambi Haggins and Kiva James from Film and Media Studies.

We are grateful to the Office of Naval Research (ONR) for funding the CSC research project "Identifying and Countering Extremist Narratives" (N00014-09-1-0872), from which this book draws much of its original impetus. Thanks to Dr. Ivy Estabrooke and Gary Kollmorgen for their encouragement and assistance. Thanks also to the sailors and soldiers who helped us complete primary research for the chapters on Iraq and Ambon, Indonesia. Their generous support of our research is a testament to their service. It should be noted that while the authors incorporate firsthand experiences with the U.S. Navy and the United Nations and secondhand experiences shared by soldiers, sailors, and Marines of the United States and other countries, and while this project received support from the ONR grant, all the analysis, opinions, and conclusions are the authors' and do not represent policies or positions of the U.S. government, the U.S. Navy, the United Nations, or any other government or non-governmental organization.

We appreciate the colleagues at the Rajaratnam School of International Studies, Nanyang Technological University, Singapore, for their invitation to and sponsorship of our participation in an international conference on rumors, including Dr. Norman Vasu, Dr. Kumar Ramakrishna, and Gregory Dalziel.

Our book would not be possible without the patient professionals of Rutgers University Press, including our editor Leslie Mitchner and series editor Patrice Petro.

Finally and most importantly, we thank our spouses for their love and support.

NARRATIVE LANDMINES

INTRODUCTION

NARRATIVE IEDs

Rumors are nearly as old as human history. . . . they impose real damage on individuals and institutions and they often resist correction. They can threaten careers, policies, public officials, and sometimes even democracy itself.

—Cass Sunstein, *On Rumors*

There is nothing that cannot be perverted by being told badly.

—Publius Terentius Afer, *Phormio*, Act IV, Scene IV

We live in a world awash in rumors. *The artificial sweetener in your diet soda can cause cancer* is a rumor that circulates with great frequency and with each introduction of new sweetener brands and chemicals. Frequently heard on street corners and right-wing talk radio, *Barack Obama was born in Kenya, not Hawaii, and is thus not a natural-born U.S. citizen* is a "birther" rumor that suggests Obama is not a lawful president of the United States. The rumor that *four thousand Jews working in the World Trade Center, warned in advance by the Israeli government, stayed home from work on September 11, 2001* implies that Jews were behind the 9/11 attacks on the United States.

Many people dismiss rumors such as these as baseless and ridiculous. But when the rumor about aspartame (and before that saccharin and before that cyclamate) influences a purchase decision in the grocery store, the veracity of the rumor itself is less critical. When the 9/11 rumor leads to anti-Semitism, its social impact is real in the sense that actions and beliefs have been affected by the presence of the rumor. If the rumor surrounding President Obama's birthplace influences a vote or garners public support for an opposition party, it becomes a strategic political campaign weapon. Even though an artificial sweetener may not seem of great importance (unless one is a soda company executive) and the President Obama rumor may seem preposterous, to dismiss rumors without considering them more seriously is a dangerous mindset. Consider that the World Trade Center rumor intersects with stories of Jewish conspiracies that have informed both Middle East and world politics for centuries. In all of these cases, the rumors have real economic, political, and social consequences.

In the course of history, there have been many rumors that have had significant consequences. Shortly after a great fire destroyed much of Rome in A.D. 64, rumors circulated that Emperor Nero was the arsonist and played his lyre as he watched the city burn. Nero's brutal response to this rumor was to shift blame to another group, the Christians, whom he sentenced *ad bestias*. During World War II, domestic civilian morale and support for the war effort in America ebbed with each new rumor about progress abroad, danger at home, or unequal sacrifice. Guided by Gordon Allport, whose *Psychology of Rumor* (1947) became a landmark study in the field of rumor research, "rumor clinics" were established in major metropolitan areas, staffed by journalists and college professors and charged with debunking rumors. Persistent rumors have also plagued large corporations. Procter & Gamble, for example, spent years battling a rumor of satanic affiliation that pointed to the company's moon and stars corporate logo, until it finally removed the logo from its consumer products in 1985. Kentucky Fried Chicken and its iconic founder, Colonel Sanders, faced rumors of tithing to the Ku Klux Klan. Curiously, other fast-food restaurants with well-known founders were subject to similar rumors. Aside from temporary revenue setbacks experienced by the restaurants, these rumors indicate more broadly that significant racial tensions still percolate in American culture and that rumors thrive in social unrest.

As these historical examples show, rumors can have real and tangible consequences. Not only do rumors occasionally influence significant events involving persecution, civic order, or corporate image; they must also be acknowledged (no matter their apparent absurdity) for how local populations perceive them. The standard in rumor studies has been for many years to define, and thus study, a "rumor" as information or belief about a situation that is of dubious veracity, a statement that does not meet "secured standards of evidence."[1] Although dubious veracity and unclear origins are central characteristics of rumors, an overemphasis on veracity and truth claims isolates rumors categorically, rather than recognizing their impact and dynamic functions, especially with regard to strategic communication contexts. At the same time, the mutability of "truth" (a concept governed significantly by perceptual frameworks) suggests that rumors must be understood in their cultural contexts. This insight points us to the question of why and how rumors circulate and, importantly, their relationships to other information and message forms prevalent in a community. Understanding how rumors participate within this arena is critical for strategic communication plans designed to frame a diplomatic cause, a business enterprise, philanthropic outreach, or any number of other activities. It is our goal to understand rumors more thoroughly within this strategic communication context.

As the epigraph from *Phormio* suggests, the manner of relating a piece of information matters as much as its content. As has been claimed in various terms by numerous scholars, but most succinctly by Walter Fisher with his metaphor of *homo narrans*, humans make sense of their world in large part through the stories they tell.[2] Underlying all narrative theory, whether born in literary criticism, used in film and media studies, or applied to psychotherapy, is the recognition of two components to narrative: *what* is told and *how* it is told. These two components construct a dual logic that shapes our understanding of the world. In chapter 1, we lay out our narratological approach to rumors. In addition to exhibiting a dual logic in their function and construction, narratives also operate as systems of subcomponents. These subcomponents include stories, characters, and rumors. Circulating within a narrative system, rumors arise from and play off of the other components present—other stories, understood histories, archetypal characters, and mythological heroes.

Although facts are important, the truth of a situation presented to any given individual has more to do with how that individual organizes available data than any objective and idealized "truth." Narrative's primary function, as we explain in chapter 1, is to make sense of a body of data, whether it is a scene in a movie, a passage in a novel, or the elements of information an individual collects about local, regional, or world events. Narrative offers a means of uniting culturally provided templates to include story forms and archetypes with data such as stories, rumors, histories, and the like. In the construction of a comprehension of events, "truth" becomes less about facts and evidence and more about coherence with pre-existing and prevailing understandings. This, we believe, is why some rumors circulate freely and widely: they are compatible with adjacent story material as well as the larger historical landscape.

Given that rumors are constructed from the components of prevailing narrative systems and local cultural artifacts, and that their anonymous origin and dubious truth claims afford them a type of concealment until their effects are known, we think of rumors as *narrative IEDs.* An improvised explosive device (IED), of course, is the feared weapon of the insurgent in Iraq and Afghanistan, constructed of locally available materials and hidden in the landscape until detonation. We see rumors as similarly *ad hoc* devices, constructed of bits and pieces of narrative systems and lying unseen to the diplomat, outreach coordinator, or business strategist until exploding and disrupting expensive and highly sophisticated communication campaigns.

Our metaphor of rumors as narrative IEDs (or, more simply, narrative landmines) is also particularly apt, given the areas of our case studies: Singapore, Iraq, and Indonesia. Why focus on these areas? Each exhibits in different ways the three intersecting subjects of this book: rumors, strategic communication, and Islamist extremism. Drawing upon the theoretical model we outline in chapter 1, chapter 2 centers on rumor-shaping attitudes about extremism, terrorism, and governmental communication within the population of a stable city-state. The case of Mas Selamat bin Kastari in Singapore also provides the opportunity to explore modes of transmission and spread of rumors through computer-mediated communication. Chapter 3 focuses on the Iraqi rumor mill, or the active propagation of multiple rumors via multiple communication platforms, during a full-scale counterinsurgency operation conducted by a foreign power, in this case the United States. Chapter 4 addresses how the world's most populous Muslim country and emerging democracy, Indonesia, recently dealt with Islamist extremism by advancing a whisper campaign against the terrorist Noordin Mohammed Top. Finally, chapter 5 attempts to connect the rumor dots that make up our case studies by returning to some of our larger theoretical arguments in order to address more forcefully the context of globalization and the Islamist extremist meta-narrative.

Notorious for terrorist attacks in the United States, Spain, London, Indonesia, and India (among many others), wrapped up in anti-authoritarian and pro-democracy protests in the Middle East, and deeply engaged with American military campaigns in Iraq and Afghanistan, Islamist extremism is one of the defining social and political features of the twenty-first century.

The contemporary moment is one of upheaval, change, and, above all, struggle for influence. Established nation-states, transitional governments, and non-state actors all compete through a combination of coercive, violent tactics and nonviolent, persuasive tactics for the opportunity to govern the world's 1.2 billion Muslims, develop international trade, and influence the course of globalization. In Afghanistan, U.S. and allied forces both wage war against the Taliban and support civil affairs projects designed to provide alternatives to Taliban rule. Representatives linked to al Qaeda regularly distribute lengthy lectures decrying the oppression of Muslim communities at the hands of Western powers, while advocating for violent measures against these perceived oppressors and their accused collaborators. They justify their call to a violent *jihad* and recruit new members by referencing specific excerpts of the Qur'an and recounting tales of Muslim heroes slain in defense of Islam.

With these incredibly high stakes and the powerful players in this global drama, what role could rumors play? Why devote a book to them? As our case studies indicate, rumors can play a significant role in the influence and allegiance of individuals and communities and the solicitation of that allegiance through communication. The continued failure of the United States and its allies to garner widespread local support for their efforts to quell sectarian violence in Iraq and supplant Taliban rule in Afghanistan exemplifies the importance of communication in affecting sociopolitical change. As the events of early 2011 in Tunisia and Egypt and across North Africa more generally show, considerable political power resides in the people. "The people," as a political entity, will pledge allegiance and, potentially, life and limb to a cause in which they believe. People's beliefs are shaped by what they know, what they think they know, and how they know it. Rumors operate in this domain, circulating as beliefs and understandings of states of affairs and intersecting with other beliefs, histories, messages, and the like in the narrative landscape.

Growing recognition of the necessity of community support for effective governance has meant that strategic communication has become an increasingly essential component of statecraft, diplomacy, and military action. Strategic communication is the construction and exchange of messages for the purpose of creating meaning (communication) in support of specific goals (strategy). The focus of this book is understanding rumors as components of narrative systems and how they affect strategic communication efforts. We draw our case studies from Singapore, Iraq, and Indonesia to illustrate the intersection of rumors with diverse strategic communication landscapes, but also to engage this study with the prevailing sociopolitical concern of Islamist extremism. It is our contention that strategic communication efforts are vitally important to garnering local political will in the efforts of governments, militaries, and non-governmental organizations (NGOs) to bring stability and protection of basic human rights to regions experiencing dramatic unrest in part fueled by violent Islamist extremism. Rumors play no small role in thwarting these communication efforts and therefore warrant a focused study aimed toward a greater understanding of their power, their function, and the possible solutions to their deleterious effects.

1

Rumor Theory

Narrative Systems and Hegemonic Struggles in Contested Populations

Every concrete utterance of a speaking subject serves as a point where centrifugal as well as centripetal forces are brought to bear. The process of centralization and decentralization, of unification and disunification, intersects in the utterance. . . .

—Mikhail Bakhtin, *The Dialogic Imagination*

Too many mistakes have been made over the years because our government and military did not understand, or even seek to understand, the countries or cultures we were dealing with.

—Secretary of Defense Robert Gates, 14 April 2006

On 20 January 2006, Mas Selamat Bin Kastari (Mas Selamat), a reported Jemaah Islamiyah terrorist, was arrested by Indonesian authorities and subsequently extradited to Singapore. After more than two years in custody, he escaped from Singapore's maximum-security Whitley Road Detention Center. News of his escape broke fast. But the government failed to explain in a sufficient or timely manner how this feared terrorist could escape from Singapore's most secure detention facility. Rumors filled the information void. Some reported that the government intentionally let Mas Selamat escape. Others suggested that he was killed in custody and that the government concocted the escape story as a cover- up. And still others claimed he had magic powers that gave him an unnatural edge over his would-be captors: he simply walked through the wall. These and other rumors were picked up by Singapore's cyber community, which fused them with a vast array of popular

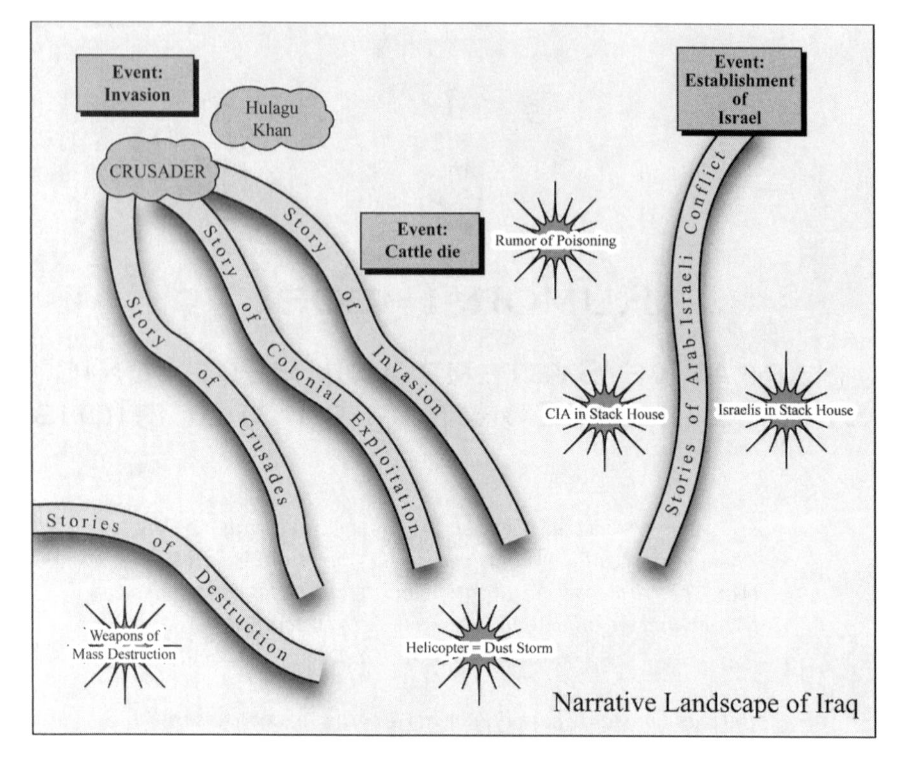

I.I. Conceptualization of interrelated events, stories, and rumors in Iraq's narrative landscapes. Figure by Becky Eden.

narratives—from Hollywood films featuring great escapes to parodies of government officials (fig. I.2).[1] The production of these virtual rumors had little to do with the particulars of Mas Selamat's escape or even terrorism itself; instead, they contributed to a growing online critique of Singapore's government.

Rumors not only capture the popular imagination of wired "netizens" in stable countries, they also advance insurgent interests in volatile regions and, as a result, thwart counterinsurgency efforts. Immediately following the 2003 invasion of Iraq and continuing through the violent insurgency and U.S. "surge" strategy that followed, a labyrinth of rumors about the motivations and intentions of U.S. forces severely hampered reconstruction and stabilization efforts (fig. I.I). Initially collected by U.S. intelligence and information operations officers in a publication titled the *Baghdad Mosquito,* the rumors became a great concern to some U.S. military commanders. Many of these rumors sprang up organically; that is, the rumors were not intentionally spread by insurgent groups but rather were repeated by everyday Iraqis living

I.2. Mas Selamat escapes from the inescapable prison.
Original creator unknown; image found on 6 November 2009 at http://xmercenaries.com/four9er/wp-content/uploads/2008/03/masescapealcatrazqq1.jpg

amidst profound social and economic upheaval. Ever the opportunists, the insurgents helped to spread these and other rumors in an effort to encourage Iraqis either to turn a blind eye to or to participate in the growing insurgency. One rumor turned a U.S. civil affairs mission to inoculate cattle at the behest of Iraqi farmers into a bovine poisoning story, which then fused with a number of other rumors, from purported links between U.S. technologies and the country's drought to reports that the U.S. invaded Iraq only for its oil. These rumors painted the United States as a colonizer less interested in the safety of the Iraqi people than in a Christian and capitalist crusade of exploitation.

Insurgents and governments alike engage in rumor-mongering. On 17 September 2009, Indonesian authorities in Central Java, Indonesia, killed Noordin Mohammed Top, a notorious Jemaah Islamiyah financier, recruiter, and bomb maker. Noordin was connected to several hotel and embassy bombings, including the 2002 Bali bombing in which 202 people were killed. After examining his body, a state forensic pathologist claimed he found evidence that the feared terrorist had been sodomized. Indonesian, Malaysian, and Singaporean media quickly picked up on the comment, speculating that Noordin, who was married to several wives, was a "sexual deviant." Rumors asserting his homosexuality began proliferating across the region. Contrary to the rumors about Mas Selamat and those found circulating in Iraq, the Noordin rumors ended up advancing the state's information campaign to paint the terrorist and, by extension, Jemaah Islamiyah as "deviant" and thus hypocritical (fig. 1.3).

Other than being related in some way to Islamist extremism, it might appear that the Singaporean, Iraqi, and Indonesian rumors have little else in common.[2] The Mas Selamat rumors conveyed an online critique of the Singaporean government, which tightly regulates broadcast media—not to mention its diverse population—more than they expressed an immediate threat of terrorist violence. The Iraq case, however, consisted of a series of rumors that ended up thwarting a counterinsurgency mission and, in the process, both supported insurgent interests and promoted a worldview complementary to that of the insurgents. Finally, there is ample evidence that the Noordin Top rumors originated as a kind of government disinformation strategy—what Gordon W. Allport and Leo Postman in 1947 called a "whisper campaign"—designed to turn the death of a successful terrorist into an antiterrorism narrative.[3] Indeed, the sociopolitical context surrounding

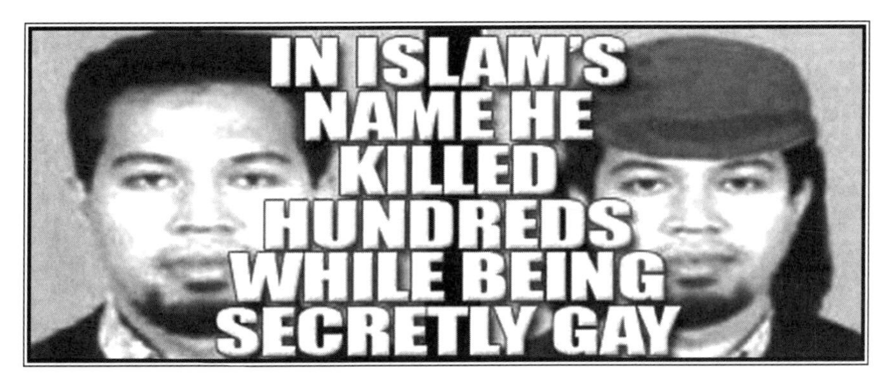

I.3. Online image that explicitly spreads the Noordin Top rumor. Original creator unknown; image found on 16 December 2009 at http://www.vexnews.com/news/6538/top-or-bottom-supposedly-devout-muslim-fundamentalist-terrorist-enjoyed-being-sodomised-between-mass-murder-missions/

each case is distinct—from a stable city-state to a country with a growing history of deadly terrorism to a war-torn country in the throes of a violent insurgency—as is the content of the respective rumors.

Yet these three cases, each of which we probe in greater detail in subsequent chapters, share a great deal in common. First, the rumors in each case ended up filling critical gaps in the flow of official information. They had the sound and appearance of news that their respective audiences craved. Second, the content of the rumors spoke intimately to the cultural sensibilities, political sensitivities, and religious principles of contested populations—the civilian populations that form the bull's-eye of resistant, insurgent, and counterinsurgent information campaigns. The rumors that make up each case might seem implausible to Western audiences, even fanciful, but they were grounded in the frustrations and fears of their intended audiences. Finally, these otherwise distinct rumors flowed freely across narrative landscapes besieged by conflicting, fractious, and volatile ideologies. Each side of the conflict—from everyday citizens to governments to insurgents and counterinsurgents—was attempting to navigate this complex landscape in an effort to influence contested populations. In short, each case reveals a key dimension of rumor origin, spread, and function during sociopolitical struggles over the right to govern.

How do rumors impact strategic communication struggles between Islamist insurgents and diverse governments? In what ways do rumors fit into and extend existing narrative systems and ideologies? For that matter, why do some rumors "stick" with a contested population and others dissipate with little more than a whisper? At what point does a rumor pose a threat to an existing government? Conversely, how can we better understand the nature and function of rumors during nascent and ongoing insurgencies?

These questions are critical at this point in history because Islamist extremism is a dominant security concern of contemporary governments from the industrialized West to the developing world. And although there is a wide range of economic, diplomatic, and cultural factors that influence the interaction between states and non-state actors and so warrant study, our research attests to the importance of rumors in today's geopolitical security environment as well. Rumors point toward anxieties, desires, and fears within a population, but they also help shape ideologies and interpretations of events and actions. Rumors, too, are a kind of grass-roots communication form, generally circulating from the bottom up, and often serve to empower the powerless. Indeed, rumors are suitable to many varieties of political expression, from violent insurgency as in the case of Iraq to political dissent as in the case of Singapore. Rumors, of course, abound in nonpolitical contexts as well (for example, the workplace or school), but our interest is in the common thread uniting diverse Islamist extremist campaigns and state responses to those campaigns.

In this book we seek to unpack the implications of rumors in a geopolitical context. We have chosen to focus our case studies on Singapore, Iraq, and Indonesia because they represent points on the scale of political unrest among diverse states in which we see ideologically charged rumors as most potent. The rumors we study in the three countries also share the common feature of a link to Islamist extremism, one of the central concerns of governments across the world. The shared traits of these three case studies, we hope, will provide the basis by which our theory and method might be usefully deployed to other locations that exhibit varying degrees of intensity of political unrest and an association with extremism in general and terrorism more specifically. Finally, we have chosen these three countries because the authors have a unique depth of experience in each. In addition to professional scholarly backgrounds in media studies, political science, and communication research, the team brings to bear firsthand regional experiences conducting counterinsurgency operations for the U.S. Army, United Nations–sanctioned observer and sanctions enforcement missions, human rights and election monitoring, as well as resident and citizen experiences. These diverse experiences help us better understand the lived context of each country—a useful requirement, we believe, to rumor research.

We seek to answer the aforementioned questions by recognizing two important features of rumors that make them a particularly volatile element within many sociopolitical situations. First, *rumors operate as part of narrative systems and circulate within narrative landscapes.* They do not arise or proliferate in a cultural vacuum, but are built from bits and pieces of prevailing narrative systems and current events. Second, *rumors spring up unexpectedly and unbidden, and circulate among everyday people.* Rumors are everyday speech and writing acts. These two qualities form the basis of our governing metaphor of rumors as "narrative IEDs." Much like their explosive cousins, the improvised explosive devices responsible for countless deaths and injuries in Iraq and Afghanistan, narrative IEDs can be created and planted by nearly anybody, require limited resources, can be deadly for those in their direct paths, and can instill fear in the people and in government forces. Also like their namesakes, rumors are a low-cost, low-tech weapon that can successfully counter elaborate and expensive government initiatives, such as outreach campaigns or strategic communication efforts.

Critical to our research interests is a desire to better understand and explain how rumors aid and hinder Islamist extremism, which is why we focus on narrative landscapes besieged by social dissent and political instability. Toward this end, this chapter sets the theoretical stage for our three case studies. We argue that rumors are, in essence, local stories that participate in larger narrative systems that, given the right mix of cultural references and ideological formations, end up volatile when placed in the service of either an insurgent or a counterinsurgent agenda. Our theoretical model and case studies grow out of the research undertaken for this book in chapters 2 through 5, as well as an Office of Naval Research grant, "Identifying Terrorist Narratives and Counter-Narratives: Embedding Story Analysts in Expeditionary Units," that we, along with colleagues at Arizona State University, received in 2009.

Rumor Theory

A review of the post–World War II literature on rumors reveals a common theoretical argument advanced most clearly by sociologist Tamotsu Shibutani in 1966: "Rumor is a substitute for news; in fact, it *is* news that does not develop in institutional channels."[4] Although Shibutani's definition is insightful and applicable to our case studies, we define "rumor" in broader terms. For us, *rumor is a shorthand term for speculation, half-truths, and misinformation in the form of stories that, to some groups, appears to offer rational cause-and-effect explanations of events.* A rumor may eventually be identified as a factual explanation of events, but its initial articulation is always based on speculation. Viewing rumors as stories that appear rational but that are steeped in speculation reveals their connection to the vast array of cultural expression circulating within a community or region—what we call the "narrative landscape." The stories and narrative systems that make up this landscape are constantly in dialogue with one another, even across time.

The spread of rumors can be nefarious, such as the Israeli conspiracy rumors noted in the preface, or with specific intent to cause difficulty for another person or group, such as those involving President Obama's citizenship. Indeed, modern political campaigns increasingly leverage mass and online media outlets to undermine and disgrace an opponent by deploying what Jayson Hardin calls "rumor bombs."[5] One example is the rumor that spread during the 2008 U.S. presidential campaign that Barack Obama is a Muslim. Though lacking any concrete evidence and countered with some initial success by the Obama campaign, the rumor continues to circulate in U.S. political discourse.[6] Harsin's analysis of U.S. politics suggests a convergence of three key elements to rumor bombs like these: contemporary journalism technologies, business practices, and ethics necessitate speed and assertion over accuracy and verification; branding and public relations practices have become central elements in both politics and governance; a "war communication" ethos, fraught with secrecy, works in concert to supplant a more transparent mode of political communication.

This metaphor of the rumor bomb is complementary to our characterization of rumors as narrative IEDs. A rumor bomb, such as the "Obama is Muslim" rumor, is much like the bomb of modern warfare: it is carefully crafted by organizations with resources and it is strategically dropped on specific targets. Harsin attributes rumor bombs to information environments marked by intensive use of electronic media. The rumors we have found in our case studies, however, are messier; they are more improvised, cobbled together from existing events, media products, and, most importantly, stories and extant narrative systems. They are not targeted "smart" bombs. Indeed, in most cases they are not aimed at a specific victim but are rather unleashed upon targets of opportunity, without regard to collateral damage, and are spread by word of mouth, traditional media, and networked platforms.

In addition to acting on nefarious motivations, people often spread rumors to satisfy a psychological need to mimic an authoritative source and, as such, appear as an authority or as a superior source. Extant studies typically point to workplace and "race" rumors as examples of capricious and value-laden rumor-mongering.[7] The provocateur, or rumor-monger, uses stories about others to inflate his/her own importance. Finally, people who spread rumors can also believe they are conveying the truth, what Prashant Bordia and Nicholas DiFonzo term a "collective explanation process."[8] David Coady takes this argument a step further by making the case that the more traction a rumor gains among a population, the greater the possibility it will contain truthful information.[9] In these cases, the rumor-monger's motivations may be centered on attempts to help a community better understand past and contemporary events.

Seen in this light, the rumor mill describes the circulation of rumors via multiple communication platforms—from sermons and speech acts to blogs and videos—among various populations. In our study, we focus on the diverse ways rumors circulate among contested populations grappling with Islamist extremism, specifically groups that reside between resistant, insurgent, and government interests. In most cases, the rumors we identify contain fragments of factual data. Their claims are unsubstantiated, yet many are rational, at least for key populations, given the narrative systems they draw upon and the sociopolitical environment in which they emerge and spread.

Rumors become a particular threat to government interests when they integrate with or invoke longstanding historical narratives that resonate with contested populations. The more a rumor speaks to the history of a population, the greater the chance it has of sticking with that population. Which is to say that, irrespective of the origin of the rumor—whether a coordinated information operation conducted by insurgents or a simple story that somehow takes hold among a discrete population—rumors aid extremist goals when they fill critical information gaps in a way that appears to offer a logical explanation of an otherwise unexplained or poorly explained event. Rumors successfully fill these gaps when they participate in, invoke, or otherwise link up with widely understood cultural narratives. This aspect of our definition complements Shibutani's view that rumors are a substitute for news while emphasizing how the information-satisfying component of rumors draws upon existing cultural narratives and ideologies.

Shibutani does not define rumors as stories that participate in and fuel larger narrative systems. Neither does the larger field of rumor research. Since Allport and Postman's seminal study of World War II rumors, scholars have instead theorized rumors from sociological, psychological, and folklorist perspectives. Throughout this body of literature there is considerable attention paid to the motivations, typologies, and broader social meanings of rumors. Although the approaches are distinct in subtle ways, three broad themes emerge that constitute what might be called extant rumor theory: (1) rumors are sense-making devices that explain conditions in the absence of information; (2) rumors express social anxieties; and (3) rumors are non-narrative.[10]

It is this last common characteristic that we think misses the mark. Distinguishing rumors as non-narrative begins with folklorists entering into rumor theorizing and trying to make useful distinctions between rumors, which they often see as non-narratives, and legends, which they often define as narratives. For example, Patrick Mullen argues that a single rumor is generally too brief and unstructured to be considered a narrative.[11] He does, however, suggest that rumors can be the kernels that grow into legends and thus narratives, further indicating that multiple rumors can coalesce into a single legend. He distinguishes legend as an unverifiable, narrative-structured piece of information that functions as a kind of cultural tradition within a specific community. Fellow folklorist Timothy Tangherlini, also working on the relationship of rumor and legend, emphasizes a narrative basis to each form of cultural expression. Although he acknowledges (but does not pursue) the possibility that some rumors may take narrative form, he also suggests that rumor "may be but a short statement."[12] Thus, Mullen and Tangherlini hint at a relationship between rumors and narrative, a relationship we think warrants expansion and focused attention.

This emphasis on the brevity of rumor is also shared by some social scientists. Nicholas DiFonzo and Prashant Bordia, for example, downplay the narratological dimensions of rumors. Like Shibutani, they tend to emphasize the topicality of rumors as a defining characteristic—the "rumor is a substitute for news" idea—in contrast to a more enduring quality of narrative. Rumors are positioned as "in the moment" and applicable to a particular situation, whereas legends entertain, teach, and explain events in the past. In fact, DiFonzo and Bordia suggest that, in the case of rumors, "a narrative cannot be present because the sense making is contemporaneous rather than post hoc."[13] By characterizing narrative as post hoc, DiFonzo and Bordia position rumors as more timely and socially relevant, but fail to explain how rumors draw on local knowledge and cultural systems to create meaning and facilitate spread.

While we agree that rumors are connected to immediate events and are timely and relevant to the moment, we do not share the viewpoint that narrative is a sense-making apparatus that arises only after events have occurred and are complete. Rather, as we discuss more thoroughly below, we see narrative as a continuous process of understanding in which external data are constantly ordered and re-ordered into patterns that make sense to people. This definition explains both the synchronic and diachronic power of rumors: they do indeed spread quickly and address contemporaneous issues—they are *in the moment*—but they contextualize these issues into an otherwise rational explanatory structure of cause and effect over time. This explanatory structure is derived from and also shapes ideology and attitudes, which are critical components when dealing with political dissent and insurgencies.

A critical dimension of rumor spread is the degree to which the story it tells connects with and is familiar in form or content to its audience. Rumors must, in some way, make sense in order to gain traction; at minimum, they must adhere to a causal logic rooted in cultural sensibilities and traditions. The narrative systems that rumors extend and enter determine the degree to which they will thrive. Rumors, most theorists agree, do not sprout and spread in a vacuum. They most often gain traction with a population when that population is under political pressure and social stress, from race riots and natural disasters to repressive government controls and insurgencies. These events invoke narrative systems that offer a host of historical and explanatory frameworks that a rumor builds upon or extends as it gains traction from individuals to groups.

Narrative Theory

The narratological features and functions of rumors give rise to the first two components of rumor theory we see operating during nascent and ongoing insurgencies: sense-making and anxiety expression. Storytelling is one of the foremost methods of organizing data about the world, one born of the sense-making architecture of cause and effect. Indeed, it is a continual and recursive process of data acquisition, pattern recognition, and comprehension. Whether fiction or nonfiction, stories set up a world, known in literary and film studies as a diegesis, or story world, containing characters, settings, events, and actions. They typically introduce a conflict that is the result of character actions or event circumstances in a particular setting. Story events take place, causing characters to react, settings to change, and new events to come about. Narrative, then, exhibits a dual logic: it is both an object we can point to (film, novel, speech, and so on) and a mental process. Narrative is the union of what is told and how it is told. A narrative consists of a system of interlocking stories, shared story elements, and specific structure.

Members of the audience, or more simply readers, make sense of characters, settings, events, and actions through their own cause-and-effect processes. These processes are themselves narrative constructions, or reconstructions, involving pattern recognition (what they see and hear in their interaction with the story) based on cognitive frameworks, cultural norms, and ideological formations. The rumors of Mas Selamat's escape from the Singaporean detention facility provide a case in point. In the absence of official reporting on the details of the escape, people were forced to speculate in order to make sense of the event, its characters, and their actions/inactions. In doing so, they told a story: *Mas Selamat (character) was a threat to the Singaporean government (setting and conflict) so they killed him (action) and then covered it up by concocting an escape (event).* Leveraging the growing popular interest in the terrorist's escape, others poached existing narratives in an effort to tell a story critical of the government: *Despite the government's (character) repressive policies (conflict), it is incompetent because it cannot keep a feared terrorist (character) from escaping (action and event) from its most secure prison (setting).* Cognitive sense-making, cultural frameworks, and resistant politics fueled the spread of online critiques of the Singaporean government—critiques spawned by rumors that provided sense-making patterns and cultural frameworks.

A narrative, then, can be defined as a system of interrelated stories that share story elements, cultural references, and a rhetorical desire to resolve a conflict by structuring audience expectations and interpretations. For this reason, in this book we use "story" to denote a particular rumor. *Mas Selamat escaped through the toilet* is a story. It links up with other stories, such as *Mas Selamat was killed in prison by the government,* to participate in a broader narrative system of government conspiracy and imply government oppression.

We use "narrative" to identify the larger framework that rumors as stories participate in and help shape. "Narrative landscape," on the other hand, is a system of narratives and refers to the complex array of narratives that circulate within a specific social, economic, political, and mediated environment—the narrative context that gives rise to rumors and in which rumors compete for prominence. In our case, the narrative landscapes under investigation include Singapore in 2008, Iraq from 2003 to 2010, and Indonesia in 2010. Each country is defined by a heterogeneous population with diverse cultural traditions; yet in each the narrative landscape includes narrative systems, stories, and rumors that can exacerbate existing political tensions and complicate their resolution, from the insurgency in Iraq to the grass-roots critique of anonymous online Singaporean dissidents.

The analyses of rumors in several extant theories are compatible with the narrative-oriented perspective on rumor we present in this book. Mullen offers the following observation about rumor in relation to its sense-making operations: "Rumor is a cognitive device which enables man to understand and cope with events which are not visibly connected; he tries to fill in missing details; he tries to explain things which are not obvious; and he tries to predict similar occurrences."[14] Compare that definition with observations about narrative by film theorist Edward Branigan: "Today narrative is increasingly viewed as a distinctive strategy for organizing data about the world, for making sense and significance," and "narrative is a recursive organization of data; that is, its components may be embedded successively at various micro- and macro-levels of action."[15] In short, the production and consumption of rumors require the same basic kinds of data-organizing, gap-filling, and predictive processes we see in both the making and the reading of films.

The theories underpinning Branigan's work are based in part on the cognitive constructivist model advanced by film historian and theorist David Bordwell. Calling his method "historical poetics," Bordwell looks at the way narrative films organize story elements, or narrative data, in relation to the way readers construct meaning from that organization.[16] Situating cinematic films alongside art, Bordwell argues that storytellers assemble a specific set of expressive options in order to guide a reader's interpretation of a film. In other words, films organize or arrange representational and story materials—from characters and events to plot and conflict—in an effort to achieve certain effects and interpretations. Conversely, film readers use the identifiable norms and conventions that make up the film to construct in their heads the meaning of the story.[17] The interaction between story elements and perceptual activity produces schemas, or mental models that are based on psychological, cultural, and ideological frameworks. Following Jean Piaget's work, Bordwell makes the case that schemas change, grow larger and at times more complex, through two complementary processes: assimilation, whereby readers take material into their mind (a rumor, a film), and accommodation, whereby they construct meaning from that material based on prior experiences (story makes sense/doesn't make sense).

Branigan and Bordwell situate narrative in the service of explaining the cognitive-constructivist processes involved in comprehending a film. Although we are not analyzing cinema as they do, the combination of seeing narrative as a strategy of data organization based on norms and conventions as well as recognizing the cognitive processes involved in interpreting a narrative is a powerful theory that helps both describe and explain the role of rumors during hegemonic struggles. Islamist extremists construct their stories in ways they hope will lead their audiences to specific interpretations and actions: a jihad (action and event) in pursuit of the Caliphate (resolution). Readers of Islamic stories reconstruct extremist narratives based on a relationship between the patterns presented in the story and their specific cognitive frameworks (what they know/don't know about Islam).

Stories are not self-contained entities. Each story is engaged in a dialogue, so to speak, with narrative systems, cultural traditions, and social ideologies. As literary theorist and philosopher Mikhail Bakhtin notes: "Each utterance [speech act, story, novel, and so on] refutes, affirms, supplements, and relies upon the others, presupposes them to be known, and somehow takes them into account. . . . Therefore, each kind of utterance is filled with various kinds of responsive reactions to other utterances of the given sphere of speech communication."[18] This dialogue ensures that stories of all kinds and lengths facilitate comprehension and meaning production in relation to larger narrative systems and within narrative landscapes; they do so in different ways and at distinct times. Seen in this way, narratives are always composed of "shorter" stories in dialogue with cultural traditions. It is our contention that rumors are a class of story operating in this dialogic process. The rumors are part of and react to cultural traditions and in so doing engage larger narratives.

Bakhtin shows us that narratives are more than a product of the story/discourse that dominates much formalist film scholarship and narratology. What is told (*story*) and how it is told (*discourse*) are critically important components, but equally critical is the fact that narratives are in dialogue with a complex array of adaptations, discourses, and ideologies. A useful example from current U.S. politics is the rhetorical strategy of conservative Tea Party activists. At the heart of their narrative is the re-articulation of the origins of American democracy from stories of egalitarianism and enlightenment to stories of deeply religious "fathers" building a new republic based on fundamentalist Christian principles. This reframing of America's political origins follows the same basic events (*story*) as the competing narrative told in most history books, but emphasizes different parts in the telling (*discourse*) and taps into contemporary cultural traditions (the rhetoric of political evangelism). By adapting foundation stories to their political agenda, Tea Party activists attempt to alter the contemporary political narrative landscape, which emphasizes, among other things, the separation of church and state.

Dialogism, then, refers to the way stories communicate with other stories and narrative systems, with other storytellers and artistic works, with a host of political and ideological movements, and, most of all, with the cultural context in which the stories originate and are interpreted. The dialogical relationship goes beyond the question of a story being influenced by other stories and narratives. As systems operating within cultures over time, stories and narratives shift and change, or adapt, as new stories enter the system and influence public expressions and social formations. In a recursive process, they provide clues as to how the public should make sense of a narrative system and, through adaptation, any new stories drawing upon and entering it.

The Qur'an provides another useful example. In the Muslim holy book there are roughly ninety references to Jesus, whom Christians believe to be the son of God and whom Muslims believe to be a prophet sent by Allah to guide Jews with a new scripture. Moreover, a surah in the Qur'an is named after the Virgin Mary, Jesus' mother, the only woman mentioned by name in the holy text. The Qur'an also draws upon revelation stories that formed the origins of the Judeo-Christian Bible. It refers, for instance, to the revelation given to the prophet Moses at Mount Sinai (the Torah); the revelation to the prophet-king David (the Psalms); and the revelation to the prophet Jesus (the Gospel). Hence, the Qur'an presupposes knowledge among its audience of the Torah and Gospels, as well as other Judeo-Christian texts, leveraging their stories to articulate the message of Allah as revealed to Muhammad. In short, the complex and intertwined holy texts of Islam, Christianity, and Judaism attempt to define the worldview of their followers and the followers of the other texts, yet are engaged in an eternal dialogue as much with each other as with their followers.[19] They contribute to each other's narrative terrain.

Using Branigan and Bordwell's cognitive constructivist model synthesized with Bakhtin's dialogical principle as a base, we see stories as formed by and participating in narrative systems that coalesce and collectively support one another, that are in dialogue with each other in an effort to shape an individual's or community's worldview (schemata). Like the stories that make up the Torah, New Testament, and Qur'an, these systems influence an individual's perspectives on a subject, participate in the dynamics of a culture, and support the development of powerful ideologies—and therein lies the under-recognized power of rumors. As stories themselves, they operate within this framework.

Too often policymakers, communication strategists, and even social scientists assume that all texts are read and absorbed identically across a population. We know, however, that individual readers frequently produce meanings that are "outside the mainstream." Humanities scholarship has long recognized this individual agency and refers to the practice of producing an alternate interpretation as "reading against the text." To read against the elements and cultural references that make up a story, the reader must read against its rhetorical grain using critical schemata developed from past experiences, education, and judgment. This process is perhaps best explained by cultural studies scholar Stuart Hall, who rejects the "textual determinism" seen in traditional Marxist, psychoanalytic, and purely Structuralist approaches; instead, he argues that the interpretation of a narrative, or its "decoding," does not follow prescriptively and a priori from the way the narrative is encoded.[20] More specifically, Hall describes three types of readings: dominant, negotiated, and oppositional. A dominant reading accepts the text's worldview without question. Muslim suicide bombers are, perhaps, an obvious example of people who have accepted a dominant reading of the Islamist extremist narrative. A negotiated reading, on the other hand, questions some of the text's ideological positions but not all of them. Tea Party members who accept the group's origin narrative critiquing "over" taxation but question the fundamentalist Christian dimension of the narrative might fall into this category. Finally, an oppositional reading begins from an "alternative framework of reference" that fundamentally rejects the text's ideological positions and worldview.[21] All social movements have their detractors in the same way that all narrative systems are questioned by select groups of readers.

There is both theoretical and practical value in developing an approach to rumors and strategic communication more generally that recognizes the agency of readers. Without such a framework, the model would not be able to assess or predict differences among heterogeneous populations accounting for education and historical experience. The model would be, like traditional Marxism and psychoanalysis, fatalistic: little could be done to subvert dominant ideologies and their narrative vehicles save for class warfare or mass catharsis. Hall's and other poststructural approaches allow for a more subtle understanding of human agency, placing it squarely in the context of culture, social formation, and experience while also identifying dominant and dominating social formations and narrative systems. We see this aspect of Hall's theory borne out in the form, function, and processes of rumor belief, rejection, and circulation.

Like Bakhtin, and implicit in the cognitive constructivist model advanced by Branigan and Bordwell, Hall gives a significant role to the decoding reader as well as to the encoder storytellers. Yet oppositional schemata are neither inherent to our cognitive frameworks nor easy to acquire. The reader must first and foremost be afforded the opportunity—the time, space, and inclination—to read against the encoded structures foisted upon them in Islamist extremist narratives, which, of course, is not always possible during conditions of extreme social and political unrest. In such conditions, people are more apt to accept Islamist extremists at their word or, as Hall might argue, construct a "dominant reading." For example, with cattle dying around them, Iraqi farmers might immediately accept the apparent logic of a rumor casting the American veterinary health campaign as a nefarious plot to poison the herds. On the other hand, in stable Singapore, citizens have greater time, security, and resources and thus can decode the Mas Selamat escape details that were encoded by the government as the act of a dangerous criminal into a parodic tale of government incompetence and outlaw hero bravado.

By considering rumors as stories that participate in and extend narrative systems, we can better identify the relationship between rumors and social formation in a specific cultural setting. The Iraqi rumors we discussed briefly above and analyze more thoroughly in chapter 3, for instance, joined with other rumors about U.S. military actions and technologies to create a cluster of rumors casting the intentions of the United States as nefarious—evidence of what many believed to be a new crusade. This belief, of course, resonated with the comments made by President George W. Bush at the outset of the "war on terrorism," when he invoked the Crusader narrative at a press conference on 16 September 2001: "This crusade, this war on terrorism is going to take a while."[22] The president literally put the "United States as Crusaders" narrative into play before U.S. forces in Iraq launched its bovine inoculation campaign. Bush's remark served to make the association between the United States and Crusaders, already in the minds of extremists and the Iraqi people more generally, easily recognizable: a literal cause (crusade/U.S invasion), effect (exploitation by infidels), and reaction (insurgency). By fitting into this same pattern, the bovine poisoning rumor both exhibited and intensified anti-American sentiment.

Abu Musab al-Zarqawi, the Jordanian terrorist who led al Qaeda in Iraq (AQI) before he was killed by U.S. forces in 2006, followed in Bush's footsteps when he invoked the Crusader narrative in characterizing U.S. intentions in Iraq. On 25 April 2006, Zarqawi was seen in a video released by AQI referencing the Crusader narrative familiar to Muslims throughout the region: "Your mujahedeen sons were able to confront the most ferocious of Crusader campaigns on a Muslim state."[23] The terrorist knew that the Crusader narrative and attendant historical memories would speak to his audiences in ways that President Bush clearly did not intend.

Narratives marshal a range of common story elements that draw upon their readers' historical experiences to facilitate diverse interpretations. This is particularly the case, at least from a historical perspective, with religious narratives. For example, the most commonly cited verse from the Qur'an verse that extremists use to counter the plethora of other verses from the Muslim holy book that call for peace and tolerance is surah 9, verse 5, known as the "Verse of the Sword": "But when the forbidden months have passed, then fight and slay the pagans [*mushrikin]* wherever you find them, and seize them, beleaguer them, and lie in wait for them in every stratagem [of war]; but if they repent and establish prayers and practice charity, then open the way for them, for God is forgiving, merciful."[24] In the extremist application, the first half of this verse is emphasized: making war on the *mushrikin*. In addition, extremists often cite a hadith (saying of the Prophet) to justify "collateral damage," or the killing of civilians, including other Muslims, when they reference a famous nighttime battle. As the story goes, one of Muhammad's followers (character) worried that he might unintentionally violate Muhammad's proscription against killing women and children because he was unable to see where his arrows might land (conflict); Muhammad replied that "they [innocents] are among them [enemies]" (action leading to the event). Extremists use this story to justify the "unintentional" killing of noncombatants residing among the enemy during battle, thereby absolving themselves of a sin prominently condemned in other verses of the Qur'an. The extremists use these two story elements together as part of the construction of a narrative system laying out conflict (with invaders, Crusaders, local governments) and response (violence).

As vehicles for ideologies, stories and narrative systems—and thus rumors—engage in what cultural studies scholars, borrowing from neo-Marxist theorist Antonio Gramsci, call "coercion and consent."[25] Coercion and consent are two of the hegemonic processes by which states and nonstate actors, in our case grass-roots movements and insurgents, struggle for the consent to govern and rule. For Gramsci, hegemony is always a tumultuous process, an "unstable equilibrium," though at critical times the struggle, and thus the narratives and ideologies that give it meaning and import, have a greater chance of effecting radical change and a rare state of total top-down dominance. This is the case, of course, during internal wars and power struggles when a government's attempt to persuade its people to accept its authority is directly threatened by an insurgency that aspires to replace it. Albeit in subtler and less immediately threatening ways, it is also the case with grass-roots opposition movements such as those we saw in Egypt and elsewhere in North Africa in 2011 and nascent insurgencies such as those spreading throughout the Middle East when the government and its policies are being critiqued and challenged by contested populations that have yet to embrace radical change. Our three case studies provide coverage of this phenomenon: Iraq is besieged by a full-blown insurgency; Indonesia struggles with an internal Islamist extremist terrorist threat; and political dissent finds subtle expression in stable but heavily censored Singapore.

A hegemonic struggle is not waged simply through what the military euphemistically calls kinetic force, or lethal targeting, though clearly coercion during counterinsurgencies is often propelled by "bombs on targets." It is also a war of ideas, of ideological coercion, where the terrain of struggle amounts to a nation's culture and identity. Which is to say that culture becomes the staging ground for narrative dominance, the site of kinetic force, and the aftermath of both. Indeed, the degree to which a contested population consents to one side or the other, the insurgents or the government, depends in large part on the array of stories and narratives marshaled by both sides, the degree to which those stories and narratives speak to the cultural history of the people, and the level of social anxiety and cultural dissonance contextualizing this dialogue—all amidst a complex political climate replete with competing political motivations and ideological confrontations. When bombs on targets will not do the trick, or when they are intended to ratchet up fear and social unrest, as is often the case with terrorism, narratives, stories, and rumors become the weapons of choice by all sides in the struggle for dominance.

Narrative Elements

Our emphasis on narrative systems requires a more precise definition of "story." Stories, we argue, consist of sequences of events involving characters in settings and are recounted for rhetorical purposes. For an utterance to constitute a story, it must have the following basic elements: time (sequence of events), space (setting), and character(s). Events shape characters and their actions; characters also shape story events. It is important to note that characters do not have to be human (or, more accurately, representations of humans). Gods might be characters. Extraterrestrials might be characters. An animal, a tree, or even a sword can be a character in a story. Moses' staff, for example, is represented as a character in a Shi'ite hadith: "It speaks if it is induced to do so. It is prepared for the one who will rise to establish the kingdom of Allah on earth. He will use it in the same way as Moses had done."[26] Usually, when a character in a story is not a human, it is depicted anthropomorphically, as is Moses' staff, so that the reader might better understand its intended meaning: "It frightens and devours things made to trick people and it accomplishes whatever commands it receives."[27]

Equally important to our definition is setting or, in cognitive constructivist terms, the spatial schemata that ranges from identifiable locations (Mount Sinai) to social situations (the time before the Kingdom of Allah on earth) in which characters reside (Moses; his staff) and story events take place (Kingdom of Allah on earth). Settings may be of historical, geographical, cultural, and political significance (Iraq). They may be referenced literally (the Whitley Road Detention Center) or metaphorically (Garden of Eden).

They can be expressed in expansive terms (Mesopotamia) or more abstractly (Kingdom of Allah).

Equally important is the rhetorical dimension of stories. Narratologists often call this the "discursive" aspect of storytelling and comprehension: stories are told to educate and entertain, and they are listened to for the same reasons. As an example of dissident discourse, Islamist extremist stories tend to be told for specific political and ideological reasons: to educate Muslims about the repressive dangers of the West; to expose the prurient culture and colonialist intentions of the West; and to inculcate Muslims into the extremists' worldview. The listener often engages terrorist stories in an effort to better understand his or her own circumstances, to determine how best to follow the principles of Islam, and to visualize a better future. This process does not mean that the extremist story automatically inculcates listeners into Islamist extremist ideologies, but it does suggest that they are in some way in dialogue with it, with their cultural surroundings, and with their fears, anxieties, and aspirations. Our colleagues in the Center for Strategic Communication at Arizona State University describe this phenomenon as "vertical integration," whereby master narratives exist in a middle ground between the level of systems of personal stories and activities (and, we would add, rumors) and broader ideological frameworks.[28] This process becomes particularly powerful when the extremists contextualize their contemporary stories within widely known narrative systems of invasion by outsiders (Christian Crusaders or pagan Tatars, for example).

Rumors fit into this system but are distinct narrative forms owing to unique characteristics of type, function, and origin. Despite the brevity noted by DiFonzo, Mullen, and others, as well as the abstraction that often removes specific characters and places or replaces them to suit the next iteration, rumors have characters, events, actions, and settings. They constitute a unique type of story because their characters are often either anonymous archetypes (apostate/tyrannous government; Western colonizers/crusaders; mujahedeen/holy warriors) or anonymous everymen (residents and diasporic citizens of Singapore; would-be terrorists in Indonesia; rural farmers in Iraq). These generalities allow for a certain malleability of the story and how it fits into prevailing narratives. When rumors have specific characters (Mas Selamat or Noordin Top, for example), this malleability is still present but often in unverifiable details or in the implied conclusions. Moreover, rumors are presented as nonfiction stories (regardless of their ultimate claims to "truth"), drawn from the real world, but their relationship to actual events is more akin to reality television and docudrama than to a journalistic news story. Reality television and docudrama are genres that strongly emphasize the discursive component of narrative's dual logic and are thus no less an ideological construction than their fictional counterparts (and arguably more so, given their rhetorical emphasis on "truth"). Like reality television, rumors appear to be about real people, events, and places. As in a docudrama, rumor verisimilitude is infused with the dramatic—even melodramatic—norms and conventions found in literature, cinema, and digital mash-ups, among other forms of expression familiar to a contested population.

Stories, and thus rumors, also contain three mutually influencing subjective elements, that is, elements that require specific cultural experiences and social frameworks to understand and make them meaningful: archetypes, story forms, and connections to master narratives. These particular elements derive from larger cultural systems, systems that comprise both the narrative landscape and the ideological fissures that mark the social lives of both storyteller and audience. In the context of political turmoil over the right to govern a contested population, this landscape and its ideological fissures constitute a struggle that defines hegemonic conflict.

Archetypes are widely recognized characters, events, and settings that recur across a narrative landscape. In other words, an archetype is a generic model of a person, event, or setting upon which other persons, events, and settings are patterned. Archetypes tend to transcend historical periods and are commonly understood by otherwise distinct cultures across time. The creation tale of Genesis shared by Judaism, Christianity, and Islam offers a variety of archetypes found in contemporary stories from all three religions. The characters of Adam and Eve, who ate from the forbidden tree, are archetypes of the fallen man and woman. The Garden of Eden is an archetype of a pristine and peaceful place that humankind aspires to recapture. And humankind's fall from grace in the expulsion from the Garden of Eden is an archetype for the loss of innocence and entrance into sin.

Archetypes are often invoked by name or by association—prophets, for example—but frequently they are unheralded and unmarked, present to be perceived should the reader or storyteller so choose. An Islamist extremist might logically ask: Is Osama bin Laden a champion, even a savior, sent by Allah to purify Islam and defeat the enemies of the religion?[29] Archetypes allow people to identify immediately with a character's struggle, for example, or a villain's treachery. When it comes to terrorist strategies, rumors have the capacity to position governments of predominantly Muslim societies as apostate (such as the Iraqi provisional authority or the kingdom of Saudi Arabia), Western governments as crusaders and colonizers (the United States and Great Britain), and terrorists as heroic agents of Islamic history (Muqtada al-Sadr, Bin Laden) or righteous heroes (Mas Selamat). Indeed, by linking with and extending established archetypes and associated narratives, rumors can facilitate sympathy for the terrorist cause.

The main Islamic archetypical characters operating in the narrative systems that contribute to Islamist extremist rhetoric include the following:[30]

Tyrant. This archetype stems from stories of the pagan Egyptian pharaohs depicted in the Qur'an. This depiction is similar to that of pharaohs in the Torah. Another story featuring the archetype is the Mongol invasion. With respect to Islamist extremism, the pharaoh has come to represent iron-handed authoritarian rulers, and Mongol kings are analogous to rulers of Muslim peoples who claim to be Muslim but do not rule their people according to shari'ah. The extremist Abdul Salam al-Faraj saw Anwar Sadat as the archetypal tyrant, dubbing him "the Pharaoh," as did Khalid al Islambouli, who, after assassinating Sadat, claimed, "I have killed the Pharaoh!"[31] As we write this chapter, some proponents of the democratic revolution in Egypt have positioned Hosni Mubarak, Sadat's successor, as a pharaoh, indicating the degree to which this archetypical figure remains central to Islamic culture.

Hypocrite. This archetype comes from stories of Muslims who have turned away from Islam, betraying in some way family, tribe, or the Ummah (the Islamic community). They are the *munafiqun* (fake Muslims) in Medina during the time of the Prophet, who are referenced repeatedly in the Qur'an. Osama bin Laden frequently characterized the Saudi royal family as traitors and fake Muslims for their associations with Western governments.

Crusader. The Crusader archetype originates in the wars fought between approximately 1095 and 1400 CE in which Christian knights from Western Europe invaded the Middle East, seeking to restore Christian sovereignty over Jerusalem. Islamic culture, and especially Muslim Arab culture, sees the Crusader as a violent invader seeking to capture rightfully Muslim lands and holy places and to destroy or subjugate Muslim peoples.

Colonizer. The colonizer is closely related to the Crusader, and the Crusader archetype is often invoked when describing the process of colonization in the late nineteenth and early twentieth centuries. Instead of employing barbaric violence with weaponry, the colonizer conducted invasion and pillaging economically, politically, and through the exploitation of resources. We see debates throughout the Muslim world about the U.S. government's interests in their natural resources, from Iraq's oil to Afghanistan's minerals.

Martyr. The hero who dies for a cause is a common archetype across many cultures. Christian (Jesus, John the Baptist, Saint Paul), Jewish (Maccabees), and Muslim (Hamza, Husayn) traditions all valorize martyrs. Islamist extremists frequently invoke this archetype in the context of their violent campaigns, including suicide attacks.

Champion. This archetype offers a heroic figure who promises to bring about Islamic revolution and reformation. Appearing in stories about the Mahdi army in Iraq and the mujahedeen in Afghanistan, Muqtada al-Sadr (Shi'a) and Bin Laden (Sunni) represent two "champions" in Islamist extremist narrative systems. Although Mahdi is an eschatological figure, a savior, and translates as "expected one," Muqtada al-Sadr positions himself as a champion to that cause (and, we would argue, implicitly as a savior). Mujahedeen is a clear reference to a champion, a "freedom fighter." Mahdi and mujahedeen storytellers reference historical victories—Sudan in the 1880s for Mahdi and Afghanistan in the 1980s for mujahedeen—that symbolize the archetypical significance of current champion figures like al-Sadr and Bin Laden, among others.

The second subjective element found in stories is what we call "story forms," which are recognizable patterns of storytelling that are easily comprehended because of their familiarity.[32] They allow people to make sense of new stories as soon as they enter the narrative system. Recognition can take shape quickly in terms of how the story is constructed, such as the Aristotelian three-act structure made especially popular across the world by Hollywood's faithful commitment to it. Another structural example is the frame tale in which a number of stories are told within a broader framework (made famous by Scheherazade forestalling her imminent execution by telling the king successive stories in *Arabian Nights*).

The patterns represented by story forms are not limited to broad story structure and more frequently combine recognizable and repeated character-to-character relationships, event sequences, and character-event relationships. A more discrete example than the Aristotelian and frame tale forms is the "rags to riches" story form common in American culture. The classic film *Citizen Kane* (1941), for example, uses flashbacks to depict the life of Charles Foster Kane. *Rocky* (1976) and its sequels, on the other hand, depict the hurdles a boxer overcomes in a series of discrete films, yet is similarly a rags-to-riches story. This story form, of course, is not unique to the United States. *Slumdog Millionaire* (2009), a film set and made in India but hugely successful in the United States, shows a streetwise Muslim slum dweller overcoming tremendous odds and obstacles to win riches through a game show. These three otherwise discrete narratives tell very different stories with different plots, events, and characters. The pattern of relationships between the characters and the events are similar, however: an underdog pulls himself up by his bootstraps to attain a nearly insurmountable goal.

A critical function of story forms is their participation as one aspect of culturally embedded, top-down schema for the comprehension of a story and its elements. New data are taken in by the audience—dialogue, settings, stylistic choices—and are placed into the comprehension template provided by the readers' previous experiences with story forms. Hence, culturally provided interpretative forms exist to guide interpretation and understanding by readers. For example, the rags-to-riches story form frames the events of Barack Obama's rise to the presidency of the United States: an individual of modest means (Barack Obama) faces significant obstacles (racism, broken home, absent father) to achieve dramatic success (the presidency) through individual talent and willpower (intelligence, political savvy, appealing message). Indeed, we can confidently assert that Obama's candidacy benefited from the comfort, familiarity, and cultural prominence afforded by this popular story form among the American people, which arguably helped minimize the impact of the rumor bomb that cast him as a Muslim and/or foreigner.

In the case of Islamist extremists, Bin Laden's speeches and public statements invoke an age-old story form dating to Saladin, an Islamic archetypal champion who successfully led the Muslim opposition to the European Crusaders in the eastern Mediterranean. Saladin is depicted as a cunning warrior who won important battles in the fight against the Crusaders, liberated Jerusalem from Christian hands when no other Muslim general had been successful, and later defended the holy city against Richard the Lionheart's attempts to recapture it. Similarly, Bin Laden cast himself as a courageous warrior fighting against a modern American-Israeli crusade to seize Muslim lands and holy places, including Jerusalem. Having succeeded in Afghanistan against the Soviets, he battled the United States and "the Jews" to free Palestine and other Muslim lands from the clutches of occupation and infidelity. It was the Crusades all over again, and Bin Laden appointed himself champion for the Muslim Ummah.

The main story forms informing extremist terrorist narratives and rumors include:

Invasion. This story form can be seen in association with the Crusader and colonizer archetypes, as well as in the framing of the modern history of the state of Israel. In all cases, an outside force of considerable power displaces Muslim control of the land around Jerusalem. The outsider's advantages of military or economic power motivate guerrilla tactics such as suicide bombing and terrorism.

Noble sacrifice. A protagonist sacrifices his or her life in a just and righteous cause in a manner that ultimately benefits his or her community, people, or nation. Islamist extremist story forms often feature a martyr archetype in the person of a suicide bomber; his or her death and the deaths of the despised infidels and hypocrites complete the noble sacrifice. Another noble sacrifice story form includes Muslims who die in battle with the enemy (for example, al-Zarqawi).

Reward. The most talked-about example of the reward story form is the promise of seventy-two virgins, which is a kind of addendum to the noble sacrifice story form. Allah grants the reward of an existence beyond comprehension, including seventy-two virgins, to the martyr who has demonstrated his piety and devotion to Allah and the Ummah regardless of the tactical success or failure of his heroic actions.

Deliverance. The community, people, or nation of the protagonist struggles in a precarious existence and must be delivered from those conditions, usually through the efforts of a prophet or a savior. This story form originated in the Moses narrative system but extends to the struggles of Muslims in Singapore, Iraq, and Indonesia, among other Islamic landscapes.

It is important to remember that the order of events structured into a particular story form—what formalists like Branigan and Bordwell call the *sjuzhet*—does not have to be chronological. This is particularly the case in Islam. The Qur'an, for example, is not organized chronologically; instead, the longer surahs generally come first. Moreover, little if anything in the text of the Qur'an guides a reader to determine the chronological order of each surah or verse (ayat). As Kenneth Cragg explains, "the Surahs, especially the longer ones, are composite within themselves as well as irregular in time, so that the continuous reader oscillates bewilderingly across the years and has, indeed, a better chance of being in historical step if he starts at Surah 114 and reads back to Surah 2, than if he lets the paging guide him."[33] Nonetheless, most Muslims believe that the Qur'an is the eternal speech of Allah, existing before time and, as such, not requiring a chronological reading. The story it tells is accessible to readers familiar with Islamic culture and history because of its connections to story forms contained in individual surahs, its reliance on recognized archetypes, and its ubiquitous place in Muslim life.

Cognitive schemas work in such a way that people can potentially reassemble the chronological events found in nonlinear story forms. The flashbacks and flash-forwards found in *Citizen Kane*, for example, work to aid the viewer's comprehension of the chronology of Kane's life. Formalists call this the *fabula*. It consists of the raw or implied events that have taken place and that are represented by way of the sjuzhet or the specific arrangement of story events. As viewers experience the flashbacks and flash-forwards in *Citizen Kane*, as well as the rags-to-riches story form it is built upon, they find it much easier to connect the fictional chronology with the personal story of William Randolph Hearst, upon whom the character of Kane is based.

In the Qur'an, the fabula consists of the historical or revelatory events recounted in the various surahs as they happened chronologically. This is an important distinction. Although the Qur'an is not structured chronologically, chronological history, or the perception of past events understood chronologically, forms the ideological fodder underpinning the Islamist extremist sjuzhet. In the Qur'an, events understood to have happened in the past—including the Exodus narrative and stories involving the Prophet Jesus, for example—predict the end of days and the return of divine order on earth.

Rumors also offer cause-and-effect events, but they often fit into Islamist extremist narrative systems in a nonlinear fashion, much like the surahs and the specific references to traditionally Jewish and Christian characters and events in the Qur'an. The Judeo-Christian references in the Qur'an are intentional; in the narrative systems crafted or simply leveraged by Islamist extremists, rumors are also wedged into place, sometimes intentionally and sometimes unintentionally, without regard necessarily to a chronological structure. For example, the former prime minister of Malaysia, Mahathir Bin Mohamad, said in a speech that because the United States has the technology to make a film such as *Avatar*, it could have faked the 9/11 attacks.[34] This claim, outlandish from an American perspective, is an intentional rumor, one introduced to disrupt the just war narrative that supports U.S. military actions in the Middle East and Central Asia. It ignores the fact that the 9/11 attacks occurred long before the special effects wizardry of *Avatar* had been developed. Even though some rumors are preposterous, easily dismissed, or operate weakly within a narrative system, other rumors provide extremists with potent rhetorical ammunition. This potential is particularly the case when the rumors form mosaics, that is, a cluster of different stories that work together to fill critical gaps in current events narratives. We discuss rumor mosaics in greater detail in chapter 3, where we show how a rumor mosaic not only filled information gaps but also invoked a historical narrative that promoted extremist ideology.

The third subject element requiring specific cultural experiences and social frameworks are "master narratives." We do not mean to imply that these narratives impose insurmountable control; nor do they represent an exclusive governing structure or scheme for a culture. Rather, master narratives are cross-cultural narrative systems deeply embedded in a contested population's consciousness (for example, tribe, race, sect, national identity) and frequently reappear over time to provide an explanatory framework.[35] They often stem directly from religious texts, such as the Torah, Gospels, and Qur'an, but also from other narrative platforms that remain meaningful across time (for example, the U.S. narrative of separation of church and state). As we noted in our brief analysis of the implicit and explicit references to the Crusades in the Iraqi rumor mill, Islamist extremists tend to rely on a specific set of master narratives to direct Muslims on how to interpret and act upon their stories. If a rumor works to that end, whether or not insurgents initially spread it, it will advance the insurgent message and, more broadly, Islamist extremist goals.

Master narratives are similar in function to archetypes in that they traverse several cultures across historical periods and are widely understood, but they, too, are not universal.[36] One culture's master narrative is another culture's story. The United States, for example, does not share many of the archetypes and master narratives circulating in the Islamic world and vice versa (in the Islamic world, for example, the Crusader archetype is an evil and violent invader; to the Western world, a Crusader is a righteous warrior or advocate). That said, some master narratives found in Islam, Christianity, and Judaism tend to be shared across larger swathes of space and time (for example, the Exodus). Though shared, common master narratives may be interpreted and produce meaning in distinct ways owing to competing religious, political, and ideological frameworks.

This diversity, of course, is further complicated by the fact that readers can and do read against the narrative's structures, strictures, and stratagems irrespective of the culture in which they reside. As Hall notes, negotiated readings are often "shot through with contradictions, though these are only on certain occasions brought to full visibility."[37] This is an important point, explaining in part why the vast majority of Muslims do not engage in or support terrorism. The readings are neither dominant nor negotiated, to use Hall's terminology, but resistant. At the same time, the notion of a master narrative also helps to explain why some Muslims find Islamist extremist rhetoric appealing.

Islamist extremists tend to rely on a specific set of master narratives to direct, implicitly or explicitly, how Muslims should interpret and act upon their specific stories. In the rumors we analyze in subsequent chapters, the master narratives encountered include:

Crusades. The Crusades sought to restore Christian control of Palestine and the eastern Mediterranean—most prominently, Jerusalem—between 1095 and 1291 through a series of military campaigns. European Christians attacked and in some cases occupied cities held by Muslims. To Muslims, the Crusaders oppressed followers of Islam, resulting in the deaths of more than 200,000 innocent civilians, until they were driven out by heroic figures such as Salah al-Din (Saladin).[38] When they invoke the Crusader master narrative, Islamist extremists are positioning contemporary Christian leaders and Western military campaigns in the Middle East as violent, extremist enemies of Islam while also predicting that Islam will be victorious. As Halverson, Corman, and Goodall note, the Crusader narrative "argues that the audience should see itself as part of the resistance, to serve as the rescuer that will repel the external enemy and restore the proper order of the world."[39]

Colonization. Colonization is closely related to the Crusades, as it is seen as merely the modern instantiation of the same process: Europeans enter into (invade) Muslim lands and exert their political power to extract natural resources (Islamic wealth and property) from the rightful Muslim owners. It is distinct from the Crusader master narrative in that it focuses on more recent historical events and, more importantly, the economic (and not simply religious) dimensions of Western oppression.

Battle of Karbala. This battle marks the split between Sunni and Shi'a Islam over the right to rule the Islamic Ummah. Husayn ibn Ali, the third Shi'a imam, refused to recognize the caliph Yazid, characterized as evil and a treaty breaker, and was slaughtered on the battlefield at Karbala by Yazid's soldiers. Husayn is popularly revered by Sunnis, but has a profound place in Shi'a Islam as a symbol of salvation, piety, and justice.

We follow the lead of Halverson, Corman, and Goodall in naming these historical events master narratives because of their repetition across time and communities. They exercise mastery over competing narratives in the culture's narrative terrain not by eliminating but rather by marginalizing these alternative narratives. This repetition suggests a high frequency of dominant encoding on behalf of authors and decoding on behalf of readers. This frequency serves to cement these narratives as central components of a community's sense of history and perspective on the world.

In sum, archetypes, story forms, and master narratives are the culturally provided, top-down schema by which a reader begins to comprehend and identify with a new story or a story positioned in a new light. As we stated earlier, rumors are a type of story and thus operate within this same system. Seen from this perspective, rumors are particularly lethal when they leverage powerful narratives that have survived to become deeply embedded within contested populations. Indeed, archetypes, story forms, and master narratives give rumors their ideological charge and potential for encouraging cultural instability.

A rumor of a pending suicide bomber that spread through Baghdad illustrates this perspective. In 2005, thousands of Shi'ites gathered to celebrate the festival of the seventh imam, Musa al-Kasim (d. ca. 799 CE), at his shrine in a suburb of Baghdad. Suddenly, a rumor spread through the crowd that a suicide bomber was present. The crowd panicked, and many people were trampled as they fled.[40] In this brief rumor story, an anonymous but threatening character (suicide bomber) is ostensibly prepared to take an action (explode) in a particular setting (town square). Importantly, this story fits into and leverages a prevailing narrative system of sectarian strife and

Shi'ite oppression by Sunnis: the U.S. invasion has upset the status quo of Saddam Hussein's restraint of Sunni violence, and thus suicide bombers run rampant on city streets. In this particular narrative system, archetypal villain and victim characters populate a generic story form of terrorist action in public places. Here, the rumor of the suicide bomber circulates within a narrative system that explains previous bombings, expresses the untenable sociopolitical state, demonstrates fear among the Shi'ite victims of past Sunni violence, and inspires extremism by Shi'ites by appealing to a desire for revenge. The narrative system aided by the rumor also undermines political stability: *Sunnis continue to target Sh'ite neighborhoods and are not to be trusted; the elected government is ineffective at maintaining security, thus an alternative must be found.*

Considering rumors in the context of a narrative system and cultural practices also helps us to understand additional elements that make rumors a special kind of story. They are often predictive or explanatory in nature: *There is a suicide bomber in the square and he will blow up himself and us; the cattle are dying because the U.S. vaccine is poison; U.S. forces continue to occupy the cities.* The form of their telling usually distances teller from source, but at the same time implicitly invokes a credible source that cannot be questioned: *I heard that . . . ; my cousin told me that . . . and his brother-in-law is a local farmer so he would know.* Once linked to a master narrative, such as the Crusades or colonization, that has been passed down through the generations by religious and tribal leaders, rumors and rumor mosaics based on this story form and invoking a clear enemy archetype provide "obvious" explanations that cannot be verified but are nonetheless steeped in cultural legitimacy.

If the ostensible source of the rumor is "official" or authoritative, such as the mayor of a local city or provincial councilmen, the rumor has greater potential for stoking public fears and anxieties. A clear example is the rumor that circulated in Baghdad in January 2010 suggesting that the government of Iraq was aware that a suicide bomber was poised to attack the same Shi'ite market near the Tigris River that had been hit in 2007 (note, too, the shared story elements with the 2005 Musa al-Kasim shrine suicide bomber rumor discussed above). The 2007 bombing killed at least 135 people and wounded hundreds more, and it remained fresh in the minds of Iraqis throughout the country. The 2010 rumor predicted that the government would not stop the bomber in order to gain further support for its crackdown on Sunni politicians. Few people hearing the rumor in Baghdad would have the contacts to follow up on the charge, which effectively separated the teller from the source in such a way that the source could not be questioned and thus the veracity of the teller could not be contested. Capitalizing on a history of suicide bombings that targeted markets in Baghdad, as well as the sectarian narrative system, this rumor effectively shut down the market, heightened already elevated fears among the citizens of the Iraqi capital, and sent authorities and community leaders on a wild goose chase for the nonexistent bomber. In the process, the citizens of Baghdad lost more confidence in their government.

Extant scholarship often discusses the explanatory nature and ambiguity-of-source feature of rumors in terms of the psychological effects for the teller and receiver and as reasons for their plausibility.[41] Yet these formal characteristics are key to identifying a rumor (to distinguish it from other stories, such as legends and gossip) as well as its points of integration into the respective narrative system. Thus, rumors are predisposed to fit a pattern of recognition (prediction/explanation) of a seemingly authentic yet unverifiable source. They take advantage of existing social anxieties because their details do not contradict anticipated patterns of cause and effect defined by generations-old master narratives as well as newer explanatory story forms: *there is clear evidence of sectarian conflict in Baghdad; Shi'ite markets have been targeted by Sunni insurgents in the past; the government of Iraq is dominated by Shi'ites and stands to gain from sectarian violence targeting Shi'ites; the Shi'ite citizens living near the Tigris River should take matters into their own hands and preemptively protect themselves against Sunni insurgents and an incompetent and corrupt government.*

These examples show how rumors function as a special class of story owing to four characteristics, all of which provide for a high degree of discursive malleability and thus facilitate easy linkage into narrative systems: (1) rumor characters are usually archetypes or semi-anonymous everymen; (2) rumors are usually very brief stories, suitable for filling informational and narrative gaps; (3) rumors have ambiguous or unverifiable origins and are of dubious or unverifiable veracity; and (4) rumors are often explanatory. This last characteristic is especially useful in positioning rumors as narrative gap-fillers, and the flexibility afforded by the other characteristics makes rumors additionally potent.

Another feature of rumors extends their systemic nature: perhaps more so than other stories, rumors frequently cluster in groups and build on one

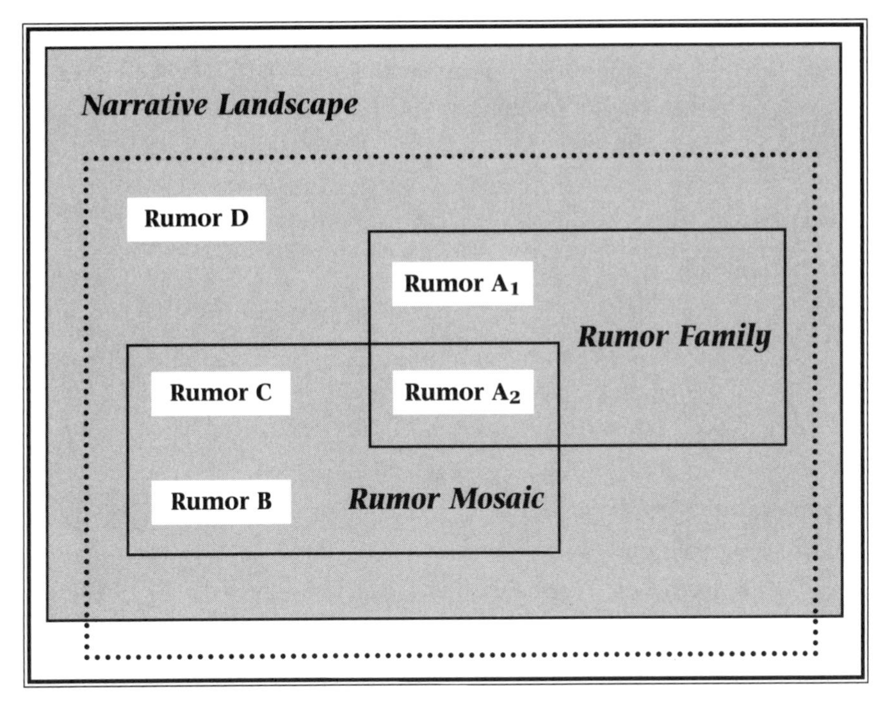

1.4. Rumor relationships within a narrative landscape.

another for their power. We have already identified two such groups. Rumor mosaics, as noted above, are clusters of rumors that have different story subjects but that ultimately cooperate in supporting a broader narrative system. Rumor families differ from mosaics in that they share a common subject or a common focus that can be traced to a common antecedent. For example, the rumors surrounding Mas Selamat's escape in Singapore constitute a rumor family, as all the rumors have Mas Selamat as the central subject and his escape from prison as the common antecedent. The rumors we analyze in Iraq, on the other hand, address cattle poisoning, secret operations, the purported presence of Israelis, and causes of drought; yet this collection of disparate subjects coalesces around the theme of destruction and exploitation by invading Americans. It is important to note that in an evolving narrative landscape rumors may exist independently or might exist in families or mosaics or both (fig. 1.4).

Understanding the connection between the narratological features of rumors, the master narratives they draw upon, and the broader cultural systems in which they thrive is a critical step to understanding the beliefs, perceptions, and concerns of particular communities. It is also critical to efforts to counter the strategic communication threat posed by extremist rhetoric, as well as to take advantage of the opportunities to facilitate resistant readings.

Conclusion

Rumors function in a narratological manner, intersecting with prevailing narrative systems and master narratives, and offer plausible explanations that reinforce certain ideological positions. As in the case of the prelude to the invasion of Iraq and the case of Mas Selamat in Singapore, rumors often operate in ways unrelated to extremism. Yet Islamist extremists are adept at using rumors to advance their ideology and thus their propaganda; even if only to show that a government is corrupt or foreigners are Crusaders. As the *U.S. Army/Marine Corps Counterinsurgency Field Manual* makes clear: "Insurgent organizations like al Qaeda use narratives very effectively in developing legitimating ideologies."[42] Like the U.S. and Iraqi governments, Islamist extremists are in a battle to win the "hearts and minds" of contested populations. To do so, they draw upon master narratives, archetypes, and story forms that speak directly to Muslims.

When social conditions are defined by trauma, calamity, and desperation—such as social unrest and insurgencies—Muslims are more likely to be swayed by Islamist extremist narratives in general and the rumors operating within those systems. The rumors we identified at the beginning of this chapter and discuss more rigorously in the rest of the book are not, of course, exclusively Islamist extremist stories. They are rumors out in the community. At the same time, they participate in certain narrative systems that have affinity with and help shape the extremists' ideology. Indeed, within hotly contested political terrains, from resistant groups struggling against a repressive government to outright counterinsurgencies, rumors "make sense," proliferate, and pose a threat to government institutions when they exploit shifting narratives, information gaps, and cultural fissures. They are particularly effective strategic tools in disrupting government information campaigns and advancing terrorist narratives, but can also be used to further government propaganda and strategic influence.

Rumors, we have argued, have *characters* (Noordin Top, suicide bombers, and so on) that take *actions* (terrorism) in *settings* (Indonesia). Together with already circulating master narratives (Christian Crusaders plundered Muslim wealth; Western colonizers exploited Arab resources; Mongol invaders destroyed Baghdad), rumors in the form of families and mosaics and other stories link together to form a narrative system that invokes powerful ideologies (the United States is evil, engaged in a crusade against the Arab world, and must be destroyed at all costs). In this way, then, rumors are stories that guide the reader to moral resolutions. In the case of Islamist extremists, the moral resolution is fairly clear: join the movement, expel apostates, destroy the infidels, serve Allah.

When rumors cluster into narrative systems advanced by "authorities," they are particularly persuasive. When these narrative systems draw upon master narratives, story forms, and archetypes, they can lead people to an already established and accepted resolution. When these subjective story elements come from religious texts such as the Qur'an, the story containing them often leaves Muslim audiences with two positions: submission or rebellion to Allah's will. In other words, Islamist extremist narratives often implicitly or explicitly call on followers of Islam to make sacrifices in the name of Allah in order to return Islam to a pure state and thus alignment with (the extremists' interpretation of) Allah's will. The rumors that circulate within contested Muslim populations influence the prevailing narrative landscape, and, we argue, these rumors can often influence the perception of existing narrative systems in favor of the extremist position, reshaping the narrative landscape to their advantage.

The case studies that form the remaining chapters of this book present rumors in distinct and diverse contexts. Yet the examples share important elements in that the rumors are linked to political dissonance in such a way that, explicitly or implicitly, directly or indirectly, they advance or hinder the Islamist extremist goal to govern Muslims under a fundamentalist structure. It is our hope that lessons from these three cases can be instructive when approaching similar situations in countries such as Pakistan, the Philippines, Egypt, and Palestine, among others.

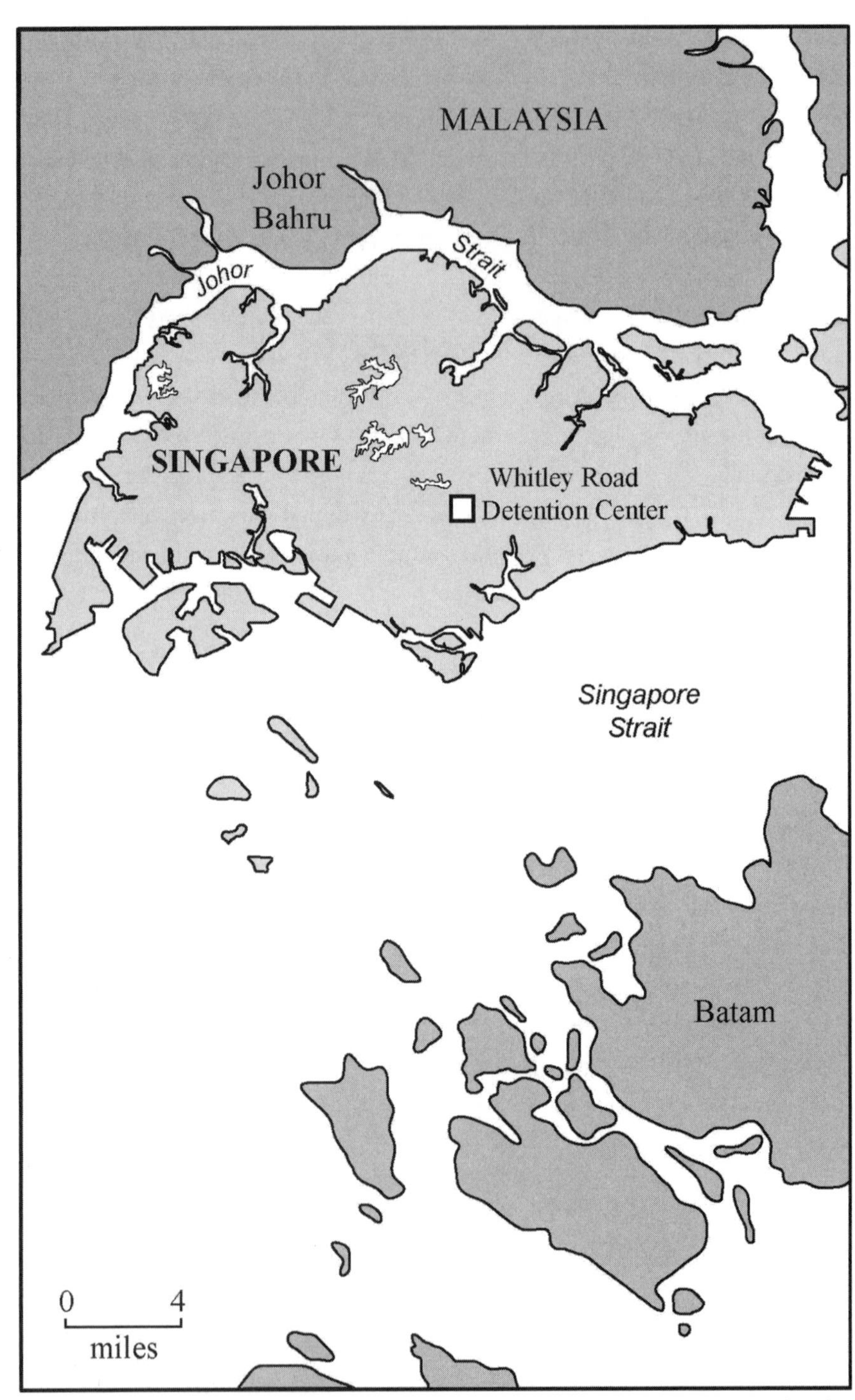
MALAYSIA
Johor
Bahru
Johor
Strait
SINGAPORE
Whitley Road
Detention Center
Singapore
Strait
Batam
0
4
miles

Becky Eden

2

Rumor Transmediation

Critical Mash-ups and a Singaporean Prison Break

For the very reason that they do express in simple and rationalized terms the uncertainties and hostilities which so many feel, rumors spread swiftly.

—Robert H. Knapp, "A Psychology of Rumor"

One interesting aspect of going viral is that when a message is forwarded, it is tacitly being endorsed by the forwarder. And when it has been forwarded by so many people, it may gain a certain degree of credibility, and in this way increase the likelihood that it will be forwarded again. "Nothing succeeds like success," and nothing gets passed on like passed-on rumors.

—Nicholas DiFonzo, *The Watercooler Effect*

On the afternoon of 27 February 2008, guards at Singapore's Whitley Road Detention Center were escorting Mas Selamat bin Kastari (Mas Selamat), one of Southeast Asia's most wanted terrorists, to the visitors' area of the center to meet with his family. Mas Selamat had been arrested two years earlier in Indonesia for using a fake identity card. He was extradited to Singapore, where he was being held without trial under the city-state's Internal Security Act, a law that gives the police and military a great deal of latitude when dealing with suspected terrorists, including the ability to hold someone without charges. Mas Selamat was suspected of leading a plot to hijack jets and fly them into targets in Singapore. He had broken out of an Indonesian prison in 2003, incurring an injury that made him limp; despite this impediment,

Singaporean authorities emphasized the threat he represented and put him in their most secure detention facility. The government had every intention of using its considerable resources to keep the elusive terrorist in custody.

As they had done during his earlier family visits, the guards at Whitley Road Detention Center brought Mas Selamat to a bathroom so that he could use the toilet and change into street clothes before meeting his relatives. Unbeknownst to his captors, the prisoner had been paying close attention to his surroundings on past trips to the bathroom and had been subtly breaking protocol—by closing the toilet stall door, for example—in order to see what he could get away with while lolling his guards into a sense of security. On this day, however, he had a more dramatic plan.

After entering the toilet stall and closing the door, he turned on the water tap and hung his pants over the stall door. He then tossed several rolls of toilet paper out of the stall window, which had no bars or lock on it, in order to cushion his fall. He climbed up and out of the window, slid down a drainpipe attached to the wall and ran across the detention center's yard. Despite his limp, he was able to escape, presumably by climbing onto a covered walkway that allowed him to jump over a fence.

Eleven minutes elapsed before the guard charged with monitoring Mas Selamat realized something was amiss and alerted superiors. Thinking that the fugitive would be found quickly near the detention center, prison officials did not notify the public for four hours. Alert Singaporeans nonetheless noted the flurry of activity in the vicinity of the detention center and blogged about it, sparking the rumors that would eventually become a kind of back channel for Singaporeans wary of official media yet interested in this important story.

Escape from the high-security detention center was previously thought impossible; Singapore prides itself on its reputation for order and is known for its zealous law enforcement. Further, the perception that Mas Selamat was such a significant threat to local and international security made his escape seem all the more fantastic. Singaporeans asked themselves how it was possible that such an important and dangerous prisoner could escape from their most secure facility. The circumstances of the escape—and the initial absence of official information—created an environment ripe for speculation; in this case, it was an ideal rumor antecedent.

One such rumor surmised that Mas Selamat had been killed in captivity and that the escape was a cover-up operation. A posting to the "Where the

Bears Roam Free" blog was typical of messages from Singaporeans both anxious and angry about the escape. The frustration of the author of the blog is palpable as he asks repeatedly how the escape could have occurred. Likening it to a Malay wayang show, in which a puppet master is behind a screen manipulating events, the blogger laments:

> I can't believe what the police is [*sic*] telling (or rather not telling) us. This is ridiculous. First, they explained that the four-hour delay in informing the public did not endanger us because he was not an imminent threat. But they then proceed to say that he is a dangerous man and even put on a global alert. . . . Damn it! Why was that info only given out now? Someone up there really, really deserves the sack now! Like I have always said, I never believed in this wayang show of fight against "terror." All this is just a show for the Singapore government to tell people that they are fighting terror, when they are completely incompetent to do so. . . . Why are they giving us information in bits and pieces? Why can't they tell us the truth, the whole truth and nothing but the truth?[1]

The comments to this post echo these pointed criticisms and speculate that Mas Selamat is already dead. A variety of seemingly logical rationales for his killing are proposed: to save money on prison expenses; the result of torture or an unknown medical condition; a covert operation by Australian special forces. In a separate post, a blogger predicted that his body would be found in a short time and that, as a result, this period of Singapore's antiterrorism fight would come to a close.

As in many highly meditated societies, the narrative landscape in Singapore is such that rumors can start, spread, and gain currency quickly. Citizens are well aware that broadcast media outlets are highly regulated and controlled by the government, resulting in a strong mistrust of mainstream television and print reporting. Add to this media environment a relatively slow response in crisis communication on the part of the government, and one can see how online rumors might seem more plausible to Singaporeans than the official news being reported or the dribble of statements released by the government. Indeed, the slow reaction of the government to the incredible escape shocked many Singaporeans, as well as foreigners.

Singapore's reputation for efficiency and order was challenged by both the facts of the escape and these rumors. In effect, these rumors operated within and disrupted Singapore's "secure state" narrative system. Along with its prominent nation-branding efforts to promote economic growth through political stability and paternal authority, Singapore is well known for what some regard as its harsh punishments for illegal activity and threats to the government. One need only think of the caning of American Michael Fay for vandalism in 1994 or the hanging of twenty-five-year-old Australian Tuong Van Nguyen in 2005 for carrying fourteen ounces of heroin into the country to recognize the stories that participate in the construction of a strongly regulated, somewhat draconian, but very secure state narrative. In the 1990s Singapore executed more people per capita than any other nation, including the United States, where the number of executions has increased dramatically over the last thirty years. Yet, unlike the United States, Singapore executes prisoners for crimes deemed less severe in other countries; trafficking in marijuana can be met with the death penalty.[2]

In addition to sanctioned executions, there have been reports of inmates dying in prisons due to inadequate access to health care, poor food, beatings by guards, and murder—all of which give some credence to the Mas Selamat death rumor. Indeed, as the case of Katu Raja shows, prisoner deaths are sometimes covered up. Raja was jailed for overstaying his visa in 2008; after collapsing on his cell floor, he was taken to a hospital, where he was declared dead. His family found out about his death via a phone call from another inmate, not from the prison or the government, thereby implicating the government in a cover-up (whether or not this charge was accurate).[3] In short, stories of harsh punishment, forceful tactics, and government duplicity in prisoner murders constitute the narrative system in which the rumors surrounding Mas Selamat would operate.

The environment in which the Mas Selamat rumors spread also grew out of mistrust of official sources and an information vacuum during a time of heightened social anxiety about terrorism. In Singapore, official sources and the mass media are at times viewed as voices of the government in an atmosphere of paternal authoritarianism and strong media controls.[4] At the same time, online media produced and consumed by everyday Singaporeans are less regulated and therefore more critical than their print or broadcast counterparts. The result is a significant amount of middle-ground, or grassroots, media content that directly or indirectly criticizes the government. We see this middle ground as the zone of contention, as counter-hegemonic, played out in narrative terms between entities committed to a particular point of view or position. In this case, the government of Singapore and its security policies stand on one side and organizations such as Jemaah Islamiyah (JI) on the other, with citizens in the middle ground. Criticism in Singapore takes many forms, from subtle venting and expressions of unease in personal blogs shared among small groups of friends to sharp-witted satire on popular websites that attract thousands of visitors a day. Because these blogs, vlogs, forums, and websites are unofficial media sources with no ties to the government, and because, in some cases, the authors of blogs know their fellow bloggers and audience in real life, there is an element of trust that is missing from encounters with official media.

These producers and consumers of online content—what new media scholars call "prosumers"—represent a significant segment of the grassroots movement in Singapore.[5] Prosumers engage in a kind of hybrid action, serving as both producers and consumers of media that result from the confluence of digital and network technologies. Unlike Iraq and Indonesia, which do not have either the economic or the technological infrastructure to support robust online activism, Singapore is a wired state in which everyday citizens can appropriate a vast library of media content, engage in interactive responses with the content and each other, and thus form a networked, online culture ripe for political discourse.[6] In fact, many Singaporean netizens are quite disparaging of the government, official media, and, as we have suggested, the circumstances surrounding Mas Selamat's escape. As such, they potentially provide a barometer for measuring support for Singapore's antiterrorism efforts.

Maintaining the support of this middle ground is crucial for these efforts. When, for example, the Singaporean government arrested members of Jemaah Islamiyah in 2001, many online prosumers lauded the action. The government's antiterrorism strategy was largely supported by its wired citizens. Although it is unlikely that many of the 2008 prosumers would consider supporting JI or other terrorist organizations, the government's delayed actions in communicating about the escape nonetheless opened a window for online citizens to link the escape of a terrorist to a critique of the government's repressive politics. The government, in effect, alienated its prosumers in a way that undermined its antiterrorist campaign.

This chapter examines the family of rumors that emerged as Singaporeans and others made sense of Mas Selamat's escape. A rumor family consists of a number of corresponding rumors that share a common subject or focus (in this case, the Mas Selamat escape) and can be traced to a common antecedent. The Mas Selamat family of rumors emerged because the official explanation and treatment of the escape challenged credulity in the minds of Singaporeans and foreigners. How was it possible that one of Southeast Asia's most notorious terrorists escaped from a maximum-security facility, especially given Singapore's reputation for order and stability? Surely, many argued, there must be some kind of alternative explanation. Netizens took on the task of creating, exchanging, and remixing their own explanations. Hence, we ask the following questions: In what ways did the reporting on the escape by official media hinder or facilitate networked responses from wired citizens? In what ways is the online content critical of the government? Do the rumors illustrate an affinity with Mas Selamat or a valorization of his terrorist persona?

To address these questions, we examine the creation and spread of rumors facilitated via emerging new and social media. We focus on prosumption, whereby rumors are appropriated, remediated, and virally disseminated across multiple media platforms.[7] We go on to discuss how rumors shape the contested information environment that marks Singapore's narrative landscape. Drawing upon the Mas Selamat case study, we examine the factors related to the mediation of breaking news stories and the cultural processes involved in the prosumption of rumors associated with one of the most important yet understudied aspects of the war on terror: finding, apprehending, and controlling the image of persons of national interest. In short, this chapter explores how online creative and versatile prosumption by non-state actors creates rumors that disrupt antiterrorism communication campaigns.

Transmediation and Virtual Resistance

Terrorism and its attendant communication efforts have moved from the fringe into mainstream daily life in recent years as governments struggle for strategic influence over insurgents and contested populations. Historically, recognition of the critical role of media in terrorism-related phenomena has focused primarily on the "theater of terror," whereby mass media amplify terror simply by reporting it to larger audiences. Secondarily, studies have focused on the so-called CNN effect in terms of the internationalization and corporatization of war journalism.[8] Attention to electronic media has shifted to a focus on the conditions surrounding warlike events, particularly fears of "netwar" via the spread of computer viruses and the eruption of cyberterrorism.[9] The recent emergence of user-generated content via participatory and social media, however, raises other significant implications for the evolving nature of mediated terrorism in general and the spread of terrorist-related rumors specifically. It allows for middle-ground participants to enter the communication fray without a heavy investment in broadcast technologies and potentially with a degree of anonymity. It represents, therefore, an opportunity for laypersons to criticize both the terrorist and the Singaporean government in the Mas Selamat case.

The effect of virtual rumors is dramatic, replete with videos, testimonials, and images with intent both to shock and to persuade. In fact, Jerrold Post, Keven Ruby, and Eric Shaw suggest that modern terrorism is information warfare, as online terrorist communications detonate “mind bombs” and “logic bombs” to further an organization’s propaganda goals.[10] As we noted in the introduction and in chapter 1, we believe that our narrative IED metaphor is consonant with this focus on information warfare, and perhaps even more apt than these other metaphors. Rumors are frequently put together with immediately available story material. Rumors blend into the narrative landscape, are often difficult to track, and can be quite damaging when they “detonate.” As stories operating in a narrative terrain, rumors compete with the stories we tell about ourselves and to one another. They are personal stories that are often saturated with fear, anxiety, and speculation. In the context of online terrorism today, which is as much about spreading ideology within a contested population as it is about instilling fear in mainstream populations and governments, rumors constitute a critical impediment to government messaging and, conversely, a potential asset to terrorist operations. As Timothy L. Thomas argues, “To jihadists, the internet is not merely a place to publish open-source material: it is a place to conduct open-source war.”[11] Given this shift toward digital platforms where extremists and sympathizers manufacture strategic narratives online, an emphasis on the virtual and viral dimensions of contemporary insurgencies and counterinsurgency studies is not only appropriate but even necessary.[12]

Yet, despite the increased attention on new media, most studies of media-related terrorism rely on an older broadcast model of direct transmission effects that is incompatible with the global and highly mediated environments that mark the twenty-first century.[13] In the traditional broadcast model, terrorism is understood as a symbolic act comprising four components: transmitter, target, message, and feedback.[14] In this model, the role of media is to coordinate the presentation of acts of terrorism as distinct spectacles. Terrorism becomes a kind of performance, a "gruesome kind of symbolic action in a complex performative field," whereby key extremist leaders assemble the more dramatic elements of terror using latent and symbolic references, including stories with actors, events, and moral endings.[15] Correspondingly, government analysts assume significant roles when terrorist activities are orchestrated and broadcast across mainstream media screens.[16] In this vein, the chief concern is the periodic but discrete application of coercion and consent by extremist insurgents on passive audiences susceptible to the aesthetics of fear that frames terror operations. Propaganda efforts by governments and extremist organizations are similarly viewed as the top-down transmission of strategic messages designed to change public opinions in a hegemonic battle to win the allegiance of contested populations.[17]

In contrast, less attention has been paid to understanding how the so-called Web 2.0, particularly social media, has facilitated changes in the nature of information warfare, altering the virtual battlefield, and how strategic narratives are constituted and spread. Understanding the changes in the narrative landscape is important for strategic communicators because the access to information afforded by new media technologies presents both opportunities and challenges to government interests. Online platforms offer opportunities for the democratization of knowledge and multiplication of sources and voices in the coverage of terrorism-related events, which may highlight aspects of truth and falsehood beyond mainstream media coverage. For example, direct reports from battlefields can disseminate via various media, from leaked photos to cell phone videos to previously unimaginable and now widespread access to media production and distribution tools such as blogs, podcasts, and YouTube videos.[18] The potential for new media to support prosumptive storytelling also allows a plethora of lay and extremist voices to construct stories that express, among other emotions, social fears and political frustrations, transforming the communication environment from one of distinct event episodes to a constant flow of transmediated images, stories, and, of course, rumors.

The Internet is an ideological force multiplier, advancing official narratives as well as rumors.[19] In the shift to user-generated content, the same people who consume what is on the Web increasingly produce it, such that traditional mass communication distinctions between producers and consumers, authors and audience, are blurred.[20] Web audiences are particularly active readers for a host of reasons, chief among them being the fact that consuming Web 2.0 also means producing Web 2.0. The creation of digital content in the contemporary theater of terror now includes new hybrid groups of prosumers, thereby facilitating individual and political awareness. Prosumers are as adept at communicating facts, falsehoods, and rumors about extremism as mainstream Singaporean media are at representing terrorist acts.

Online prosumption involves ongoing development of "unfinished" artifacts in the open information commons. Prosumers adopt and adapt content, including text, photos, and video, changing both its visual presentation and its meaning. As Henry Jenkins argues, the convergence of old and new media produces transmedia storytelling, "as consumers are encouraged to seek out new information and make connections among dispersed media content."[21] Unlike the top-down dissemination of narratives and messages found in traditional broadcasting, transmediation involves additive and iterative forms of consumption and integration of multiple media forms as audiences engage with media and with each other to create new texts—read against the dominant and dominating text—on varied media platforms. Practices of continuous development, recycling, and extension of content include forwarded email, digitally altered images, digital remixes, and video mash-ups of samples without permission from copyright holders and/or the original author(s).[22]

With the blurring of lines between traditional media and Web 2.0 technologies that enable the transmediation of images and ideas, the construction of a rumor for purposes of political intervention involves the appropriation and circulation of texts from otherwise distinct sources. These multidirectional texts become compelling ideas, catchphrases, graphics, or stories that generate virus-like imitations and reproductions that do not have to be exact in order to reinforce traditional and emerging belief systems. Like mutating chain letters, the (re)circulation of altered media stories may be conceived as a viral code that works to influence a society's agenda—particularly among online participants, who tend to connect to ideologically similar websites. The result is a kind of echo chamber that reinforces political beliefs.[23] Under wartime fears and social anxieties, transmediated stories such as rumors conceivably help some online participants protest against mainstream media practices and representations and thus vent their dissent.

The creative and resistant possibilities of this web of practices lead to different kinds of representations and truth claims. As we will show, new media content constructing the Mas Selamat escape rumors, which used satire, songs, dance, and imagery, may be especially popular in the political environment of Singapore and in the context of the battle to eliminate extremist terror. Populations in Singapore and neighboring countries question political power behind the shield of parody by producing, remixing, or sharing alternative reports involving critiques of mainstream media and the government.

Online rumor-mongers poach and recombine popular culture products, engage in negotiated readings, and thereby provide contested populations with a common knowledge framework and a space in which to engage national security issues and government politics. As James Scott argues, lay communication networks represent "weapons of the weak" under oppressive conditions of social change. Subordinate classes enact middle-ground resistance, consenting in the open and resisting online. They do not engage in open rebellion but rather fight back in prosaic and constant struggles that are not significant enough to invite state retaliation.[24] Scott's ethnographic research in Malaysia highlighted various forms of quotidian resistance, where peasants engaged in subversive practices (including rumor-mongering, character assassination, false deference, and sabotage), contested social hierarchies, and reclaimed a more acceptable and equitable equilibrium. In this way, rumors function as resistance practices that help contested populations express their frustrations and critiques without great risk to their livelihoods. Hence, in light of the potential of new media to support the transmediation of news stories and vernacular prosumption of rumors, it becomes important to understand the multiple transmediated (re)presentations of rumors, including how they unfold, connect, and spread over time, as a kind of barometer of public opinion, public support, and ideological affinity for government, antigovernment, and extremist positions.

Singapore presents an interesting social laboratory for the study of mediated rumors because the country is one of the most wired nations in the world. More than three-quarters of the population is online, with 81 percent of those households having access to the Internet and almost the same percentage using broadband and wireless connections, which are readily available throughout the island state.[25] In addition, the political environment provides a context whereby online participation plausibly serves as an outlet to resist state power and the strong, even authoritarian control of the mainstream press. The political landscape has been dominated by one-party rule and a communitarian ideology guided by economic pragmatism in the four decades since Singapore gained its independence from British rule and broke away from a brief merger with Malaysia. Although challenges for regulating media exist amid the contrary forces of an open economy and sophisticated technological developments, freedom of speech is constrained via multiple formal and informal methods, from licensing and libel laws used to stifle media content, to social pressures that reinforce Confucian cultural norms of deference to authority and respect for and loyalty to leaders.

Indrajit Banerjee and Benjamin Yeo argue that Singapore's citizens are depoliticized due to these laws and norms and other social engineering practices by the state.[26] Yet researchers have found that Singapore-based and Singapore-focused websites authored by both mainstream and fringe groups function as sites of resistance.[27] This fact raises interesting questions concerning the potential of social media practices to facilitate political debate and spur grassroots activism in an otherwise tightly controlled society. We must caution, however, that our conclusions come with some caveats concerning the reach of our research, as well as the applicability of our research to other cases. Lars Willnat and Annette Aw, for example, note that political communication research in Singapore is rare due to restricted opportunities to conduct this kind of research, and the problem is compounded by the small research community and the limited financial and institutional support from the government and the private sector.[28] Indeed, there is little research in and on Singapore that examines the role of new and social media in the construction and dissemination of rumors that parody or criticize governments in the context of national security and the war on terror.

Our analysis draws upon data collected from a triangulated methodological approach.[29] Specifically, we conducted a detailed content analysis from both scientific and humanist perspectives of multiple media materials (websites, flyers, television and newspaper reports, and social media sites) that covered Mas Selamat's escape and the subsequent hunt to re-arrest him. We undertook more than one hundred hours of ethnographic observations of online textual, audio, and visual content to reach data saturation. In order to understand how media stories about the terrorist leader spread, we viewed web pages, blogs, and forums to develop a reliable picture of the transmediation of images and ideas associated with Mas Selamat's escape. Quantitative measures, such as determining the most popular YouTube videos related to Mas Selamat, were enabled through YouTube's sorting filter. Data were acquired largely via hyperlinks provided by chronologically catalogued sources, reflecting the archival and weblike nature of electronic media. To obtain additional contextual information, we also contacted six bloggers and YouTube video creators who were key agents of prosumption, as well as academics in regional think tanks who were actively studying the communication strategies employed by the Singaporean government and its citizens. Two of the co-authors, Pauline Cheong and Chris Lundry, who are multilingual, analyzed content in English, Malay, and the local variant known as Singlish (English, Malay, Mandarin, and Hokkien words spoken according to Chinese grammar rules). In our examples, we have reproduced the original language as closely as possible and have analyzed the rumors and transmediated mash-ups via constant comparison and multiple readings of the texts.

The Mas Selamat "Escape" Narrative

The establishment of JI in the early 1990s represented a change in extremist strategy from a national resistance movement to an international organization with connections to al Qaeda. Although some groups labeled as terrorist in Southeast Asia have parochial goals, JI is heir to the Darul Islam movement that emerged in Indonesia in the 1940s and actively fought the government through the 1950s with the goal of creating an Islamic state. Many high-profile members of JI received training in Afghanistan following the 1980 Soviet invasion, including Mas Selamat.[30] In the aftermath of the 9/11 attack on the United States, JI increased its activities in Southeast Asia. There have been several attacks in Indonesia, perhaps most notably the 2002 Bali bombing that killed more than two hundred people.

In the crackdown following the Bali bombing, Indonesian authorities arrested Mas Selamat in February 2003 on immigration offenses. He served eighteen months in jail, after which he lived in Singapore but traveled throughout the region. He was arrested again in January 2006 in Java for using a fake identity card and was extradited to Singapore the following month. Authorities housed him in the maximum-security Whitley Road Detention Center without filing charges. He was accused but not charged with plotting to bomb foreign embassies and crash airliners into Singapore's Changi International Airport.

As we noted at the beginning of this chapter, roughly two years later Mas Selamat broke out of the detention center. Following the escape, Singapore tightened security in the city-state by mobilizing the Gurkhas, the govern-

POLICE NOTICE

Call 999 immediately if you see him
若你发现此人请即刻拨 999 通知警方
Telefon 999 segera jika anda melihat dia
இவரைப் பார்த்தால் உடனே 999-ஐ அழைக்கவும்

Mas Selamat bin Kastari

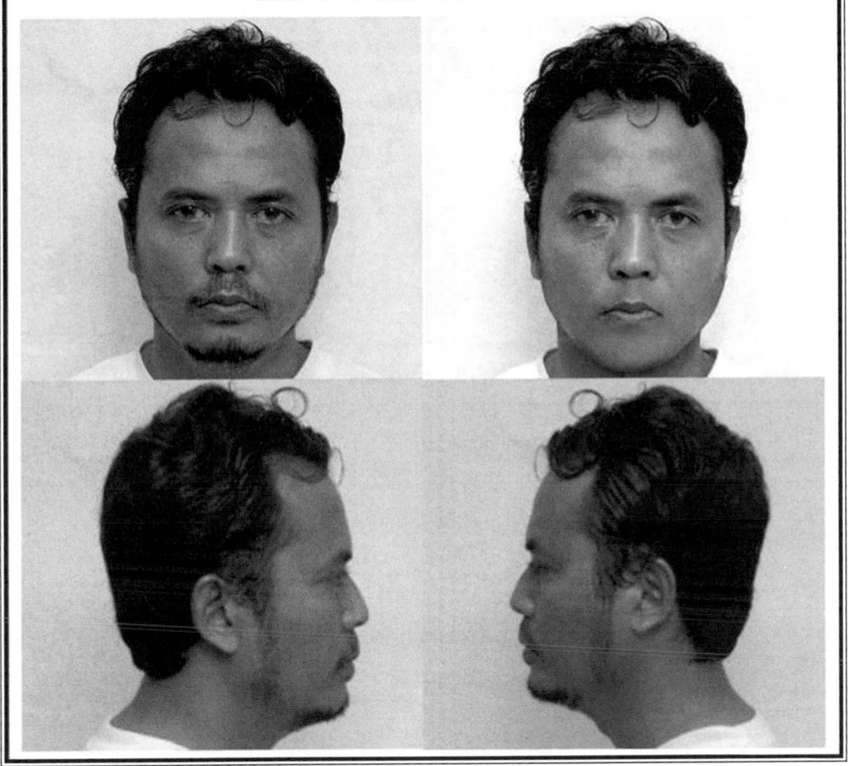

2.1. Mas Selamat bin Kastari wanted poster.
The original wanted poster was created by the Singaporean national police and circulated widely online; see, for example, http://lifeisfullofsurprises.wordpress.com/2009/05/ (accessed 6 November 2009).

2.2. One of many satirical wanted posters circulating online. Image created by TalkingCock.com: http://www.talkingcock.com/html/article.php?sid=2487 (accessed 6 November 2009).

ment's elite guard and counterterrorism force. Additionally, a navy and coast guard cordon ringed the island, and security on the bridges linking Singapore to Malaysia was increased. Singaporeans were also subjected to roadblocks and random vehicle searches. A classic version of the "wanted" poster appeared on light posts at street intersections, in bus and train stations, and in traditional print and broadcast media (see figure 2.1). Yet Mas Selamat was deft enough to flee Singapore and evade arrest for more than a year, even though a cash reward of S$1 million (US $717,000) was offered for information leading to his capture.

Malaysian police eventually arrested him in Johor Baharu on 1 April 2009. In the fall of 2010 he was held under Malaysia's Internal Security Act in a detention center in Kamunting, Perak. He was subsequently handed over to Singaporean authorities toward the end of September 2010. At the time of this writing (spring 2011), three of his relatives have been convicted in court and sentenced to jail for harboring the terrorist leader and aiding his escape from Singapore to Malaysia.[31]

The escape of Mas Selamat is the most sensational story in the recent history of the Singaporean government's attempts to identify and eliminate terrorism within its borders and throughout the Southeast Asia region more generally. Despite the terrorist leader's relatively low profile prior to his escape, he became the leading news story in Singapore following his escape.[32] In other words, the escape and the government's actions afterward turned this would-be terrorist into an international star.

It took the Singaporean police four hours to make an official announcement of Mas Selamat's escape through online and broadcast media. Whether the government was trying to stave off panic or was overconfident in its ability to capture him, four hours is very long time—especially in a wired country like Singapore. In four hours Mas Selamat could have left the small city-state, contacted colleagues, and found a hiding place in Malaysia or Indonesia. As revealed in November 2010, Mas Selamat stayed with family members in Singapore, who aided his subsequent escape to Malaysia. This revelation spurred another series of embarrassing questions for the government.[33]

Singaporeans were exhorted to be on the lookout for Mas Selamat and to contact the police if they saw him; they were given information regarding his clothes, his limp, and the disguises he might adopt. Reflecting the region's ethno-linguistic mix, these messages were published in English, Chinese, Tamil, and Malay, Singapore's official languages, and later in Thai, Bangladeshi, and Burmese to appeal to migrant workers. Three days after the escape, Singtel, M1, and Starhub, the three telecommunications companies in Singapore, sent multimedia messages to 5.5 million mobile phone users with a wanted picture of the escapee.[34] The words and images associated with these official media regarding the escape became the basis for the prosumption of subsequent rumors (see figure 2.2).

News of Mas Selamat's escape and the wanted poster were also distributed internationally. Authorities in Singapore's closest neighbors, predominantly Muslim Indonesia and Malaysia, distributed posters in bus terminals, airports, and ports. The day after his escape, Interpol (the International Criminal Police Organization) issued an Orange Notice (an urgent worldwide security alert), sent electronically to its 188 member countries with details of the escape. On 2 March the alert was upgraded to red (arrest on sight, approved for extradition) because in the three days since his escape he could have left not only Singapore but also the region.

In the days following the escape, most official local news outlets, such as the *Straits Times*, downplayed the details of the escape and emphasized the continuing search for the terrorist. Mas Selamat was portrayed as an imminent threat to both the city-state and its citizens. News coverage shifted the threat perception from the potential for large-scale acts of terror, such as the bombing of international embassies or Changi Airport, to individual acts of criminality. For example, television news featured interviews (later posted to YouTube) with residents who expressed fear that the accused terrorist would break into their homes. Minister Lim Swee Say described the incident as a test in "inter-racial cohesion" that Singaporeans passed with an "A+."[35] Public calls for the resignation of Wong Kan Seng, the Minister for Home Affairs and Deputy Prime Minister, were muted or non-existent in mainstream media. But amid increasing online demands for resignations of those in charge of Mas Selamat's detention, Minister Mentor Lee Kwan Yew agreed that complacency among security staff led to the escape. At the same time, he stressed that all Singaporeans were in a way culpable and could learn a lesson from the episode.[36] The government wanted all attention focused on Mas Selamat and the apparent threat he posed to individual citizens rather than on the escape itself and the failure to keep him in prison. This attempt to control the narrative surrounding the escape was successful in official media but failed in unofficial online media, allowing the latter to become the source of alternative news for Singaporean netizens and also allowing the spread of unsubstantiated rumors that altered the escape narrative in ways the government feared.

Online rumors posted on multiple blogs and social media sites focused on alternative explanations behind Mas Selamat's "miraculous" escape from Singapore's most secure and feared detention facility. In addition to the rumor that he had been killed in captivity and that the escape was an attempted cover-up, several others circulated. Some suggested that he was allowed to escape so that he could be followed and lead law enforcement to more JI members. Others argued he was still in captivity and this was some kind of civil defense test. A particularly popular rumor suggested that Arab supporters of JI and al Qaeda had paid bribes to secure his release. Another rumor suggested that the escape was meant to divert people's attention away from a looming budget crisis. One rumor posited an agreement between Mas Selamat and the Singaporean leadership: he would be freed, but only if he promised never to return to Singapore. And others said the infamous terrorist leader used some kind of black magic (*ilmu tinggi*) to escape.[37]

Rumors also circulated about his fate after the escape. Some speculated that he was hiding in Singapore with members of a JI cell. Others posited that he had escaped to Malaysia or Indonesia. And still others had him hiding out in a forest and foraging for food and shelter. These rumors all had some degree of local plausibility, which is essential if a rumor is going to stick with a population, and constituted a rumor family that generated furious activity in the days and weeks following the escape.

On 28 February, American resident and Singaporean dissident blogger Gopalan Nair asserted that an escape from Whitley Road was impossible, that there must be an alternative explanation. He surmised that Mas Selamat must have had help and that the escape was almost certainly financed by "the Arabs" and enabled by Singaporean corruption.[38] This story is consistent with Nair's unrelenting portrayal of Singapore as a kind of banana republic, with corruption tainting even the highest levels of government. Comments on the post echo both this rumor and the rumor that Mas Selamat was killed in captivity.[39] Implicit in this rumor and the many like it is a damning critique of the government as incompetent and hypocritical. Online comments on various forums, for example, called for an overhaul of the prison surveillance systems and the resignation of key government ministers, who were criticized as being negligent and incompetent in both the search for Mas Selamat and the maintenance of national security.

In light of the paucity of information put out by Singapore's mainstream media regarding the escape itself, the creation and spread of rumors inside and outside Singapore served to fill critical information gaps with otherwise plausible explanations. Media reports for the first week were silent on how such a dangerous detainee escaped from custody. As Cherian George notes, the shallow coverage made any attempt to follow the mainstream media "frustrating and farcical"; even international news sources reported on the knowledge gaps on the key question of how Mas Selamat escaped. According to George, "The Associated Press news agency quoted the brief Ministry of

Home Affairs statement about in the third paragraph of its report, adding immediately after, 'It did not say how he escaped.' Similarly, Canada's CBC said in the third paragraph of its report, 'the statement did not say how he escaped.'"[40] The *New York Times* stated that "Singapore has one of the tightest security systems in the world, and the government gave no details on how he escaped."[41]

Other international news sources further fueled speculation by publishing rumors online. For example, *Kompas*, an Indonesian broadsheet, posted stories speculating that Mas Selamat was killed by Singaporean security forces before the news of his escape, thus suggesting the escape story was concocted as a cover-up. Another said that he had been secretly extradited to the United States (as fellow JI member Hambali had been, following his arrest in Thailand). Yet another rumor claimed that he was selling noodles in Riau Province near Singapore. Finally, a rumor said and that he had reconnected with other terrorists, including Noordin Top. These rumors formed a rumor family that indirectly served the interest of JI and the disinterest of the government. Aside from the clear danger presented by the possibility of Mas Selamat rejoining his terrorist comrades, the rumor of him as a noodle seller—a common and mundane job, but also a very public one—undermines the credibility of the Singaporean and Indonesian police in their effort to locate him.

The conspiratorial charge of this rumor family served as a sense-making device for netizens interested in how and why Mas Selamat escaped. The rumors that the terrorist possessed extraordinary strength and magical powers may seem absurd and tenuous, yet these rumors were prolific on multiple media platforms and also appealed to the imagination and fears of a citizenship searching for explanations within an information vacuum. And among many local Malays—and some Chinese and Tamil residents—belief in the supernatural and the magical is not uncommon.

Rumor texts in this case were multimodal. Using material from popular films such as *The Limping Man, V for Vendetta, Transformers, Catch Me If You Can, Crouching Tiger, Hidden Dragon,* and *Escape from Alcatraz,* bloggers created a narrative pastiche (for examples, see figures 2.3 and 2.4).[42] The use of these movies not only grounded the fugitive story in popular stories but also implicitly linked Mas Selamat to plot structures featuring an archetypal and righteous, but persecuted, protagonist. In *The Limping Man,* for example, an American veteran with a limp (Lloyd Bridges) is wrongly suspected of murder

2.3. Mas Selamat becomes a hero of popular culture.
Original creator unknown; image found on 6 November 2009 at http://xmercenaries.com/four9er/wp-content/uploads/2008/03/catchmeifyoucan2002moviez1.jpg.

2.4. Another transformation of Mas Selamat into a popular hero.
Created by Miss Loi (screen name); found online at the Joss Sticks blog: http://www.exampaper.com.sg/study-break/crouching-terrorist-leaping-maiden (accessed 23 November 2009).

in England, questioned by Scotland Yard, and then subjected to surveillance while he tries to clear his name. By associating Mas Selamat—a man with a limp who has been subject to state surveillance for nearly a decade—with a sympathetic film character, this rumor family valorizes Mas Selamat and elides his criminal past. In *V for Vendetta* (based loosely on the story of Guy Fawkes), the protagonist commits acts of terror against an unjust state in the name of fomenting a revolt. Notably, in *Transformers* and *Crouching Tiger, Hidden Dragon,* the protagonists possess superpowers that allow them to morph physically and perform gravity-defying feats in their resistance to evil persecutors.

As our examples might suggest, prosumers consumed the news and rumors regarding Mas Selamat and linked them to popular films in order to produce subversive mash-ups that conveyed rumor material and meaning that implicitly connected Mas Selamat's escape to a story form of righteous victory and deliverance. Instead of being tainted as the enemy of the state, Mas Selamat is glorified as a hero battling the government and international security systems. And like rumors, these transmedia texts took on lives of their own, spreading rapidly, albeit electronically, beyond word of mouth.

Games were also part of the story's transmediation. On 18 March, Pac-Mat, a parody of the arcade game Pac-Man, was created for online visitors to the website TalkingCock.com (figure 2.5).[43] Consonant with the mercurial nature of prosumption, Pac-Mat was later upgraded to version 2.0 with added levels of difficulty, reflecting breaking news of more targeted searches for Mas Selamat. As of this writing, the site had received more than 16,250 hits.[44] In the game, the player controls Mas Selamat's movements around a maze of rewards and obstacles as he tries to avoid capture by police, military personnel, Gurkhas, and ministers of state. In a surprising twist, his disguises change with every level of the game to reflect rumors surrounding his disappearance, such as his hiding in plain sight as a noodle (*mee*) seller. Through interactive gaming, the search for Mas Selamat takes on added layers of meaning via "cultural reproduction,"[45] as media consumers are placed in the fugitive's position and learn rules that contain direct and oblique references to rumors embedded in alternative interpretations of this conflict.

Beyond the inventive and humorous elements of prosumer remixes like these, rumor texts concerning the incredible triumph of Mas Selamat over the massive security and military capabilities of the state connect to the familiar core message in narratives featuring heroes who achieve victory in

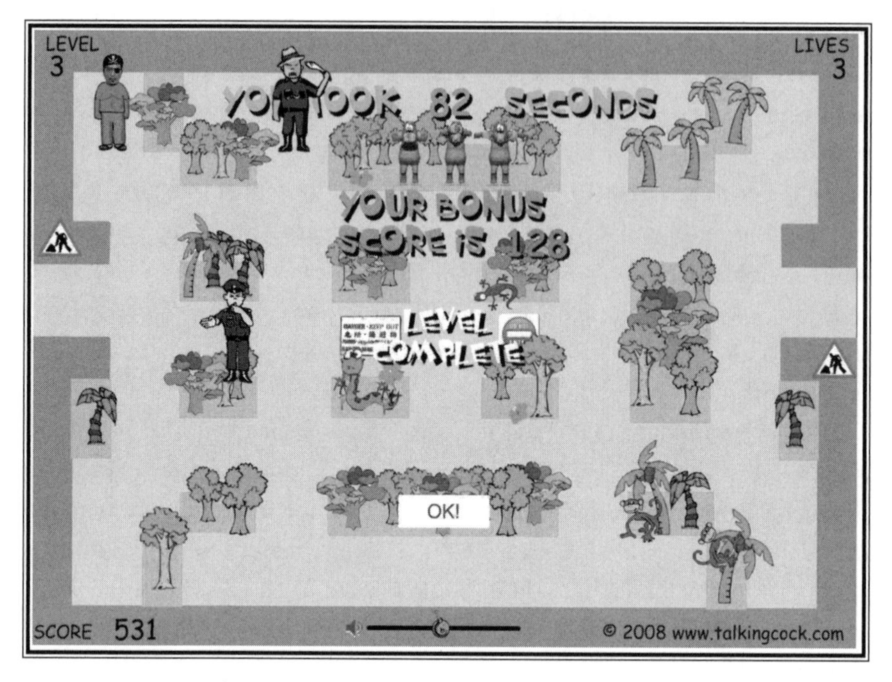

2.5. Mas Selamat as Pac-Man and Singapore government officials as the hapless ghosts. Screen grab of the Pac-Mat game created by TalkingCock.com and found at http://www.talkingcock.com/html/games/pacmat.html (accessed 12 November 2009).

battle against all odds. In this case, texts featuring his hero status invoke the story form of a miraculous victory, which echoes a master narrative in Islamic history that is familiar to most Muslims in the region. In the Battle of Badr the Prophet Muhammad led a small and ill-equipped army of some three hundred Muslim believers against a superior army of one thousand pagan warriors from the city of Mecca. Miraculously, with the aid of Allah and His angels, Muhammad's small army defeated the pagans and their false gods. Here, the significance of Mas Selamat's escape is amplified via these connections to larger miraculous narratives in religious literature as well as popular culture, which may explain the fast transmission of his story across various media platforms in a culture familiar with these master narratives and story forms.

With direct implication for government credibility, rumors making up the escape mosaic included attempts to construct demeaning allegations to tarnish the reputations of the state's agents, including the integrity of ministers of state. It appeared that the official version of Mas Selamat's story was difficult for many Singaporeans and others in the region to swallow, as calls for the resignation of Deputy Prime Minister and Minister of Home Affairs Wong Kan Seng percolated on the Internet. Beginning the day of the escape, bloggers wrote much more critically than official media about the escape. Before the day had ended, the story was spreading virally, with commentators questioning the official version of events, countering it with their own versions, and calling for Wong's resignation because of his negligence and incompetence. For example, several bloggers agreed that leaving security up to the police, the military, and the *gahmen* (government) was a mistake.[46] Some commented that the escape was an inside job and that Mas Selamat received help from the security forces. Comments in some blog posts ratcheted up the rhetoric and surmised that a Jemaah Islamiyah sleeper cell was hiding in the Singaporean government.[47] Other bloggers volunteered to quit their jobs and look for the terrorist themselves in return for the minister's million-dollar paycheck. These rumors function as resistance tactics that rest upon character assassinations of political leaders. They use exaggerations to defame public authorities and present an unflattering picture of the state and its lax security systems. And while they denigrate the state and its leaders, they provide fodder to the rumor-mongers intent on censuring state authorities.

In addition to the blogosphere, YouTube quickly became a hub for the prosumption of Mas Selamat rumors. Almost immediately after broadcast, clips of television newscasts covering the escape were posted to YouTube, a practice that continued for several months. In a week's time, streaming video creations, including parodies of these news clips, were being created and disseminated by prosumers in Singapore, the Southeast Asian region, and farther abroad. Table 2.1 presents a snapshot of the ten most-watched YouTube videos according to their content and the number of views and comments, which illustrates the diffusion of these videos (as shown by shared links and rising numbers of hits on YouTube videos). For instance, numerous videos were created by prosumer Abelislove. His videos, also posted on his blog, portrayed Mas Selamat as disguising himself in multiple forms to escape: as toilet paper, as a cat afraid of dogs, as a street dancer, as a gay man escaping to reunite with his lover, and as a snake dancer. In making these (and other videos), Abelislove propelled the rumor mill into the fantastic, where the line between a rational/psychological explanation for unusual events competes

Table 2.1. Top Ten YouTube videos and Prosumption Artefacts Related to Mas Selamat (as of January 2011)

Rank	*Title*	*Creator*	*Date*	*No. of views*	*No. of comments*	*Theme*
1	Mas Selamat Kastari —Toilet Escape Video	Abelislove	3/2/08	171,279	273	Humor: MSK target of parody
2	Mas Selamat Kastari —Street Dancer	Abelislove	3/2/08	65,112	123	Humor: MSK target of parody
3	The Mas Selemat Story	Singapore-democrats	3/21/08	48,198	100	Criticism; Opposition party mocks government
4	Mas Selamat Kastari —Confession of a Terrorist	Abelislove	3/1/08	42,023	137	Humor: MSK target of parody
5	Mas Selamat was last seen wearing this	Huaqing	3/4/08	32,277	82	Rebroadcast of *Straits Times* news
6	Manhunt Day 2 —SAF join police to search for JI escapee	Huaqing	2/28/08	26,930	137	Rebroadcast of *Straits Times* news
7	Mas Selemat —How he hurt his leg	Abelislove	3/4/08	23,225	35	Humor: MSK target of parody
8	Escaped Singapore Terrorist by Hot CNA Reporter	Foodmore	2/27/08	22,841	61	Rebroadcast of New Asia
9	Mas Selamat Kastari —Short video taken by inmate	Abelislove	3/2/08	21,933	20	Humor: MSK target of parody
10	Mas Selemat —Fear of dogs	Abelislove	3/2/08	19,313	65	Humor: MSK target of parody

with a supernatural explanation, generating confusion on the part of the reader.[48] The corpus of mash-up videos focusing on Mas Selamat's escape offers the range of explanations and allows viewers to decide their own attitudes, shaped by their reactions to the visualizations.

Prosumers also spread rumors by commenting on emerging media content as the story was retold through songs broadcast online. For example, the "Mas Selamat Song (Where Did You Go)" was posted twenty-four days after the escape as a karaoke video with original song lyrics that reflected current events, speculations, and rumors, all accompanied by official images of Mas

Selamat. This remix was popular (more than 14,200 views), but the comments on it reflected a wide spectrum of opinions, including broader criticism of the Singaporean government, insults directed at Singaporeans (some of which were later flagged as spam and removed), tributes to people who spread the word of the escape, insults and praise directed at the escapee and even to other posters, bloggers, and content creators. For example, commenter pigchopp heaps vitriol on Singaporean citizens, the government, and the "Mas Selamat Song (Where Did You Go)" songwriter Greywolf8029: "Grey, u are a no life noob faggito down in the faggito hole. Go crawl back there. Mas Selamat owns, he and his muslim suicide bombers will own Singapore and you F@GITOTS!!!!!!!!!!"[49]

These posts demonstrate not only the varied opinions Singaporeans had concerning the escape and the responsibility of the authorities, but also the international attention attracted by the escape rumor family. Some Malaysians and Indonesians feel targeted by Singaporeans for being poorer or less developed, or for their countries' internal political and social problems, and the escape provided a means for them to strike back. Thus the responses also demonstrate the unpredictable nature of transmediation and the ability of prosumers to shift the topic in myriad ways.

Conclusion

This chapter contributes to a broader understanding of the social and political implications of new media for strategic communication and social influence in the contemporary battle over contested populations. Changing Web 2.0 conditions, we argue, are now such that strategic communication related to terrorism is not primarily just a struggle between nation-states managing their media and influence.

Indeed, our analysis of the Mas Selamat case suggests that mediated conflicts can be further understood in terms of prosumption practices among contested populations, embedded in geopolitical vulnerabilities and dependencies. The case of Mas Selamat gives an account of the conflict between political elites, official media representatives, and lay publics over the disputed developments, rumors, and alternative interpretations of the escape of a key terrorist in Southeast Asia. As the bulk of research on the mediatization of war has largely represented views from the West, this chapter contributes to data on mediated rumor mosaics and communicative conflict from a non-Western perspective.[50]

Instead of outright protest, prosumption activities demonstrate play with mainstream texts (news broadcasts and popular films, for example) in the creation of alternative texts that incorporate cultural icons, Internet memes, and rumors. These alternative media texts express critical communication and yet exist within unobjectionable bounds, a communication zone where authors are not easily found or held accountable and punished for their digital remixes. Contemporary media technologies allow citizens in the middle ground, those without the power to affect state action or government-approved media production directly, to mash up mainstream content with creative contributions and generate resistance messages. Amid state strategies and civic militarization, these forms of resistance serve various tactical communication goals to mock public officials, raise public consciousness about failed national security politics, and entertain and persuade participants to alternative ideologies. In a context where official media are silent or lack credibility, the transmediation of rumors allowed alternative speculations to enter into sociopolitical discourse, opening up possibilities for the public expression of social anxieties. In this case, blogs that disseminated rumors of Mas Selamat were not just disruptive tactics but also a means of collective sense-making and coping, given the limitations of mainstream media reports. Greg Dalziel also argues that rumors surrounding the Mas Selamat case reflected how Singaporeans came together in narrative sense-making amid pervasive ambiguity, which is "a testament, perhaps, to the cohesiveness of Singaporean society and the strong sense of national identity."[51] He suggests that a moderate amount of rumor-mongering may be useful to build social trust and civic participation, in this case to raise awareness of terrorism collectively as well as draw attention to the perceived mismanagement of a national crisis by the government.

Our study also extends the accompanying concept of transmediation (more commonly associated with the merchandising and branding of popular media content) to critical grassroots responses toward terrorism. In addition to news coverage, as we have shown, the Internet was utilized to support the transmediation of rumors to fill information gaps and obliquely voice social critique. This study not only showed the methods by and through which terrorist-related images and ideas are appropriated and subverted by lay commentators, but also revealed the chronological development and social conditions in which these messages gained traction. Although the full extent of transmediation practices was impossible to ascertain, these results suggest that computer-mediated communication can act as unofficial "digital backchannels" in the information arena of terrorism.[52] Digital backchannels, like online rumors, serve to fill a gap in an immediate information vacuum following a crisis. Their influence is apparent in a man-hunting event like the Mas Selamat case because social media interactions often leave digital traces that persist and diffuse in the public sphere, as evident in the prosumption texts that can be retrieved from YouTube and blogs months after the terrorist's escape.

The longevity and long tail of prosumption texts is further evidenced by the increased views of these YouTube videos and blogs after the November 2010 investigations revealed the collaboration of Mas Selamat's relatives in his escape. Mainstream news reported that the terrorist was sheltered in his brother's home and, interestingly, highlighted how his niece also assisted him by destroying his clothing, applying makeup, and securing a headscarf (*tudung*) to disguise him as a woman. Critiques by netizens quickly appeared online, in many cases reviving rumors associated with Mas Selamat's feminine disguise and the mistakes committed by the relevant security agencies. For instance, Muhammad Hydar questioned why local authorities could not have disguised themselves "with brightly dyed hair and skinny jeans to blend in" with the crowds in their hunt for Mas Selamat and further demanded that the minister and relevant agencies disclose more information on the latest investigation of the escape, including "the exact shade of lipstick" used by Mas Selamat.[53] Fresh prosumption texts have also circulated on blogs, including a comic strip that illustrated the different approaches of the Singaporean government ("Comb the jungles") and three counterterrorist experts ("Check his family").[54]

A related implication of the ability of new media to generate critiques and pose challenges for counterinsurgency and diplomatic efforts is its capability to network multiple actors to facilitate immediate as well as long-term social change. Prosumption rumor texts became inspirations for others, so that organic reproductions of these texts became more resistant to attempted censorship of online media spaces. Evidence of online collaboration among prosumers was found as bloggers appropriated elements from other sites. As such, dynamic production and reception processes aided the "spreadability of values," to gain "greater resonance in the culture, taking on new meanings, finding new audiences, attracting new markets, and generating new values."[55] Because video remixes with political themes draw upon popular

2.6. Mas Selamat mashed up with a television tale of wrongful imprisonment and ingenious escape. Image created by SimplyJean (screen name) and available at http://blog.simplyjean.com/2008/02/29/toilet-break-4-mas-limping-terrorist-selamat/ (accessed 6 November 2009).

cultural referents, they can significantly alter the ways in which people perceive and remember public authorities and events. For instance, Minister Wong Kan Seng was renamed "Wong Can't Sing," which taints his credibility as a senior leader of homeland security. Furthermore, the "Toilet Break" image created by SimplyJean the day after the escape (figure 2.6) has become indelibly associated with the Mas Selamat escape through its viral spread online and its eventual coverage in the mainstream media.[56] In this way, the prosumption of terrorism-related stories points to its possible impact on perceptions of terrorists and state agents among citizens of a nation-state, its diasporic community, and its international allies.

Apart from being expressions of resistance, online remixes have growing functional importance for strategic communication even as computer-mediated communication has increased the complexity and informal nature of cross-cultural exchanges. Government-supported agents seeking to understand public sentiment toward the nation-state could look to new media and mediated rumors as a strategic indicator for prevailing social anxieties as they implement cultural diplomacy and prescribe appropriate counter-insurgency solutions. Indeed, the Mas Selamat case appeared on various web-sites, including terrorist or Islamist media. Two days after the escape, Indonesian blogger Abu Bakr praised the escape as good news for "lovers of jihad" and called for prayers to aid in his escape from the "dogs of the Singaporean government":

> All praise to God, thanks be to God, chant to God our brother Mas Selamat Kastari has gloriously freed himself from the grip of the Singaporean police yesterday afternoon. The country that often beats its chest with pride with its sophisticated technology and its tight security has been crippled with the head of Jemaah Islamiyah Singapore who has been said to walk with a limp.[57]

The Indonesian website Ar-Rahmah, the owner of which was recently found guilty of charges that he sought funding for the JI terrorists responsible for the 2009 Jakarta bombings (and his father was a mentor to Mas Selamat), published a story five days after the escape noting the international ridicule that Singapore faced, including the online parodies. In an article entitled "The Insolence of Singapore Becomes Explosive Material," author "Fadly" quotes Singaporean blogger Philip Chua: "no prisoners have escaped from terrorist prisons in the West or at Guantanamo, much less one implicated as the leader of a terrorist network active in a neighboring country."[58] These examples show how grassroots remixes are given credence by terrorist sympathizers, who framed the escape as a victory for their cause and a defeat for the unjust Singaporean government and enemies of Islam. A better understanding of prosumption practices may give law enforcement and governments the ability to react and restore their credibility by countering these messages. For this reason, Steven Marks, Thomas Meer, and Matthew Nilson propose that government agencies should supplement their use of classified information with open-source information online as actionable intelligence.[59] Seen in this light, the multidimensional digital rumor mill should prompt further research in strategic influence and payoffs at the micro level as well as in popular culture's ability to shape perceptions and credibility of nation-states in the ideational struggles to mobilize popular support in today's increasingly mediated environment.

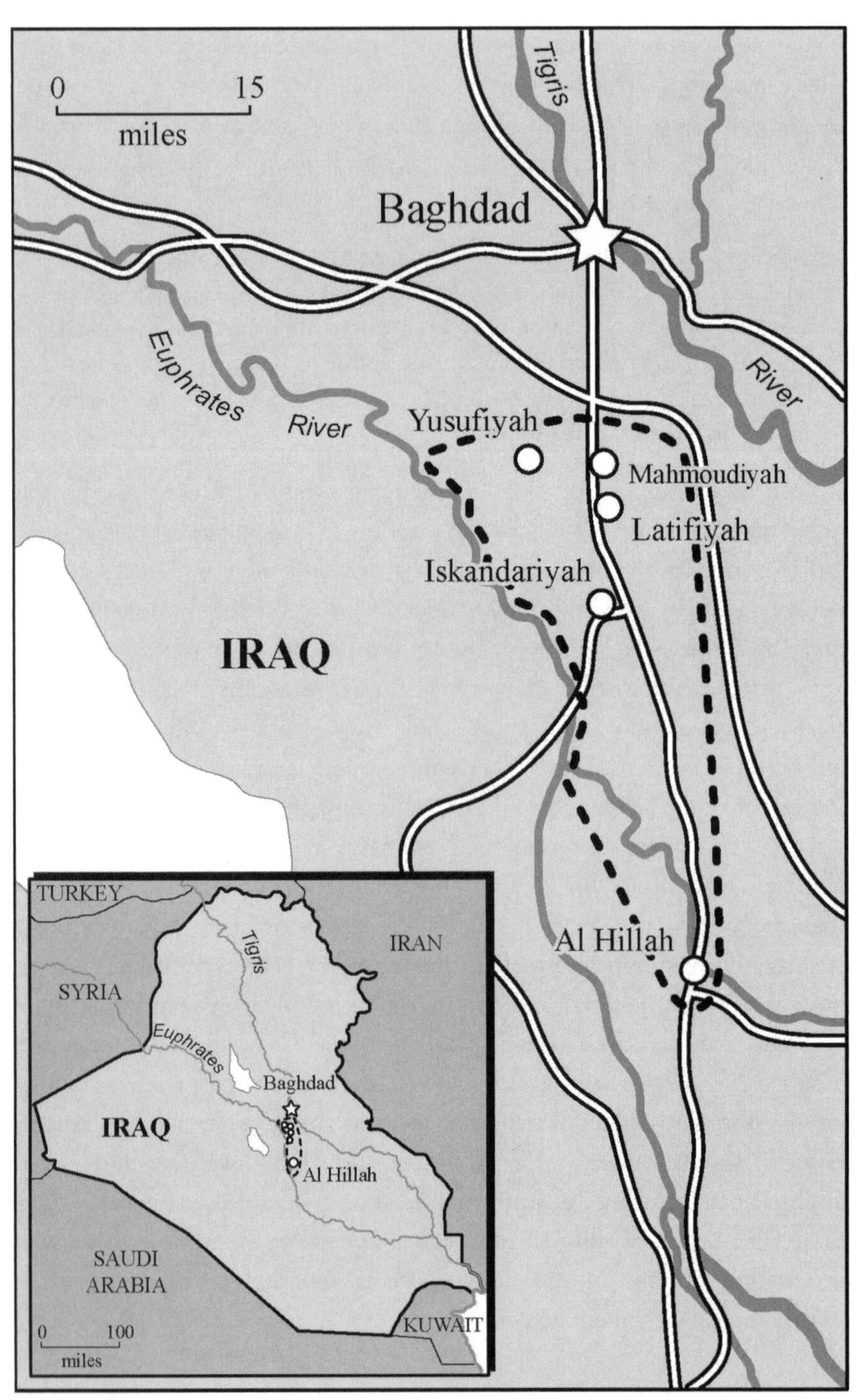
0
15
miles
Tigris
Baghdad
Euphrates
River
River
Yusufiyah
Mahmoudiyah
Latifiyah
Iskandariyah
IRAQ
Al Hillah
TURKEY
IRAN
SYRIA
Tigris
Euphrates
Baghdad
IRAQ
Al Hillah
SAUDI
ARABIA
KUWAIT
0
100
miles

Becky Eden

3

Rumor Mosaics

Counterinsurgency Operations in Iraq's Triangle of Death

The first, the supreme, the most far-reaching act of judgment that the statesman and commander have to make is to establish . . . the kind of war on which they are embarking; neither mistaking it for, nor trying to turn it into, something that is alien to its nature. This is the first of all strategic questions and the most comprehensive.

—Carl von Clausewitz, *On War*

Insurgent organizations like al Qaeda use narratives very effectively in developing legitimating ideologies.

—U.S. Army/Marine Corps Counterinsurgency Field Manual

In 2005, Multi-National Force–Iraq (MNF-I), the military command overseeing U.S. and coalition forces in the war-torn Arab nation, began a bovine inoculation campaign to improve the health of cattle throughout Iraq.[1] Although the intent was to stabilize the food supply and increase the return on investment for local cattle ranchers and dairy farmers, the inoculation program was also a key element of an information operation to counter insurgent violence and propaganda. At this stage of the war effort, the insurgents, who were mostly foreign jihadists, Ba'ath Party loyalists, and disgruntled Iraqi soldiers, had severely degraded counterinsurgency communication efforts by U.S., coalition, and Iraqi forces. These measures ranged from early information campaigns designed to portray U.S. and coalition forces as liberators to later efforts at building consensus and support among the civilian population for the nascent Iraqi government. MNF-I was seeking ways not only to defeat the insurgents in battle but also to overcome the political mindset that interpreted insurgent activities as beneficial and MNF-I actions as detrimental to the well-being of local and regional populations. The vaccination campaign was a key pillar in what amounted to a narrative countermeasure attached to a civil affairs operation.

Yet soon after the inoculation campaign began, a rumor spread throughout Iraq that the Americans had embarked on a sinister plot to starve the Iraqi populace by poisoning livestock.[2] The conspiratorial charge and dramatic structure of this rumor appealed more to imagination and fear than to thoughtful reflection and questioning at a time when official news sources inside Iraq were either silent or lacked credibility. Indeed, for farmers already wary of the U.S. and coalition presence, wracked by fear of societal and political instability, and suffering livestock losses to disease and a rapidly dwindling water supply, the bovine poisoning rumor explained the deaths of the herds, predicted future loss and gloom, and linked the cause of the their current woes to the U.S. invasion and occupation. It provided a target for pent-up frustration, anxiety, and fear that led some farmers to turn a blind eye to insurgent activities and others to participate in violence. MNF-I's information operation and civil affairs mission backfired. The insurgents gained narrative ground at a critical juncture in the war effort.

The bovine poisoning rumor posed a local challenge for counterinsurgency and diplomatic forces in the area. At the same time, it dovetailed with three other rumors: (1) American helicopters cause more and larger debilitating sandstorms by kicking up enormous amounts of dust; (2) American forces and weapon systems contribute to the drought by using up water reserves and by creating sandstorms; and, most important, (3) America invaded the country to steal Iraq's oil. By linking with other rumors concerning the environment, the bovine poisoning rumor advanced the widely held belief that the United States cared little for the Iraqi people and had invaded Iraq to exploit its natural resources. Seen in this light, this cluster of rumors posed not only a local threat to a civil affairs outreach effort but also a larger geopolitical—and hence strategic communication—challenge for the U.S. and Iraqi governments.

Given the everyday violence Iraqis experienced after the U.S. invasion, the explanation implicit in the bovine poisoning and associated rumors was plausible and even rational. With the country's political, economic, and

3.1. Rumors rampant in the local populace claimed that U.S. helicopters created additional dust storms. U.S. Navy photo by Mass Communication Specialist 1st Class Jackey Bratt.

physical infrastructure decimated in the aftermath of "shock and awe," two significant factors led to these rumors making sense: first, recent experience had created a population filled with anxiety over safety, access to resources, and economic stability; second, official and trustworthy communication keeping the populace informed about government progress was inconsistent to non-existent. In this anxiety-ridden information vacuum, the story presented by the bovine poisoning rumor made sense: *U.S. forces in Iraq are engaged in a crusade, destroying our land and livelihood, and something, even violence, has to be done to stop it lest our families go hungry and our country fall permanently into the hands of infidels.* Ground truth gave way to grounded lies, impeding reconstruction efforts in the battle to win the support of contested populations such as rural farmers and Iraqi civilians more generally. In short, an otherwise local rumor with relative plausibility rushed into a knowledge gap during a period of extreme violence and political uncertainty, became linked to an array of existing rumors about U.S. forces and intentions, capitalized on a lack of official information, and, in the end, provided a means to express and inflame local, national, and regional fears and frustrations.

Often dismissed as unimportant or even silly by many U.S. and allied commanders and government officials, rumors represent significant obstacles and raise several fundamental questions for counterinsurgency operations. In what ways do rumors indicate or predict rising social unrest and violence? In what ways are rumors susceptible to insurgent manipulation and propaganda? How do rumors that, on their face, seem too fantastic to be credible nonetheless gain traction among a contested population and, in the process, lend credibility to insurgent propaganda? Finally, how can strategic communicators achieve their tactical and strategic goals in a communication landscape besieged by rumors that appear rational to contested populations?

In this chapter we offer an analysis of rumor mosaics—the interlocking systems of related rumors that function to support broader cultural narratives—that were circulating in Iraq and most notably in the famed "Triangle of Death" in 2009.[3] Unlike a rumor family, where all participating rumors share a common subject and antecedent (such as the Mas Selamat escape), rumor mosaics are composed of a diverse, seemingly unconnected number of rumors that do not share a single antecedent. Mosaics are formed when otherwise diverse rumors cluster around and end up advancing narratives that are widely understood by a specific community. When forming to advance a master narrative, and particularly the master narratives linked to Islamist extremism, rumor mosaics end up appealing to local interests in a way that impacts geopolitical goals. In the case of Iraq, some of the rumors Stephanie Kelley identified in 2005 (see below) and those that constitute our case study in 2009 leverage and propel the Crusade and colonization master narratives, thereby positioning the United States as a Christian force interested in converting the country in its image (democracy) while pillaging its resources (oil). The master narratives also position the participants in the nascent Iraqi government as hypocrites, thereby adding a considerable challenge to their strategic communication goals.

We select the counterinsurgency operation in Iraq as a case study not only because of the ongoing conflict there but also because of the shifting narratives employed by strategic communicators to frame the invasion, occupation, insurgency, and surge. The war in Iraq began as a traditional armed conflict between nation-states but quickly transformed into a nontraditional counterinsurgency battle among occupying forces, a newly established national government, and a mélange of non-state actors. Strategic communication becomes a greater challenge, yet even more critical, in the rugged landscape of armed political struggle between states and multiple non-state actors. The metaphor of a narrative IED is particularly insightful here, as it expresses the preferred non-kinetic weapon of insurgents in Iraq. Like their kinetic cousins, rumors in Iraq during the counterinsurgency were easily conjured up by using local material. They were unpredictable and, though many missed their targets, often deadly, as the bovine inoculation campaign illustrates. Narrative IEDs can slip past force protection measures and eviscerate carefully crafted strategic communication campaigns.

Narrative Networks

In Iraq, rumors have a long history of influencing popular perceptions and cultural sensibilities.[4] Stephanie Kelley, an Air Force intelligence officer who tracked the spread of rumors during the height of the insurgency, notes: "Iraqis have long employed rumor as a credible information source and reflection of the mood on the street, suggesting that naturally occurring, readily available rumors are an ideal guide in the battle for hearts and minds in this conflict."[5] Kelley sees rumors as valuable open-source intelligence, revealing the attitudes, anxieties, and morale of the Iraqi people.

Kelley surveyed 966 rumors collected in Iraq in 2003 and 2004 and categorized them according to traditional rumor-study typologies of motivation (fear, hostility, wish, and curiosity) and subject (government/politics, quality of life, insurgency, military, terrorism, and so on). She found nearly equal instances of fear rumors (33.7 percent) and hostility rumors (35.7 percent), and U.S. forces were the most common target of these rumors. The two most prevalent rumor subjects were government/politics (26.6 percent) and quality of life (18.1 percent). This broad-scale categorization paints a picture of the attitudes of the Iraqi populace and highlights areas of significant concern. For example, Kelley classified as "hostile" a rumor that U.S. forces intentionally cut off electrical power to Iraqi neighborhoods because it targets the United States in the area of citizen quality of life. Government leaders can draw from this example that the unstable power grid is of particular concern and stirs local hostility toward the U.S. presence. Kelley's findings offer a useful snapshot of the mood of the Iraqi people at the time (notably, anxiety and resentment). "The fact that there are almost as many fear as hostility rumors is extremely telling when one considers the large number of sectarian divisions that exist," she writes. "Groups have been played against one another for decades under Saddam, who exploited religious, ethnic, and tribal divisions to protect and reinforce his own power."[6]

Although Kelley's approach provides important information about the populace, it does not tell us much about the rumors themselves or why some posed an explosive threat to strategic communication and civil affairs efforts while others petered out without so much as a spark. Understanding the storytelling elements of a rumor in relation to its historical context, or what might be best described as a specific narrative landscape, is key. As noted in chapters 1 and 2, the term "narrative landscape" means the sense-making ordering of data and information that shapes an individual's or community's viewpoint.

The Iraqi narrative landscape had undergone a bombardment of rumors long before the ones identified by Kelley came on the scene. A well-established example is the rumor spread in the 1990s by Saddam Hussein that his country had stockpiles of weapons of mass destruction (WMDs). Hussein apparently spread this rumor in an effort to intimidate his neighbors, particularly Iran. After the Iran/Iraq war of the 1980s, which essentially resulted in a stalemate, the dictator remained wary of Iranian influence and intentions in Iraq. Extending a historical tension between Persians and Arabs and adopting the strategic communication language that defined the Cold War between the United States and the Soviet Union, he described his WMD program as a kind of "mutual annihilation" threat. This strategy was more bluff than threat, however, as Hussein's WMD program was largely dismantled after the 1990–1991 Persian Gulf War by U.S. and United Nations (UN) inspectors. But U.S. news coverage and government reports suggesting that Hussein was thwarting inspection efforts in a bid to retain a WMD capability added strength to the rumor's persistence.

The American people were also influenced by these rumors. Advanced by Hussein's foes in exile, namely, Ahmed Chalabi and the Iraqi National Congress, Hussein's WMD rumor picked up considerable credence after 9/11 and in the wake of the U.S. announcement of its intention to invade the country if the dictator did not destroy the stockpile in 2002 and 2003.[7] Consisting of half-truths, misrepresentations, and lies from defectors deemed credible by a few inside President George W. Bush's administration, these rumors gave the United States the pretext to invade the country, despite reports from Hans Blix, head of the UN Monitoring, Verification and Inspection Commission, as well as from select U.S. intelligence agencies that Iraq's stockpile of chemical and biological weapons had been largely destroyed by UN inspectors—and that the country did not possess the technical means to build or deliver a nuclear weapon.[8] As became evident after the invasion, Blix's report was accurate: U.S. forces failed to find evidence of an active program or of stockpiles of WMDs, let alone a nuclear capability.[9]

Hussein's rumor campaign simultaneously prevailed and backfired. The United States, not Iran, posed the greatest threat to his rule, as rumors of his WMD program formed a key communication strategy supporting the rationale for the 2003 invasion. The Bush administration chose to believe the Hussein/Chalabi rumors to be credible and used them as a platform for preemptive war. Not only did the U.S. government base national security policy decisions on rumors, it incorporated these rumors into its strategic communication efforts. For example, on 8 September 2002, National Security Advisor Condoleezza Rice appeared to engage in classic rumor-mongering when she said on CNN, "We don't want the smoking gun to be a mushroom cloud."[10] President Bush repeated the notion that Hussein possessed nuclear weapons, or was close to having this capacity, in a speech he gave in Cincinnati, Ohio, a month later. After invoking the memory of 9/11, a common rhetorical strategy deployed by the president and administration officials, Bush said: "Knowing these realities America must not ignore the threat gathering against us. Facing clear evidence of peril, we cannot wait for the final proof—the smoking gun—that could come in the form of a mushroom cloud."[11] The smoking-gun motif was also broadcast by General Tommy Franks, head of U.S. Central Command, a little more than a month after the president's remarks. On 12 November, Franks warned the American population that inaction could result in "the sight of the first mushroom cloud on one of the major population centers on this planet."[12] In all of these cases, high-placed U.S. government officials advanced unverified information ("we cannot wait for the final proof . . .") in vivid and alarmist terms ("mushroom cloud").

The Bush administration's WMD narrative, whether based on rumors perceived to be facts or intentionally created, was not the only one it offered as justification to invade Iraq.[13] Vice President Dick Cheney also engaged the media with tales of a link between Hussein and al Qaeda before 9/11, connecting the terrorist group, which was known to be working toward its own WMD capability, and a dictator who, in the 1980s, actually used chemical weapons against a Kurdish village in his own country. For example, on *Meet the Press*, the vice president offered the following carefully crafted statement to host Tim Russert's question, "Is there a connection?":

> We don't know. You and I talked about this two years ago. I can remember you asking me this question just a few days after the original attack. At the time I said no, we didn't have any evidence of that. Subsequent to that, we've learned a couple of things. We learned more and more that there was a relationship between Iraq and al-Qaeda that stretched back through most of the decade of the '90s, that it involved training, for example, on BW and CW [biological and chemical warfare], that al-Qaeda sent personnel to Baghdad to get trained on the systems that are involved. The Iraqis providing bomb-making expertise and advice to the al-Qaeda organization.[14]

The vice president did not make the link explicit, but his answer made a direct connection seem likely, with the result being a persuasive, though ultimately falsified case for preemptive invasion.[15]

The dramatic performances and rhetorical flourishes of Rice, Bush, Franks, and Cheney took advantage of a heightened level of social anxiety among U.S. citizens after 9/11. Indeed, the image of a mushroom cloud painted by the top leaders in the U.S. government extended a Cold War narrative, thereby capitalizing on deep concerns held by Americans and the world more generally about nuclear war. It also piggybacked on contemporaneous stories about nuclear proliferation in general and the sale of nuclear secrets by Pakistani scientist Abdul Qadeer Khan and rogue figures in the former Soviet Union to terrorist groups more generally. Forming a kind of metonymy, the mushroom cloud image and the alleged connection between Hussein and al Qaeda stoked fears and anxiety across the United States that led to an otherwise rational justification for an invasion designed to stop an imminent attack, thereby demonstrating how authoritative sources lend credibility to narratives that are spun out of rumors.

The Bush administration's shifting narrative about Iraq sustained a rumor mosaic that explicitly painted Hussein as an imminent threat and implicitly as the force behind 9/11. On its face, the mosaic was plausible and its support among Americans rational: *al Qaeda did attack the U.S. on 9/11; Hus-*

sein had used chemical weapons on his own people; a known terrorist, Abu Musab al-Zarqawi, resided in Iraq during the 1980s; the intelligence agencies of U.S. allies agreed that Iraq was capable of unleashing a mushroom cloud of terror; a preemptive invasion is justified lest we suffer another 9/11. Today, of course, many scholars, journalists, and government agencies have forcefully argued that the administration's case was "sexed up,"[16] with questionable evidence reported as definitive and with carefully crafted media campaigns linking Iraq to Osama bin Laden's terrorist group. In any other context, the campaign would be regarded as propaganda. It certainly was viewed that way by many Iraqis.

Our point in reviewing this material is to show that an almost endless reserve of rumors in Iraq during Hussein's reign and prior to the U.S. invasion served to misinform the Iraqi and U.S. people, not to mention their leaders, while intimidating neighbors and allies alike. As the rumors Kelley identified in her report and the bovine poisoning rumor we discussed at the top of this chapter might suggest, the U.S. invasion and occupation had the effect of putting a torch to those rumor reserves.[17] With both the U.S and Iraqi people softened up for the invasion, the result was a geopolitical information disaster that subsequent counterinsurgency operators had to manage in an effort to quell rising social unrest and insurgent violence in Iraq and beyond.

We focus on Iraq not only because the invasion and occupation are defining events of the early history of the twenty-first century, but also because the study of rumors there brings to light lasting lessons for strategic communication, public diplomacy, and military operations. During periods of heightened social anxiety, such as in the United States after 9/11 and in Iraq before and after the invasion, rumor-mongers have a greater chance to advance their strategic communication agenda effectively if they can make plausible connections between otherwise distinct events, offer an explanation that reflects social anxiety, and predict a resolution that promises to allay those anxieties. Indeed, rumors have the greatest likelihood of impeding strategic communication efforts during times of social upheaval and political instability, driving wedges between constituent populations, between populations and their governments, and between governments and their allies.[18] This is especially the case when competing forces work to keep rumors and rumor mosaics alive and focused on advancing their respective agendas.

Crucial to understanding the ideological functions and effects of rumors is recognition of their operation within relevant narrative systems. Assessing rumors with a cultural and narrative-based approach not only aids in understanding what rumors do but also helps to identify how and why they circulate, repeat, and, most important, impede strategic communication. As we will show, although rumors circulate freely in society as otherwise credible stories and in some ways are cross-cultural in that all cultures engage in rumor-mongering, rumors are a critical, yet underestimated and understudied, threat to counterinsurgency operations—particularly when the counterinsurgency force, in this case the U.S. government, is believed by a host nation's population to be engaged in its own propaganda campaign to conceal or recharacterize an agenda of oppression and subjugation.

Rumors are not discreditable ideas circulating aimlessly in a population. As we suggested in chapter 1 and in detail above, they are significant participants in the narrative landscape. They fit into this landscape singly, in families, and in mosaics, further "clarifying" the picture for uninformed, suspicious, and downtrodden populations. These populations can draw upon a wealth of historical experiences, understood and remembered through narratives, many of which end up sounding strikingly similar to what they are experiencing at the moment.

The post-9/11 U.S. population had every reason to believe that Iraq was poised to launch a WMD attack on its soil, thanks to the statements of its leaders. Explanations of the 9/11 attacks did not seem to make sense: *How did a rag-tag bunch of terrorists from Afghanistan penetrate our defenses with limited resources and destroy the Twin Towers?* This anxiety plus an information gap bred numerous rumors (*9/11 was an inside job; the Twin Towers were brought down by explosives; the terrorist act was orchestrated by Israel,* and so on) and lent plausibility to the notion of Iraqi complicity and/or cooperation with al Qaeda. Conversely, the Iraqi people had every reason to believe that the United States was orchestrating a propaganda campaign to justify an invasion that would secure their oil fields. Their country did not perpetrate the 9/11 attacks, and for decades there was great resistance to fundamentalist Islam in the government and populace at large. A network of rumors informs this history and narrative landscape, making the job to "win hearts and minds" a particular challenge for counterinsurgency communicators.

Rumor Minefields

During counterinsurgency operations rumors potentially undermine strategic communication, diplomatic outreach, information operations, public affairs, and psychological operations. The WMD rumors discussed above illustrate the capacity of rumors to influence national security and international relations, as well as state power and control, but we think they are more tangible, more addressable, and potentially have more immediate impact at the local level. Easily created and spread by insurgents, disaffected communities, and other impoverished groups, they are among the "weapons of the weak"—discreet and seemingly ad hoc IEDs that can radically disrupt carefully crafted and expensive operations because of their simplicity and the tendency of commanders to dismiss them as lies or gossip. At the same time, rumors are often indigenous and organic, rising within a population of their own accord, and, as such, can be taken as a strategic indicator of prevailing social anxieties and the shaping of worldviews. Insurgents are able to exploit the rumor mill, gaining a tactical and a strategic edge, especially in environments of information uncertainty where there is limited access to institutional media, where institutional media lack credibility, or where institutional media legitimize a rumor by presenting it as fact.

The rampant spread of rumors during periods of upheaval and uncertainty and their cultural reverberation in the midst of national crises pose particularly thorny problems for strategic planning and communication efforts. Broadly speaking, strategic communication is the production, transmission, and exchange of messages for the purpose of creating meaning (communication) in the service of a specific goal (strategy). For counterinsurgency operations, in which the military partners with governmental and non-governmental organizations to achieve political stability in the face of violent campaigns by non-state actors, strategic communication functions to allay public fears, keep citizens informed, and, in the end, facilitate broad support for and confidence in the national government while weakening support for adversaries.[19] As Sebastian Gorka and David Kilcullen summarize: "If a strategy is the plan by which a nation's goals are related to the means at its disposal to achieve those goals, strategic communications are the tools we use to garner support for that plan and the vision behind it, and the tools used to undermine an enemy's ability to obstruct us in achieving that vision."[20]

Or they fail to do so. As we suggested above, strategic communication is not restricted to pro-government forces. Terrorist groups such as al Qaeda engage in highly effective communication strategies that include the dissemination of narratives that, as the epigraph to this chapter notes, "develop legitimating ideologies." For example, even though the vast majority of Muslims do not believe the Qur'an permits terrorism, Islamist extremists are particularly adept at justifying violence against innocent people—including Muslims—by linking their cause to divine intervention. The killing is justified because the larger cause of jihad is based on specifically selected passages from the Qur'an and hadith that extremists interpret as a divine sanction for violence under grave circumstances. Crusades and colonization against Islam, along with passive cooperation with Crusaders and colonizers by local Muslim populations, serve to justify, in the name of Allah, extreme actions by Muslims against innocents and fellow Muslims.[21]

During times of national crisis such as the invasion and occupation of Iraq, insurgents are more easily able to entice contested populations into a kind of complacency, even tolerance, for kinetic IEDs targeting U.S. and government forces by exploiting mass unrest and anxiety with highly effective yet selective narrative IEDs. For example, Abu Musab al-Zarqawi, the Jordanian terrorist who reportedly formed al Qaeda in Iraq (AQI) and had been waging jihad from Jordan to Afghanistan to Iraq, picked up on Bin Laden's 1998 fatwa titled "Jihad Against Jews and Crusaders," which requires Muslims to kill Americans, both civilian and military.[22] This fatwa explicitly invokes the Crusader master narrative and positions the United States as an occupying, exploitative, and evil force. With this narrative in circulation, the bovine poisoning rumor gained additional rhetorical power, given the impact of the U.S. invasion on the country's infrastructure and collective psyche, and aided the insurgent cause while degrading the efficacy of the inoculation campaign.

Not all rumors become imminent threats to counterinsurgency efforts; most fail to gain traction and thus do not stick with a contested population. For example, Kelley's study of 966 rumors circulating in Iraq between 2003 and 2004 included examples ranging from the innocuous to the deadly. Yet most of them were not observed in circulation during 2009, when co-author Bernardi was in Iraq. Nonetheless, even if many rumors are duds on the battlefield, during a particularly tense crisis they can fast become a force multiplier for insurgents. This outcome is especially the case when rumors link up to form mosaics that complement or extend insurgent propaganda. When it comes to rumors and counterinsurgency operations, there is a lot at stake.

The bovine poisoning rumor illustrates the challenge faced by military personnel when grappling with the myriad rumors circulating on the battlefield of ideas. To begin with, the rumor's archetypes, plot, and ideological charge played to local Iraqi fears rather than rational thought and action. In this rumor, the U.S. forces fill the archetypal villain role, a role previously played by Crusaders, Mongols, and early twentieth-century colonialists. The plot of the bovine rumor fits into the basic pattern of invasion, subjugation, oppression, and exploitation articulated by the Crusader master narrative. In the bovine poisoning rumor, the plot elements are simple: *U.S. forces administer medicine to cattle; cattle are observed to die in the region.* There is no evidentiary basis for a causal connection; but the similarities shared with existing narratives circulating in Iraqi culture (and Arab and Islamic cultures more broadly) gave the bovine rumor a causal logic. In the Crusades, Westerners came, attacked, pillaged, and destroyed; in the contemporary situation, the bovine rumor implies that the United States came, attacked, pillaged, and destroyed. This story fits into a familiar pattern for local residents. It makes sense.

Notably, there was no single antecedent or provocateur promulgating the bovine poisoning rumor; rather, many versions or retellings of it were in circulation. This anonymity makes this rumor and other wartime rumors a particular challenge to track, assess, and thwart. As rumors fragment and cross various modes of expression—from word of mouth to mosque sermons to print and visual media—they gain legitimacy among contested populations. As explained in chapter 2, understanding the formal complexity, cultural specificity, and spread, or transmediation, of rumors is the first step toward assessing the threat they pose to counterinsurgency efforts.

It is important to keep in mind that, as we noted in chapter 1, a rumor does not necessarily have to be a lie to be classified as a rumor; some rumors contain truthful, plausible, and factual information.[23] Indeed, some studies show that the more acceptance a rumor attains, the greater the possibility that it contains truthful elements.[24] Generally, people are less likely to repeat a rumor if they know it to be untruthful. As David Coady explains, extending Tamotsu Shibutani's use of natural selection as a metaphor to describe this phenomenon: "There is 'competition' between different rumours (and different versions of the same rumour) in the sense that some will survive and spread while others will die out. Finally, which rumours (and which versions of rumours) survive and spread is not entirely arbitrary. In other words, there is selection pressure."[25] The notion that the survival and spread of a rumor indicate a truthful claim suggests that information operators and host-nation public affairs offices should saturate contested terrains with accurate and timely information. Doing so might not advance strategic messaging—as in the case of accurately reporting civilian or collateral casualties in a timely manner, for example—but the communications will serve as obstacles to the flow of rumors that occur in information vacuums. In other words, there may by short-term consequences to adhering to the U.S. military public affairs creed of "maximum disclosure, minimum delay," but the long-term consequences of "minimum disclosure, maximum delay" can prove fatal for counterinsurgency goals.[26]

Strategic communicators would also do well to remember that the narrative systems circulating in a culture define what is "truth" for local constituents far more reliably than what is labeled as truth by counterinsurgency forces. Although Coady and Shibutani both offer insightful arguments about the relationship among rumors, traction, and ground truth, they miss a critical point essential to the study of rumors during counterinsurgency operations: in times of sociopolitical crisis replete with violence and existential threats to sovereignty, rumors survive and thrive on anxiety. Indeed, these kinds of threat rumors are often extended or initiated by rumor-mongers interested in facilitating greater anxiety and instability. Insurgents, familiar with the culture and the narrative ecosystem in which rumors evolve, actively spread rumors that they have concocted or that have arisen organically and serve their interests in order to advance their strategic messages. This does not mean that the content of the rumor is untrue; but it certainly also does not mean that, if it survives, as did the bovine rumor, it is likely to be true.

While seemingly contradictory to Shibutani's and Coady's conclusions, this phenomenon is actually indicative of the cultural relativity of truth. Rather than fixed as black or white, true or untrue, fact or falsehood, the concepts of plausibility, believability, and truth are shifting and malleable, shaped in large part by experiences, traditions, and knowledge systems. The meaning of "truth" is often a key feature of hegemonic struggles like the one pitting radical Islam against the West today. This puts a slightly different spin on a well-known aphorism, usually attributed to U.S. Senator Hiram Warren Johnson in a 1918 speech, "The first casualty when war comes is truth." In today's battle with Islamist extremism, truth is both the rationalization for war and the obstacle to peace.

We think it is more useful to look at rumors as sharing the dual logic of a nonfiction narrative in that they have the "meaning" of the rumor and the "telling" of the rumor that align as "truth" until proven otherwise. This approach is consistent with narratology, which, as we also noted in chapter 1, posits that a narrative consists of both content (the story, or what happened) and telling (the discourse, or how it was told), and that both combine to create the narrative.[27] As narratives, rumors feature actors experiencing actions and events in specific settings at specific times. They go on to explain events through simple cause/effect strategies. In the process, they foretell outcomes; in the context of counterinsurgency operations, these are outcomes that, if not averted, promise to bring grave consequences for contested populations. Seen in this light, the truth or falsehood of a rumor is tangential to the meaning it conveys.

In counterinsurgency situations, rumors are particularly explosive when they coalesce across common themes to form a mosaic. As we suggested in the beginning of this chapter, rumor mosaics consist of a number of otherwise unrelated rumors that draw upon master narratives that appeal to local interests in a way that impacts regional and even national politics. In the bovine poisoning example, the rumor mosaic includes stories that *the United States poisoned cattle, American helicopters created large dust storms, American technologies caused the drought,* and *the United States invaded Iraq to pillage its oil fields.* The moral of these stories, or the rhetorical glue that binds them as a mosaic, goes something like this: *the U.S. Crusaders have little regard for the people or future of Iraq and are interested solely in the country's natural resources.* As rumor mosaics such as this one gain momentum, they end up portraying American forces and interests as an existential threat to the people the United States is trying to protect and to the host nation it supports. Thus, these rumors contribute to a point of view that the Americans and the cooperating government of Iraq, not the insurgents, are the enemies that the people must defeat.

Rumor mosaics can more easily spread beyond national borders to become a geopolitical threat when they evoke particularly powerful master narratives. As we noted in chapter 1, master narratives are systems of stories that circulate across historical and cultural boundaries and express a desire to resolve archetypal conflicts through established literary and historical forms. Because they are deeply embedded within a particular culture and because they are repeated in a labyrinth of cultural texts and contexts, master narratives are particularly powerful systems shaping opinions, perspectives, and ideological leanings. The master narratives supporting Islamist extremism include stories of invasion and occupation, such as those of the

Crusades or the Tatars; stories of martyrdom, such as the Battle of Karbala; a narrative conveying a reversion to primitive pagan barbarism called the *jahiliyyah*; as well as a narrative of pious opposition to an exploitative tyrant, the Pharaoh.[28]

The bovine poisoning mosaic implicitly invoked the Crusader master narrative in which non-Arab/non-Muslim invaders plunder Arab lands for their riches while proclaiming allegiance to a higher power and a more righteous religion. The wanton killing of livestock and the imposition of privation through drought in this mosaic parallel the slaughter of Muslims by Christian soldiers of the First Crusade. The accusation of economic exploitation parallels the nineteenth-century reworking of the Crusader narrative in the form of colonization. The twenty-first-century rumor mosaic illustrates the transhistorical nature of master narratives: the system grows and accumulates contemporary stories that retell the same archetypal conflicts. This master narrative of invasion, destruction, and exploitation eventually defined the U.S. occupation across Iraq and, even more problematically, the Islamic world, undermining U.S. strategic messaging and, as a result, U.S. strategic planning and vision. More important, the association of the bovine rumor mosaic with this Crusader master narrative enhanced its threat: rumors that activate, catalyze, and extend this historical and widely understood narrative about foreign invaders are both more problematic because of their implications and more widespread because of their narrative fidelity. In other words, because they follow the same pattern and underlying message as the Crusader narrative, these rumors will find widespread traction and belief because they reinforce a prevailing narrative of invasion and exploitation. Hence, the rumor involves a kind of circular logic: it is rational and seemingly truthful, given historical narratives and official information gaps.

The power of narratives like these during counterinsurgency operations is echoed by the *U.S. Army/Marine Corps Counterinsurgency Field Manual*, which grew out of U.S. military failures during the occupation stages of the Iraq war: "The central mechanism through which ideologies are expressed and absorbed is the narrative. . . . Narratives are central to representing identity, particularly the collective identity of religious sects, ethnic groupings, and tribal elements."[29] The *Manual* goes on to emphasize the centrality of narratives in the struggle to win hearts and minds and makes clear that, despite insurgent lies and distortions, in this battle of ideas the U.S. military's best munitions are facts and truth.

A strategy that depends on "truth" to deal with rumors, however, fundamentally misunderstands both the nature of rumors and the geopolitics of truth.[30] Narrative comprehension and adoption proceed as individuals make patterns from available data (stories, actions, and the like); flooding a communication landscape with information may overwhelm existing narrative patterns and generate new narratives (possibly to the advantage of counterinsurgents). Truth is a malleable concept, influenced by prevailing narratives and worldviews as much as by facts in evidence. Procter & Gamble discovered that truth had little effect in combating rumors in the early 1980s about its satanic affiliations. Despite a telephone hotline and media campaign offering proof (or truth) that debunked the rumor, public attention and negative publicity continued to plague the company and finally led corporate leadership to remove the company logo (part of the rumor-mongers' evidence) from its products in 1985.[31]

Debunking the falsity of content and the falsity of origins seems to have been the primary effectiveness of World War II "rumor clinics" run by Gordon Allport and Robert Knapp.[32] But responding to a rumor threat like the Procter & Gamble situation or the bovine poisoning rumor with a truth strategy that worked in World War II—the same strategy advocated by the *Counterinsurgency Manual*—overlooks how rumors play into prevailing narratives that shape the interpretation of the world and that rationalize a conflict as divine. For believers and disseminators of the Procter & Gamble rumor, evidence or data (star patterns in the logo, reports of admissions of satanism by corporate leadership) fit into a narrative template present in American subcultures that casts suspicion on corporations in general and seeks malevolent explanations for individual success. Similarly, the evidence of dying cows apparent to Iraqi farmers solidified the narrative of invasion and destruction; newly observed behaviors and actions (U.S. representatives administering veterinary medications) became comprehensible in terms of the prevailing narrative: poison. On the other hand, reasoned counterarguments to fear-based rumors in the U.S. civilian population may have been successful because a desired/prevailing narrative was one of American success and victory, and the rumors were countering, rather than supporting, a prevailing narrative. The key, then, for strategic communicators is to understand the processes that create individual and cultural "truth perspectives," such as recognizing the role that rumor mosaics play in these perspectives.

Rumor Politics

The power of insurgent rumors to disrupt or hinder counterinsurgency goals and to create competing versions of the truth is seen in the case of U.S. Special Forces (SF) operating in the southeast side of Al-Hillah, Iraq, the apex of the Triangle of Death. The teams of SF soldiers, sailors, and airmen occupy a modest compound on the outskirts of this city of approximately 400,000 people. The compound is called Stack House in internal U.S. documents and communications. Signifying the symbolic as well as strategic value SF places on the facility, it was named for Sergeant Major Michael B. Stack (U.S. Army Special Forces), who was killed in the area on 11 April 2004. The Iraqis, on the other hand, call the compound Beit Wazir, which means "the minister's house." It was originally built to house ministers from Saddam Hussein's Ba'ath Party. It was abandoned after the U.S. invasion, and it is now owned by the Iraqi Ministry of Interior and contracted to the U.S. military.

SF teams have lived and worked in the discretely fortified compound since 2004. Although they are capable of killing insurgents in battle, their primary mission after the Iraq Security Agreement Act of 2009 is to train the Hillah Special Weapons and Tactics unit (SWAT), an elite Ministry of Interior police force under the regional leadership of Brigadier General No'aman Jawad. As is often the case with the SF mission, particularly for the Green Berets who currently reside in the compound, the U.S. soldiers share the risks associated with counterinsurgency activities with their Iraqi partners as they pursue terrorists in an effort to stabilize the city. Yet, despite the strategic value of the facility and the U.S. presence to Iraqi security forces, the SF team is under constant threat of being kicked out by local politicians and business leaders so that, ostensibly, the facility can be used for other purposes. Rumors play a significant, if not determining, role in a constant struggle to legitimize and thus maintain the U.S. presence in the city.

According to the U.S. commander of Stack House in late 2009, Captain Ted Morton, 10th Special Forces Group, U.S. Army, as well as Hillah SWAT constables,[33] three rumors coalesce to threaten public support for the team: (1) the compound is occupied by Israelis; (2) the compound is occupied by the U.S. Central Intelligence Agency (CIA), which tortures Iraqis by using waterboarding and other techniques; and (3) Hillah SWAT is a puppet militia for the U.S. forces residing in the compound. Amounting to a family of rumors, which we call the Stack House rumors, these stories are articulated in local newspapers, radio programs, and television coverage, not to mention con-

3.2. Brigadier General No'aman Jawad discusses security operations around Al-Hillah with CNN's Cal Perry. Photograph by Daniel Bernardi.

versations in mosques and other public places.[34] In fact, this rumor family is pervasive throughout all strata of local Iraqi society; according to Captain Morton, even the mayor of Hillah thought that Israelis occupied the compound.[35] Both Captain Morton and Brigadier General No'aman note that the rumors end up disrupting civil affairs missions—including school refurbishment projects, park and recreational projects, and humanitarian assistance—that are designed to improve the daily life of the local population while increasing public support for both U.S. and Iraqi government forces. Local residents consider these missions to be covert operations, much as they suspect the occupation of the compound. The SF teams describe these civil and public affairs efforts as aimed toward "working themselves out of a job" (that is, leaving Hillah and Iraq secured from internal threats, able to protect itself from external threats, and with sufficient municipal, social, and political infrastructure), which, ironically, is what many of the residents and politicians actually want. In circular fashion, however, the rumor mill keeps them and their SWAT trainees on the job under potential kinetic and ideological threat.

The SF teams and their Iraqi SWAT partners responded to these rumors in concerted ways. In 2004 and 2005, when the Israeli rumor dominated the local rumor mill, Stack House experienced a high number of direct assaults from insurgents in which U.S. and Iraqi soldiers were killed and wounded. The SF teams at Stack House responded to those attacks with lethal methods, and also with non-lethal operations. They embarked on an information campaign, deploying civil, information. and public affairs teams to engage in medical and media outreach programs, which, according to Captain Morton, "really worked to dispel that rumor." In the last twenty-four months, there has not been a single mortar attack on Stack House.[36] But even if the lethal consequences of the Israeli rumor were defused, the rumor itself lingers and has meshed with the CIA and puppet rumors that continue to circulate in the Hillah area in 2010 to impose a non-lethal but nevertheless deleterious influence on counterinsurgency operations in the area.

Although Captain Morton and his SWAT partners feel at times they are fighting an uphill battle against this complex of rumors, their constant efforts to engage the population through civil, information, and public affairs activities—in short, through strategic communication—has resulted in a kind of unstable equilibrium. "There is constant talk about evicting the team among the local population," the captain told us, "but to date no legal course of action has been initiated." The team continues to train Hillah SWAT, which has steadily grown as a force capable of securing the city from insurgent violence, but not from propaganda. The SF teams, their chain-of-command, and Brigadier General No'aman consistently negotiate with local politicians and Ministry of Interior officials to keep the U.S. forces in the compound, and the SF teams continue to marshal non-kinetic resources in support of that goal.

The Hillah Stack House rumor family, replete with conjoined archetypes, merges with a rumor mosaic that tells a familiar story to the Iraqi people: *American occupiers are interested only in Iraq's resources to the peril of its people* (colonizer); *they engage in torture and support Israeli interests in keeping Iraq weak* (Crusader); and *the government of Iraq is ineffective in combating American interests or, worse, is merely a puppet government* (apostate force/traitor). And this story connects implicitly but in powerful ways to master narratives that define Iraq's history. In 1258 Hulagu Khan, for instance, led his Mongol army in the destruction of Babylon and the massacre of hundreds of thousands of Mesopotamian residents. "Hulagu" is an epithet still in circulation for invading leaders. It was even invoked by Osama bin Laden in 2002, referring to the roles of Colin Powell and Dick Cheney in the 1991 invasion of Iraq.[37] Furthering the support of the puppet rumors, the master narrative of Hulagu Khan concludes with Mongol governors ruling over Islamic lands. These governors converted to Islam but still ruled in accordance with *Yasa*, the Mongol code, and were thus perceived as apostates and puppets of the Tatars.[38]

Abu Musab al-Zarqawi invoked this master narrative as a justification for killing Muslims in Iraq in an intercepted letter to Bin Laden:

> The Qur'an has told us that the machinations of the hypocrites, the deceit of the fifth column, and the cunning of those of our fellow countrymen whose tongues speak honeyed words but whose hearts are those of devils in the bodies of men—these are where the disease lies, these are the secret of our distress, these are the rat of the dike. "They are the enemy. Beware of them." Shaykh al-Islam Ibn Taymiyya spoke with truth and honesty when he said—after he mentioned their [Shi'a] thinking toward the people of Islam—"For this reason, with their malice and cunning, they help the infidels against the Muslim mass[es], and they are one of the greatest reasons for the eruption of Genghis Khan, the king of the infidels, into the lands of Islam, for the arrival of Hulagu in the country of Iraq, for the taking of Aleppo and the pillage of al-Salihiyya, and for other things."[39]

Here Zarqawi quotes a prominent imam to lend credibility to a master narrative, one also invoked by Osama bin Laden, thereby justifying the deaths of Iraqi Muslims in pursuit of the U.S. Hulagu in the lands of Islam. This letter illustrates the narrative landscape within which the insurgents operate comfortably and in which the bovine poisoning rumor and the Stack House rumor family circulate.

The narrative of the Crusades, with an emphasis on Christian warriors attacking Muslim lands and extracting Muslim wealth, also reverberates to this day throughout the Islamic world, enhanced by the majority Christian status of the United States and its coalition allies. In fact, the Crusade master narrative and its attendant rumor mosaics were exacerbated in Iraq in January 2010, when it was widely reported that the sights on high-powered rifles used by the U.S. military were inscribed with passages about Jesus from the New Testament, including 2 Corinthians 4:6: "For God, who commanded the light to shine out of darkness, hath shined in our hearts, to give the light of the knowledge of the glory of God in the face of Jesus Christ."

Like the Hulagu master narrative, the Crusade narrative survived World War I and World War II as the British determined the territorial borders of Iraq, and it is easily extended in narrative terrains such as the Iraq invasion and the Hillah Stack House occupation. The Stack House rumor family builds upon these narratives, speaking to the local people in meaningful ways while also implicitly and explicitly aiding the insurgent information campaign by propelling a rumor mosaic; and that campaign links to Bin Laden's global jihad via Zarqawi's deft use of powerful narratives justifying violence in a religion whose majority of members decry violence against the innocent and, especially, innocent Muslims. How else do you fight a crusading force bent on spreading Christianity through violence and plunder against the will of Allah?

Rumor Gaps

As the Stack House case suggests, the rumor mill can pose a significant impediment to effective economic, social, diplomatic, and military development—the pillars of counterinsurgency operations—by invoking longstanding narratives. Whether the goal is to develop cooperative relationships between non-governmental and governmental agencies or to implement counterinsurgency strategies, the effort to mobilize popular support in today's media-saturated environment is nothing short of a communication challenge, one made all the more complex when there are gaps in the flow of credible official information. In fact, the rumor mill is a particular challenge in the fight against terrorism and, more important, against the spread of extremist ideology in places fraught with historic instability like Hillah.

Combating the rumor mill is even more challenging when the intentions of an organization or government (and the accompanying justifications, explanations, and other strategic communication content) shift and change over a short period of time and especially when those intentions are found to be based on erroneous assumptions or, worse, geopolitical distortions. With respect to Operation Iraq Freedom, counterinsurgents often appeared tongue-tied when denying rumors like the bovine poisoning tale or the Israeli/torture story because their words, not their deeds, were juxtaposed with the shifting U.S. narrative for the invasion and occupation of the Arab nation: from weapons of mass destruction to establishing freedom and democracy in the Middle East to nation building. These shifts create gaps in narrative coherence when explaining the U.S. invasion and occupation, which interferes with comprehension. The rumor mosaics then fill the gaps with culturally credible explanations.

As chapter 1 stressed, narrative is fundamentally a process of comprehension in which information fills patterns and creates relationships that facilitate sense-making. Whether the input comes from scenes in a movie, sequences in a novel, events on the ground, or rumors, these narrative elements are fit into comprehension patterns, or *schema*, by viewers, listeners, and community members. These patterns are constructed with an internal logic developed by the story, the audience's expectations, and the narrator. When story elements violate this internal logic or the storyteller lacks credibility and fails to perform to expectations, the narrative itself lacks cohesion; either a new pattern must be applied or new story elements added to complete the picture. This is the window of opportunity for rumors to flourish during counterinsurgency operations.

This phenomenon is especially likely when contradictions appear in the dominant narrative. The gap between the rhetoric of promoting human rights and the actuality of the Abu Ghraib torture case, for example, creates the space for other torture-related rumors to develop. In fact, the Abu Ghraib narrative frames many of the rumors circulating in Iraq and has become a kind of master narrative in itself. Despite the open prosecution by the U.S. Army of the perpetrators of the crimes that occurred at the prison, the story—and particularly the near-pornographic images of torture, murder, and humiliation—lingers in places like Hillah. The gap in narrative cohesion still exists (the gap between a pattern fitting the United States as liberator/protector and the events of Abu Ghraib), allowing for the plausibility of the "Stack House as CIA torture compound" rumor to grow; it ends up fitting nicely into the historical pattern of occupation and exploitation established by the historical record and the master narratives indigenous to the region. In turn, the plausibility of this rumor confers veracity on the others: *the compound is inhabited by Israelis; Hillah SWAT is a puppet of the United States, which is exploiting precious Iraqi real estate and resources.* As a result, this family of rumors supports the conclusion, at least rhetorically, that the United States invaded Iraq for its natural resources. *Why else would the United States perpetrate the Abu Ghraib and bovine-poisoning incidents? Why else does the United States continue to occupy valuable property like Stack House inside key cities?* Where narrative coherence and alignment are lacking, rumors fill the gaps.

3.3. American and Iraqi partners discuss a mission inside Stack House. The secrecy surrounding the otherwise innocuous building exacerbated the rumors connected to it. Photograph by Daniel Bernardi.

The shifting narratives around U.S. involvement in Iraq (invasion justification, Abu Ghraib abuses despite rhetoric of human rights) complicate efforts to combat rumors and rumor mosaics. Their inconsistency creates gaps and provides an opportunity for a semblance of narrative cohesion born of conspiracy theories and rumors offered up by insurgents and media pundits alike. The shifting narratives reveal contradictions and knowledge gaps, thereby introducing a high degree of contradiction (even hypocrisy) on the part of the U.S. and Iraqi governments into an already complex and unstable information environment. As a result, strategic communication practitioners working in governmental and non-governmental organizations, whose interests are not always aligned, continually fight an uneven war of words against extremist campaigns of lies, distortions, and half-truths designed to undermine host nation officials and institutions. With contradictions prevalent in the narrative landscape, community members have difficulty achieving a consistent understanding of political and military events around them. Rumors participate in the narrative system by providing a kind of explanatory cohesion that leads to comprehension.

Narrative provides a meaningful structure for these rumors to become politically powerful, and the narrative systems in which they flow, particularly religious systems, give them popular credibility. This combination means that narrative and the systems it supports are key to our understanding of rumor threats and of the cultural context, including the counterinsurgency struggle for consent to rule, in which they arise and circulate. Rumors, then, are best understood as specific elements functioning in narrative landscapes. They circulate singly, as families, and as mosaics in specific cultural conditions. As unrest and public anxiety ferment, rumors spread, form mosaics, and threaten stability operations. The more the counterinsurgency narrative shifts, the more apparent its contradictions, the wider the gaps, and thus the greater the opportunity for insurgent narratives to fill those gaps.

Conclusion

Practitioners of strategic communication are forced either to grapple with or to ignore the narratological and cultural dimensions of rumors. In times of cultural strife and social conflict, rumors have the greatest potential for influencing contested populations, threatening an already unstable social order, and challenging the legitimacy of a government regardless of the rumors' validity or even plausibility. We believe our study of rumors circulating in Iraq points to this conclusion, and our theory laid out in chapter 1 predicts it.

It is important to note that we are far from the first researchers to focus analytic energies on the Iraqi rumor mill. The circulation of rumors in Iraq has been a potent source of frustration to diplomatic, military, and governmental efforts throughout the country during the U.S. invasion and occupation, and the rumors have received sporadic attention from various organizations. The study closest to ours in terms of data set and application is Stephanie Kelley's 2004 Master of Arts thesis.

Kelley's study is insightful and filled a gap at the time of its publication, as no concentrated effort had yet been made to address the rumors hindering the coalition forces, U.S. efforts at stabilizing the region, and the nascent Iraqi government. Nonetheless, the phenomenon of rumors deserves a great deal more attention, particularly in places such as Afghanistan, Pakistan, Yemen, the Philippines, and Indonesia, where Islamist insurgencies coercively engage contested populations in an effort to win their consent to extremist rule. These are also locales where rumors and rumor mosaics influence the prevailing narrative landscapes in which strategic communication professionals must operate.

Rumors are a particular type of story, one that feeds on social anxieties, fears, hopes, and dreams and is fueled by gaps of information. Rumors are particularly influential, indeed powerful, during counterinsurgencies. They get their political charge from the master narratives that give them cohesion and the ideologies that exploit existing cultural and political fissures. When rumors coalesce to form a mosaic, the threat is even greater. As is the case in Iraq, rumors during counterinsurgency operations constitute their own sort of dangerous triangle, bounded by sociopolitical upheaval on one side, gaps and contradictions in official messages and narratives on another, and master narratives that explain current situations in religious, cultural, or historical terms on the third side.

Taken out of context and out of the communication landscape of Iraq, the bovine poisoning rumor seems silly. Why would U.S. forces poison cattle when far more efficient means of killing livestock are available, if that was their goal? But concentrated within this dangerous triangle, a triangle of death, so to speak, the poisoning rumor takes on greater power and significance. Framed by inconsistent explanations for the U.S. presence (produced by both the U.S. government and the new Iraqi government) and circulating within an anxiety-laden, contested population dealing with armed insurgents and foreign militaries, the bovine rumors participate in narrative systems offering models of understanding and comprehension of this confusing state of affairs. Dying cattle point to other ecological difficulties, such as drought. Culturally resonant master narratives that keep stories of invasion, occupation, and destruction fresh offer cause-and-effect structures by which to understand these troubling circumstances, and the rumor mill becomes energized, stifling government attempts at regional stability and quality of life improvements.

Outreach and stabilization efforts also suffer as a result of the Hillah Stack House rumors. Again, the triple threat of sociopolitical upheaval, inconsistent official narratives, and coherence with master narratives increases the potency of this rumor mosaic. Hillah itself is within the so-called Triangle of Death, one of the most unstable and violent regions within Iraq, with a civilian population seeking answers, allegiances, and, above all, safety. In the aftermath of the atrocities of Abu Ghraib, it comes as no surprise that rumors questioning the activities and behavior of any U.S. forces would circulate widely, and especially rumors that resonate with the archetypal figures of the Crusader and the traitor. In the gaps between the abuses at Abu Ghraib and the purported message of American defense of human rights, the rumor of Hillah Stack House as a CIA torture compound penetrates and undermines the U.S./Iraqi security and civil affairs partnership. The prevailing narrative system provides the sense-making explanation of why the Iraqi SWAT forces utilize the Stack House compound as well: just like the *Yasa* leaders left behind after the thirteenth-century invasions, these constables are apostates, traitors, and Iraqi/Arab/Muslim in name only.

Far more than silly and untrue stories, these rumors are strategic communication landmines, narrative IEDs put together on the fly—sometimes specifically by insurgents, sometimes arising of their own accord—from local cultural materials. And when the conditions are right, they can explode, inflicting metaphorical harm to information operations and counterinsurgency communication strategies and literal harm to the soldiers, sailors, airmen, Marines, diplomats, politicians, and NGO representatives working toward stability and security. Rumors, however, do not discriminate with regard to which side of a political divide or insurgency conflict they affect. As the next chapter will show, rumors can work to the strategic communication advantage of an established government attempting to maintain the safety and security of its citizens in the face of a terrorist threat. Like those studied in this chapter, these rumors activate, catalyze, and extend prevalent cultural narratives, including those popularized by extremists.

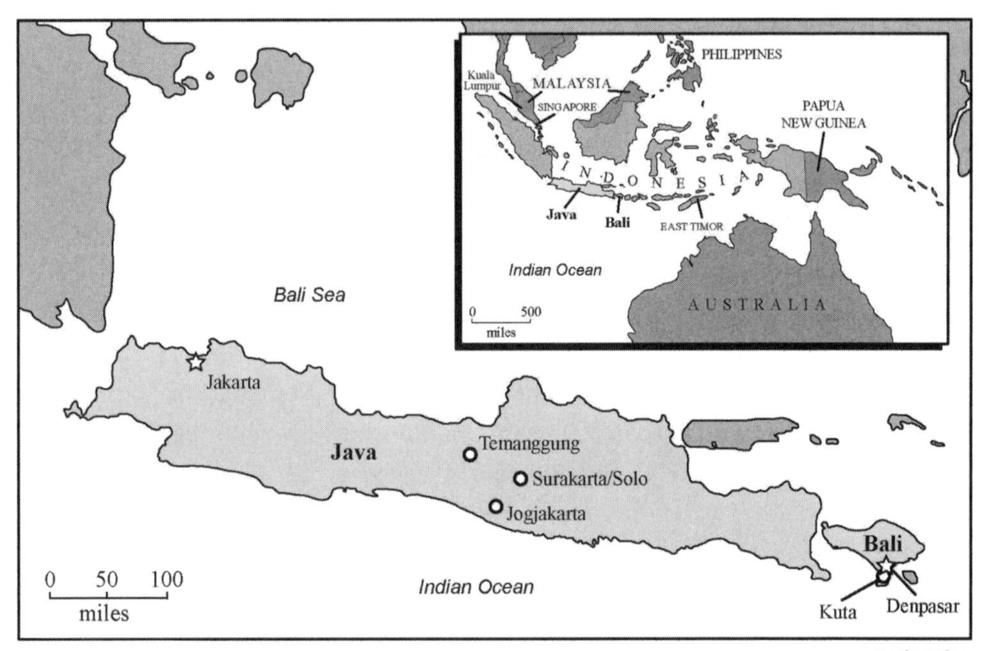
PHILIPPINES
Kuala Lumpur
MALAYSIA
SINGAPORE
PAPUA NEW GUINEA
I N D O N E S I A
Java
Bali
EAST TIMOR
Indian Ocean
A U S T R A L I A
0 500
miles
Bali Sea
Jakarta
Java
Temanggung
Surakarta/Solo
Jogjakarta
Bali
0 50 100
miles
Indian Ocean
Kuta
Denpasar
Becky Eden

4

Whisper Campaigns

State-Sponsored Rumors and the Post-Mortem (De)Construction of an Indonesian Terrorist

The idea that simply hearing a rumor repeatedly might raise one's level of belief in it is slightly unsettling. And yet this appears to be the case.

—Nicholas DiFonzo, *The Watercooler Effect*

Death is better than life in humiliation! Some scandals and shames will never be otherwise eradicated.

—Osama bin Laden

Noordin Mohammed Top, a notorious Islamist extremist working in Southeast Asia, had successfully evaded police for years while simultaneously directing deadly and large-scale attacks against Indonesian and Western targets. He is believed to be one of the masterminds of the 2003 Marriott Hotel bombing in Jakarta, the 2004 Australian embassy bombing in Jakarta, the 2005 Bali bombings, and the 2009 Marriott and Ritz-Carlton Hotel bombings in Jakarta. Noordin's ability to evade capture despite being one of the most wanted terrorists in the world, let alone Southeast Asia, was the subject of numerous rumors emanating from various sources.[1] These rumors increased with each act of terror or with police activity aimed at killing or capturing him. Sightings of Noordin were rumored through face-to-face communication, by official media, and even on YouTube. Some rumors cast him as a satanic figure, others as an Islamic savior. Like Mas Selamat, Noordin became a kind of celebrity. And as with today's Hollywood stars, his celebrity status was partly due to the Indonesian rumor mill.

When Indonesia's antiterrorism police force Densus 88 surrounded the house of suspected terrorists on Friday, 8 August 2009, and killed the inhabitants, reporters for Televisindo stated that police were 80 percent certain they had killed Noordin. This assertion set off more rounds of rumor and speculation, as well as several YouTube videos, which announced the "last moments of Noordin Top."[2] Some comments on these YouTube videos advanced the idea that he had actually escaped, others that he was martyred; some comments supported the work of Jemaah Islamiyah (JI) and other terrorists, but most condemned them. How the police arrived at "80 percent likelihood" that he was killed is unknown, although there was speculation that the man killed in the action yelled to police that he was Noordin.[3] The corpse in question was taken to Jakarta for a forensic exam and DNA testing, and over the weekend many Indonesians believed that Noordin was dead. It was not until the following week that an official announcement admitted that the body was not that of Noordin. The government was embarrassed.

Noordin eventually did meet his demise at the hands of the government in an antiterrorism assault in Central Java a little over a month later. Although his death ended some rumors, it spurred new ones. In fact, a particularly salacious rumor about his sexual proclivities originated from official sources: first, a police spokesman, Nanan Sukarna, at a press conference; second, a University of Indonesia forensics expert, Mun'im Idris, during a quick interview after Nanan's press conference. These state officials revealed that forensic evidence pointed to years of repeated sodomy, indicating that Noordin was gay or bisexual. The charge of sodomy and the implication of homosexuality were printed in national papers, reported in news broadcasts, and circulated by online media.

In Indonesia's heteronormative culture, which regards gender identity and roles as innately aligned with biological sex, the rumors associated with the slain terrorist implicitly cast him as a sexual deviant. Although homosexuality is tolerated in Indonesia (there are no laws outlawing it in this predominantly Muslim country, for example), it is considered by JI and other extremist groups operating in the region to be an abomination. In this light, the sodomy rumors ended up supporting the government's information war against Islamist extremism. Indeed, the post-mortem sexual construction was particularly damning to groups like JI, which Noordin represented, that espouse a virulently homophobic version of Islam. The story of Noordin's homosexual deviance cast doubt among Islamist extremists and potential converts about his piety and suitability as an Islamic martyr.

Owing to Noordin's Malaysian heritage, the rumor also became a weapon used by Indonesian nationalists. Indonesians often find themselves at odds with their neighbor over perceived slights or attempts by Malaysians to appropriate Indonesian cultural artifacts and territory. This anger manifests itself in several ways described later, including a rumor that cast Malaysians as deviant by leveraging national and regional stereotypes in a way that exacerbated geopolitical tensions. As such, the rumor about Noordin Top shows how transmediation can lead to the appropriation of a message and images that are used in a host of information operations supported by or reinforcing a state's strategic communication efforts.

The Indonesian rumor environment is distinct from those we have already discussed. In chapter 2 we showed how "middle-ground" netizens of Singapore created and spread rumors about a fugitive terrorist in attempts to express distrust and disapproval of their governing agencies and official media. In chapter 3 we showed how Iraqi insurgents try to further their goals by spreading rumors detrimental to counterinsurgency and the host-nation information operations. In both cases, the sources behind the rumors took advantage of information gaps, social distrust of official media, and political discontent with the respective authorities in order to fuel a rumor mill steeped in a specific hegemonic conflict over governance. This chapter will examine rumors that originate from a third source, the government itself, which also plays a hegemonic role in the nation's struggle for narrative dominance. In the Indonesian context, the rumor mill was aided by a relatively free media environment that generally supports the government's anti-terrorism efforts.

If rumors serve the interests of both insurgents and middle-ground participants, might governments also be served by the use of rumor in their strategic communication campaigns? And might both the mainstream media and new media prosumers, wittingly or unwittingly, aid the government through their reportage and mash-ups? Indeed, how do governments contending with Islamist extremism leverage their resources to spread information that disrupts extremist threats to the state and its political interests? And how do media outlets and technological platforms assist in that practice?

The practices of the Indonesian government provide a view into how governments engage the rumor mill to advance their strategic communication goals. As we noted in the introduction to chapter 1 and develop more fully here, Noordin was positioned as a sexual deviant in order to discredit him, his legacy, and the JI movement in Indonesia. Rumors were the vehicles by which this communication outcome was achieved, with the antecedent essentially being a whisper campaign: a covert method of strategic communication whereby rumors are spread about a specific subject in such a way that either the source of the rumor, in this case a government, is not readily detected or the information is so plausible as to defy suspicion of official propaganda. As Robert Knapp noted in 1944, "Propaganda through rumor has the further advantage of not being easily discernible as 'propaganda.'"[4]

In an unusual twist, the covert nature of this campaign derived from its overt beginnings. The government's very public announcements gave the information an official, truthful appearance. Yet, as we will show, the statements had the same degree of ambiguous veracity as Mas Selamat's magical powers or the bovine poisoning rumor. Thus, while this whisper campaign did not conceal the source of the original rumor (results of the forensic autopsy), it did conceal the facts of the matter (absence of scientific connection between anal deformity and sexual practice) and thus made the seemingly irrelevant message (a terrorist is alleged to be gay) both relevant to its consumers (the Indonesian citizenry) and detrimental to its opposition (JI is hypocritical). In addition, the prurient nature of the rumor added to the whispering quality of the information campaign. Built upon official police announcements, a forensic report, and a political climate that resists attempts to curb homophobia, the whisper campaign successfully facilitated the spread of a rumor that consequently undermined this terrorist leader's legacy as a martyr.[5]

Birth of a Terrorist, Hints of a Whisper Campaign

Noordin Mohammed Top was born in Kluang, Johor, Malaysia, on 11 August 1968. He turned toward terrorism in 1995 while a graduate student at Universiti Teknologi Malaysia, where he attended lectures at the Lukmanul Hakiem pesantren (Islamic boarding school) run by Abdullah Sungkar, the co-founder (along with Abu Bakar Basyir) of the terrorist network JI. He joined JI in 1998 and became the director of Lukmanul Hakiem. The school closed when the Malaysian government cracked down on JI in 2002, and Noordin left for Indonesia.[6]

JI's campaign of violence in Indonesia reached a new height that year with the first Bali bombing on 12 October 2002. The bombing killed more than two hundred people, most of them Australians, in the tourist region of Kuta. Several JI members were arrested in the aftermath, including Abu Bakar Basyir, Ali Imron, Ali Guffron, Imam Samudra, and Amrozi. Another suspected plotter, Hambali, was arrested in Thailand on 11 August 2003. Abu Bakar Basyir served twenty-six months after being found guilty of conspiracy; Ali Imron was sentenced to life in prison; and Hambali remains imprisoned by the U.S. government as an enemy combatant at Guantanamo Bay.[7] On 9 November 2008, Ali Guffron, Imam Samudra, and Amrozi were executed by the Indonesian government for their involvement in the Bali bombing. Although Noordin was thought to be the mastermind behind the Bali bombing and subsequent attacks, he managed to evade arrest. This, of course, added to his celebrity-like reputation as a skilled terrorist.

By 2009, according to the International Crisis Group (ICG), Noordin was operating more autonomously, although he continued to identify himself as a JI member.[8] The ICG speculated that he perceived himself as the "true JI," willing to carry out attacks despite the heightened security following the Bali bombing and subsequent attacks; Abu Bakar Basyir, on the other hand, toned down his rhetoric justifying violence following his two stints in prison.[9] In other words, while the leadership of JI began to take a less virulent stance, Noordin's extremist activities increased. In fact, he is thought to have coordinated several attacks subsequent to the Bali bombing, including the 17 July 2009 attacks on the Ritz-Carlton and Marriott hotels in Jakarta, which killed nine people. Following the bombing, an announcement describing a new JI offshoot—Tandzim al Qo'idah Indonesia—was posted on the Internet and attributed to Noordin.[10] The choice of name was a conscious effort to link Noordin's group to al Qaeda, another organization that rationalizes attacks that target Westerners and other enemies but that kill Muslim civilians as well.

Following the 17 July 2009 Jakarta bombings, Indonesian police—including the elite Densus 88—ratcheted up their operations in search of Noordin and other terrorists. The 8 August raid in which police mistakenly identified the man killed as Noordin made the government wary of another such error. Following the 17 September raid on a house near Solo, Central Java, announcements about the death of Noordin were muted until they could be verified. After the bodies were taken to Jakarta for DNA testing and identification by family members, the terrorist's death was officially verified on 19 September, two days after the raid. The results of a subsequent forensic exam were announced on 30 September. It was this exam that led to the rumor that Noordin was a sexual deviant.

In a 30 September press conference, police spokesman Nanan Sukarna said that forensic investigators had discovered evidence of anal trauma consistent with sodomy, a charge that would lead most consumers of this information to connect Noordin to homosexuality. The same day, forensics expert Mun'im Idris told reporters that there were "irregularities" with Noordin's corpse, and he later verified that they pointed to sodomy. According to Mun'im, Noordin had a funnel-shaped anus, and this indicated passive sodomy. A *Jakarta Globe* story that day sent the story viral: "'There is an anomaly in Noordin's anus because it is shaped like a funnel,' said Mun'im Idris, a forensic pathologist from the University of Indonesia. 'It indicated that somebody had sodomized him.'"[11] The nation's most widely read English-language newspaper connected the dots that were implicitly but rather didactically laid out at the press conferences.

From this point on, rumors spread that Noordin was homosexual. *Why else would someone as strong as Noordin engage in repeated anal sex if he was not gay?* Yet unlike the Mas Selamat escape and Stack House torture rumors, the "Noordin Mohammed Top is gay" rumor has no origin conundrum; it was clear that state authorities started it. The only uncertainty was whether the originators were spreading a story they knew to be false (that is, he did not have a funnel-shaped anus but they said he did to facilitate a rumor that he was gay), or whether they did find an anomaly, believed it proved scientifically that he engaged in repeated sodomy, and thus announced what they thought was a fact. We think the latter is improbable for reasons we explain below; but either way, the fact that the forensic results were announced to the press, and the manner in which they were announced, points to a deliberate information operation by the government.

Nanan's announcement was made in front of reporters at a press conference held at police headquarters. Irrespective of the forensic examiner's subsequent statement and scientific knowledge, this staging suggests a concerted whisper campaign. Additional evidence, albeit indirect, for a whisper campaign is that, oddly, Nanan made the following statement after informing the reporters of Noordin's apparent anal trauma: "This is the doctor's secret. Indeed I do not know who was stating this. It has to be kept secret, it cannot be announced. There is a code of ethics. It is a problem of visum etrepesum [sic: repertum]."[12] One might ask for whom the announcement was intended if not the public? Why disclose something to reporters if you do not expect it to be published and spread? Why breach an ethical code in the first place? Nanan did not make the statement on deep background, where the reporter is asked to protect the identity of the source. This was a far more conspicuous leak.

The whisper campaign came replete with homophobic ideologies that resonated with its target audience. A minority of Muslims argue that homosexuality is not inconsistent with Islam, but most view it as somewhere between transgressive and a capital sin.[13] Our point, of course, is that Islamists such as Noordin claim that they represent a supposedly pure Islam antithetical to homosexuality and that Muslims who do not accept their version of Islam are not practicing the true faith. For example, the spiritual leader of JI, Abu Bakar Basyir, calls for homosexuals to be stoned.[14] Aziz Abdulrahman, a member of Islamic Defenders Front (FPI), calls gays and lesbians "moral terrorists" who "should be banned from the East Java province."[15] Just as for fundamentalist Christians,[16] the path to righteousness for Islamic fundamentalists includes the condemnation of homosexuals. The accusation of sodomy against Noordin nullified his Islamist credentials in the eyes of many Muslims and rendered him a *munafiq* (hypocrite). The state's use of a stereotype and an Islamist master narrative became the cornerstone to its successful whisper campaign.

The narrative elements of the Noordin case are both similar to and distinct from the Bush administration's justification for preemptive war with Iraq, discussed in chapter 3, which also smacked of a whisper campaign. The suggestion of mushroom clouds resulting from Iraq's purported stockpile of WMDs worked in the same way as Nanan's less-than-subtle positioning of Noordin as gay in that both statements leveraged national anxieties about terrorism and stereotypes about the Other (Arabs for the U.S. market, homosexuals for the Indonesian market). Yet, unlike statements from the Bush administration, Nanan's case was not built on past stories of similar charges from multiple sources (other governments agencies, different governments, defectors, and so on). It came from one source, seemingly out of the blue, and it was not challenged by the national press.

Nanan's inference was disseminated uncritically by the reporters who attended the press conference. *Surya Online,* for example, was discreet in its coverage, but quoted Mun'im as saying there were "peculiarities."[17] The flagship paper of eastern Indonesia, *Pos Kupang,* also quoted Mun'im, but more directly: "Yes, there is damage to Noordin's anus."[18] Perhaps the best example of the nod-and-wink game is the reporting from *Kompas,* Indonesia's most respected national newspaper: "Nanan: The Matter of Noordin's Anus Has to Be Kept Secret," the headline blared in an unattributed article.[19] The story of Noordin, by its very nature, was irresistible to the Indonesian mass media and their public. It was titillating in the way it maligned a notorious terrorist by creating a particular version of the Islamic hypocrite master narrative—the sexual deviant—but ironically vulgar in the way that it also announced the secret. And it was cloaked in the "breaking news" drama of a state secret being revealed by the paper and its gumshoe.

By the following day, the story had mostly disappeared from mainstream media, displaced by stories about the magnitude 7.6 earthquake off the coast of Sumatra that killed more than a thousand people. Online, however, the story spread rapidly. As we show below, rumors of Noordin's sexual proclivities continued to percolate in other sectors of the Indonesian media. The mainstream news cycle shifts to breaking news. The online news cycle, however, endlessly circulates and repositions the news in multiple forums and formats, which is what makes it an idea platform for a whisper campaign.

Truth to the Rumor?

In the Noordin case we have a collection of rumors about a terrorist leader's sexuality with an identifiable origin (official forensic reports). In addition, we have evidence allowing us to interpret the origin of the rumor as a whisper campaign by the Indonesian government. We see a smoking gun that points to, at the very least, a complex narrative struggle that involves a host of ideologies: from homophobia to criminality; from gender politics to national identity; and from sexual deviance to Islamic fundamentalism. It is important, we think, to examine the medical facts surrounding this case briefly, as well as the history of associations of anal deformity with certain behaviors in order to understand the motive, ideology, and eventual success of the "Noordin is gay" whisper campaign.

The link between sodomy and anal physiology can be traced to Auguste Ambroise Tardieu (1818–1879), a prominent forensic medical scientist and the "leading medical expert on pederasty in France."[20] In describing the physical harm associated with what is often called active and passive sodomy, or the one who penetrates the anus and the one who is penetrated, he noted that complementary physical deformities manifest in the sodomites' sex organs. In the case of the passive sodomite, Tardieu claimed to have found evidence that the anus becomes severely damaged over time, taking on a fundibuliform (funnel-shaped) form: "The characteristic signs of passive pederasty . . . are the excessive development of the buttocks, the infundibuliform deformation of the anus, the relaxation of the sphincter, the effacement of the folds [of the anus], the crests and caroncules around the circumference of the anus, and the extreme dilation of the anal orifice."[21] Tardieu's claims about sodomites extended to their outward appearance as well. He noted that the habitual sodomite could be identified by "curled hair, made-up skin, open collar, waist tucked in to highlight the figure; fingers, ears, chest loaded with jewelry; the whole body exuding an odor of the most penetrating perfumes; and in the hand, a handkerchief, flowers, or some needlework; such is the stranger, revolting and rightfully suspect physiognomy that betrays the pederast."[22] For Tardieu, homosexuality was a choice that led to a range of both physical deformities and cosmetic indulgences.

The identification of sodomites was important to Tardieu and the French government because sodomy allegedly indicated moral and intellectual deficiencies, which led to criminal behavior.[23] The scientist had access to prisoners in French jails, which is where he conducted most of his research, and this body of evidence led him to what amounts to a circular argument: finding cases of sodomy among criminals and then arguing that sodomy led to crime. For Tardieu, homosexuality and criminality were intimately linked.[24]

Despite Tardieu's reputation as a prominent scientist, his conclusions were by no means universally accepted. Many contemporary and subsequent forensic experts, including Tardieu's successor, Paul Brouardel, disagreed with his conclusions and published criticisms of his work.[25] Some of Tardieu's contemporaries, including the American forensics expert Charles B. Kelsey, recognized fundibuliform anus as a congenital defect, which became the scientific consensus.[26]

The interest in identifying homosexuals through an analysis of their sex organs was related to the attempt to identify criminals through their sexuality. Tardieu's position was such that doctors trained in his techniques were most often employed in criminal cases to identify pederasts.[27] Despite modern evidence and medical training to the contrary, homosexuality remains linked to criminality broadly and to immorality specifically in some societies. In the case of Indonesia, as the Noordin rumor suggests, these links seem to lie just below the surface of popular discourse among various segments of the population, perhaps even among members of the medical profession, as Mun'im's forensic report suggests.

This association is also found in other Islamic societies, especially those in which homosexuality is a crime. In what Human Rights Watch calls a "fully technologized violation of the subject's integrity, dignity and privacy," Egyptian doctors continue to test the anuses of suspected sodomites. In addition to using techniques that build on Tardieu's methods, they incorporate manometry (to determine pressure in the anal cavity) and electromyography to determine whether someone is a passive or active sodomite. Indeed, Egyptian Deputy Minister of Justice Dr. Ayman Fouda was at pains to stress that these methods did not exceed the standards set by Tardieu but merely elaborated on them: "We don't discard Tardieu's criteria, and I do not mean that the funnel-shaped anus is not a sign of habitual use. I mean that electromyography is more exact." In response to this article, Robert Nye, professor of the history of sexuality at Oregon State University, told Human Rights Watch: "I have never heard of such a wild notion as mapping the electrical conductivity of anal tissue."[28] The director of the Lesbian, Gay, Bisexual, and Transgender Rights Project of Human Rights Watch found an Arabic-language World Health Organization report entitled *Forensic Medicine and Toxicology* (1993) that echoed Tardieu's criteria, save for the funnel-shaped anus claims: "See how the WHO . . . condones categorizing consensual sodomy as a 'crime,' and calls for tortuous expeditions around the anus to prove it. Tardieu endures."[29] Some Islamic countries, unlike those in the West, still adhere to these notions.

At the same time, other experts have noted the baseless nature of Tardieu's claims. Professor Lorna Martin, a forensic pathologist at the University of Cape Town, calls Tardieu's conclusions "bizarre and antiquated . . . rubbish. . . . It is impossible to detect chronic anal penetration" except in cases of injury resulting from nonconsensual sex.[30] Nye refers to Tardieu as "utterly discredited" and the Egyptian examinations as "horrific in the extreme."[31] Like the scientists who looked at the studies supporting the American and European eugenics movement, which sought to find morphological evidence supporting the belief that "mongoloid" and "negroid" races were inferior to "caucasoids," these scientists discovered ideology behind Tardieu's conclusions.[32] This is not to suggest that the condition known as funnel anus does not exist—it certainly does—but rather that it is not caused by sodomy. The condition is congenital and makes up 3.5 percent of all low anorectal anomalies. It leads to constipation and a condition called megacolon, which requires surgery. Some scientists suggest that there is a connection between funnel anus and embryologic and genetic etiology.[33]

Although the connection between the physical condition of funnel anus and sodomy is spurious and clearly homophobic, two important questions remain in our effort to understand the motive and valence of the Noordin Top homosexuality rumor. First, did Noordin have a funnel-shaped anus? No subsequent forensic examinations were undertaken in Indonesia or in Malaysia after the corpse was repatriated there. Consistent with Islamic tradition, it was buried quickly. But more to the point, the results of the postmortem alone would not prove that the terrorist engaged in homosexual acts or that the police and forensic examiner were not trying to facilitate the spread of a salacious rumor. Second, did Mun'im Idris know that purported science linking fundibuliform anus to passive sodomy has been discredited? This question remains unanswerable at this time, as our repeated attempts to reach Mun'im Idris in Jakarta were unsuccessful.

Regardless of the actual state of Noordin's physical condition and the spurious connections between funnel-shaped anus and sodomy that Mun'im Idris may or may not have been aware of, the accusation was made publicly by both a police spokesman and a forensics expert. Moreover, no mainstream media outlet publicly challenged the assertion that funnel anus is caused by sodomy (although some speculated that a funnel-shaped anus could be the result of an attempt to hide explosives). The police spokesman and forensic expert intentionally floated the notion that Noordin, a celebrity terrorist with a movement that was gaining support among contested populations, was homosexual. What remained to be seen was if and how the story would gain traction, and whether it would link homosexuality to terrorism and, as a result, taint the reputation of Noordin, JI, and Islamist extremism more broadly.

The Story of Homosexuality in Indonesia

Like the Old Testament, the Qur'an directly addresses homosexual sex. In telling the story of Lot, the Muslim holy book states: "We also sent

Lot: He said to his people: 'Do ye commit lewdness such as no people in creation (ever) committed before you? For ye practice your lusts on men in preference to women: ye are indeed a people transgressing beyond bounds.'"[34] The Qur'an also has the verse: "What! Of all the creatures in the world, will you approach males, and leave those whom Allah has created for you to be your mates? Nay, you are a people transgressing (all limits)!"[35] Scholars differ in their interpretations of these verses, as is the case with many others, but these are frequently invoked to condemn homosexuality.

Compared with other predominantly Muslim countries, Indonesia appears tolerant, even accepting, of homosexuality. Historically, there has been little violence targeting homosexuals as a group, and people usually react to non-heterosexual expressions of gender and sexuality, such as transvestism, with humor.[36] Yet, although Indonesia is not as homophobic as other Muslim (and Christian) nations, it is, as anthropologist Tom Boellstorff explains, a heteronormative or "heterosexist" society: "Heterosexism refers to the belief that heterosexuality is the only natural or moral sexuality. It does not imply the gut level response that homophobia does; for instance, a bureaucratic structure may be heterosexist but it cannot be homophobic. It operates on the level of generalized belief and social sanction, rather than on an emotive plane." Boellstorff concludes: "The 'tolerance' of homosexuality exists only because Indonesians keep these practices secret and do not publicly proclaim homosexual identities."[37]

In his analysis of the classic work of Javanese literature *Serat Centhini* (compiled between 1616 and 1814), Benedict Anderson points to the commonplace nature of bisexuality and homosexuality among Javanese and other Indies natives. "Male homosexuality at least was an unproblematic, everyday part of a highly varied traditional Javanese sexual culture," he argues. This cultural practice was noted by Dutchmen up to the end of the colonial era, in fact, and apparently viewed with abhorrence. Interestingly, after independence in 1949, Indonesians claimed that bisexuality and homosexuality were unheard of until the arrival of the Dutch and were a result of their immoral influences.[38] In our view, this historical revisionism further indicates the heteronormative basis of modern-day Indonesian national identity. It also reflects a broad pattern among postcolonial states to try to distinguish themselves from their former overseers by portraying perceived social ills as having been introduced by the colonizer.

Acceptance or rejection of homosexuality has gone through several phases since the colonial period. Boellstorff writes of the dearth of material on homosexuality in the Dutch East Indies, at least until the second and third decades of the twentieth century. Homosexuality was in the Dutch colonial penal code—based on Dutch national law—but in the context of sexual assault and pederasty (the article retains its original number, 292, in the modern Indonesian penal code). In the context of homosexuals becoming visible in Surabaya and elsewhere, he notes a crackdown on homosexuality in the late colonial period, including the famous persecution of German painter and Bali resident Walter Spies.[39] Among Indonesians, Dédé Oetomo, a co-founder of the Indonesian gay rights group GAYa Nusantara, notes a duality in the perception of homosexuality in the late colonial era, when, for example, future first president Soekarno cross-dressed in Javanese ludruk performances while at the same time condemning the gay Dutchmen who came to watch.[40] The irony, of course, is that we see something similar operating in the "Noordin is a homosexual" rumor: a government unwilling to condemn homosexuality outright but willing to exploit homophobia for its political ends.

Following Indonesian independence, homosexuals began congregating in groups in parks, although they were not open about their sexuality. When the attempted communist coup d'état and counter coup of 1 October 1965 occurred, members of Gerakan Wanita Indonesia (the Indonesian Women's Movement), who were associated with the Communist Party, were accused of being lesbians as well as having sexually mutilating the corpses of the military officers killed in the early hours of the struggle.[41] In fact, the organization promoted a "puritan" morality.[42] Interestingly, this persecution did not apply as directly to men. Nonetheless, gay men became more careful and in some cases stopped congregating in parks, although over time they have become less guarded.[43]

Gay rights groups began emerging in the early nineties, a process that was accelerated with the onset of Indonesia's democratization. Yet, despite the increasing openness and visibility of homosexuality in Indonesia, gays and lesbians there remain less assertive than those in some other countries of Southeast Asia, particularly Thailand and the Philippines, preferring to keep their activities private and not seeking recognition of their status by the government.[44]

Concurrent with the rise of gay rights groups has been the increasing visibility of religious fundamentalism, including groups with anti-gay agendas such as the Islamic Defender's Front (FPI) and the Betawi Brotherhood Forum.[45] GAYa Nusantara, Indonesia's best-known gay rights group, has a video clip on its website showing members of the FPI pressuring hotel managers to refuse to allow a gay and lesbian conference at a hotel in Surabaya, and another shows FPI members storming a gay and lesbian meeting in Depok, West Java, intimidating, chasing out, and attacking participants while police stand by idly.[46] In 2010 these groups, as well as the theologically conservative Majelis Ulama Indonesia (Indonesian Ulema Council), threatened violence toward the organizers of a gay film festival in Jakarta and asked that the government intervene to stop it.[47]

The tolerance of the culture and the intolerance of religious and some political groups produced a duality practiced by homosexual men who marry and have children, essentially submitting to a heteronormative culture while simultaneously continuing to conduct illicit sexual affairs with men. This culture is entwined with the Indonesian national character in such a way that to be gay is to be a failed citizen. Richard Stephen Howard describes the pressure exerted on and felt by gays in Indonesia to marry and have children: "These 'roles' become embodied in individuals as an assumed divinely inspired, natural character (*kodrat*). A man, therefore, 'becomes a man' by getting married, being a good husband, and eventually being a good father. Marriage is a key step in the fulfillment of kodrat . . . when a man marries, social and cosmic stability are thought to be reinforced."[48] In this context, the rumor that Noordin engaged in sodomy with men while maintaining heterosexual marriages is plausible, given this understanding of public versus private sexuality. Thus, the rumor that Noordin maintained a low-profile homosexual lifestyle fits into the narrative landscape of Indonesian heteronormative nationalism; it is familiar and believable within Indonesian culture. However, it would be particularly damning and discrediting to the legacy of Noordin Top, an Islamist extremist who supposedly adhered to a very strict—and homophobic—interpretation of Islam.

Muslims who oppose homosexuality often express this sentiment in the overall context of support for Islamic law and a shift in the Indonesian state to reflect its predominant religion. "The homophobic reaction of these Islamic youth groups appears not as a specifically religious response (those attacked were not in mosques or demanding religious recognition)," Boellstorff explains, "but rather as a reaction to feelings of *malu* (shame) associated with representations of the nation."[49] Needless to say, there are no gay—

or at least gay-identifying—heroes in Indonesian national mythmaking. Rather, there is often an undercurrent of heterosexual virility, as embodied by the facts and rumors circulating around President Soekarno's infamous womanizing. Soekarno (1901–1970) is regarded as the founder of the nation and still revered by Indonesians. His escapades with women other than his wives were public secrets and in many Indonesians' eyes bolstered his image as a virile man standing up to both the West and the communist East.[50] There are also gender ideologies at play in this history of homophobia, as accusations of passive sodomy emasculate the hypermasculine terrorist. One assertion by Islamists in Indonesia and elsewhere is the need to protect Muslim women from the degenerate and immoral influences of the West. And, if the Indonesian narrative concerning the Dutch spread of homosexuality is believed to be true, Noordin himself has succumbed to the immoral influences of the West, making him a hypocrite. JI condemns the lifestyles associated with the West, including "consumerism, free sex and homosexuality, the consumption of drugs and alcohol, satanic music, pornography, and the threat of Norwegian nudism," and argues that it must wage jihad against them.[51] As an accused passive sodomite, Noordin is feminized and rendered weak; his external image—a jihadist engaged in a holy war, a manly protector of the virtues of women—is inconsistent with his internal feminized image. As such, he is perceived to be psychologically imbalanced and, hence, not a true Islamic warrior. Indeed, as we show below, an Airlangga University psychiatrist weighed in on his perceived condition and deemed him psychopathic (of course, that conclusion could have easily been made simply by the fact that he murders innocents in large-scale acts of terrorism).

The accusation is also consistent with the portrayal of Noordin as an outsider not belonging to the Indonesian nation. This element of the accusation is perhaps the easiest for the Indonesian audience to understand; after all, Noordin was a Malaysian citizen. Indeed, it is within three converging contexts—gender/sexuality, religion, and national identity—that we can better understand the implications of the posthumous rumors spread about Noordin, their success in reducing his legacy from martyr to deviant and in the process tainting national pride, and thus the success of the state's whisper campaign. In effect, the state mobilized stereotypes of homosexuality, national antagonism with Malaysia, and the cathectic anxiety over anal sex in order to undermine the Islamist extremist narrative associated with one of its heroes.

Transmediation of Top Stories

Although the mainstream Indonesian press backed off from the "Noordin is gay" story shortly after initiating it, rumors spread online and the story thrived.[52] Here, too, the rumors were received without question; the dominant position first offered by the state, and then by the mainstream media, went unchallenged. This response makes the Noordin case distinct from the Mas Selamat case, where resistant interpretations of official statements resulted in a virtual critique of the state itself. In the Noordin case, the state was not a player in the narrative but its beneficiary.

According to Yahoo, the term "Noordin M. Top" was the most searched term in Indonesia for 2009.[53] Although we are not asserting that the rumors following his autopsy are what caused his name to be the most popular search term, the rumors certainly contributed to interest in him. Other reasons include: the 17 July Marriott and Ritz-Carlton bombings, for which he was blamed; the online announcement attributed to him, in which he claimed responsibility for the bombings and announced the formation of a new extremist group; the reports about his supposed death in August; and, of course, the reports concerning his actual death in September. Despite the spurious science on which the claim was based, the sodomy rumor was picked up and broadcast by blogs and other online sources. Although it is impossible to pinpoint the effect of this story on the popularity of the search term, it is highly plausible that rumors about Noordin fueled the popularity of online searches related to him.

The transmediation of the Noordin story began through repostings of the original news stories, often with commentary. The day after the announcement, the al-Yaasin website, a blog that focuses primarily on Islamic topics, posted sections of the *Kompas* news articles about the rumor. The blog entry also incorporated unattributed comments from psychologists at Surabaya's Airlangga University, who speculated about Noordin's psychological condition. His heterosexual relations with women were described as "torture," and, in the fashion of Tardieu, his alleged homosexuality was blamed on his "psychopathic" condition.[54] The article also cites University of Indonesia criminologist Adrianus Meliala as stating that it was unlikely that the shape of Noordin's anus was caused by an illness or birth defect. Within one day of the announcement, Noordin Top was already being characterized as a deviant in the Indonesian blogosphere.

— 4.1. Transmediated images of Noordin Top, including as American singer — Michael Jackson and Indonesian reggae artist Mbah Surip, along with two images feminizing the terrorist. Original creator unknown; image found at http://idekonyol.wordpress.com/2009/09/01/idekonyol-penyamaran-noordin-m-top-lagi/ (accessed 16 December 2009).

Other supposed experts chimed in as well. In a 2 October online story in *Detik Health* entitled "Funnel Anus Is a Sign of What?" Professor Wimpie Pangkahila of the Faculty of Medicine at Udayana University stated that indeed a funnel-shaped anus is a sign of repeated sodomy. "This is what separates normal people from bisexuals, and that shape cannot appear with just one or two acts," he stated. "Ooo, it can be years to make a shape such as that." The same article states that bisexuality can be a result of damaged chromosomes but cannot be detected under normal circumstances.[55] These conclusions by "experts" were circulated widely in the Indonesian media landscape.

Given the nature of the rumor and the medium of its spread, the online commentaries quickly turned to parody and crude jokes. Bloggers began to acquire and manipulate official images of Noordin (from, for example, his wanted posters), changing them to feminize Noordin by giving him a *jilbab* (headscarf) or long hair or by adding rouge to his cheeks. Others made multiple images of Noordin, some feminized, others simply for humor, including

— 4.2. Transmediated images of Noordin Top, including feminized images. —
Original creator unknown; image found at Milk vs. Juice blog:
http://milkvsjuice.wordpress.com/2009/09/19/nurdin-m-top/
(accessed 16 December 2009).

4.3. Transmediated images of Noordin Top that reflect various musical styles. Original creator unknown; image found at http://www.kaskus.us/showthread.php?t=2385624 (accessed 16 December 2009).

4.4. Mash-up of an official image of Noordin Top, depicting him as a woman carrying a bomb. The caption reads: "Only a coward is brave like this, we are not afraid!!!" Original creator unknown; image found at http://www.supermance.com/noordin-m-top-pun-pakai-ilmu-psikosibernetik/ (offline; accessed 16 December 2009).

4.5. Transmediated official images of Noordin Top, reflecting various cultural references. Image created by bungandy (screen name) and found at http://bungandy.net/post/169735840/noordin-m-top-collection-2010-hahahaha (accessed 17 December 2009).

Noordin as Robocop, lead vocalist of the American hard rock band Guns N' Roses (Axl Rose, who remains popular in Indonesia), a pirate, and a clown, and Noordin as devotee of various musical styles (emo, rock 'n' roll, punk, and dangdut, an indigenous Indonesian pop music influenced by Indian and Middle Eastern music). In a particularly potent example of transcultural transmediation, a mash-up image of Noordin as legendary pop icon Michael Jackson also began circulating after the terrorist's death and the government's press conference. This mash-up brings to the legacy of Noordin Top the same gender ambiguity that marked Jackson's physical transformations, as well as the persistent rumors of pedophilia and homosexuality.

Indonesian prosumers also appropriated images associated with the transmediation of the February 2008 Mas Selamat escape story. The mock wanted poster, purportedly showing Mas Selamat in a variety of ridiculous disguises, was copied by Indonesians following the rumor of Noordin's demise in August; they added images of Noordin but retained many of the elements of the poster. In other words, images associated with Mas Selamat became a meme, resulting in a kind of memetic isomorphism.[56] For example, figures 2.2 and 4.6 illustrate how rumors utilizing similar frames of reference may spread within culturally close contexts and related mediated spaces online. From this example, it is clear that Indonesians were aware of the Mas Selamat case and that online communication concerning terrorism is a transnational phenomenon (this is also clear from the examples below concerning the Noordin case as a proxy for Indonesian attacks on Malaysia).

Although the target of the Mas Selamat poster was primarily the Singaporean government, which was taken to task for allowing such a high-profile prisoner to escape, the target of the Noordin poster is clearly Noordin himself, in an attempt to malign him posthumously. Whereas comments on the Singaporean blog clearly and explicitly target the Singaporean government, the comments that follow the Noordin image do not mention the Indonesian government, but rather point to the ridiculousness of Noordin's "new looks." This treatment of the JI celebrity chips away at the image of the group as pious. At least online, JI (as represented by Noordin) was slowly but clearly being positioned as a hypocritical organization. After all, if one of its key leaders was gay, questions must be asked about the organization itself. *Are the other leaders gay? If not, how could they not know about Noordin's supposed homosexuality? Are other JI members gay?* Noordin was a very important figurehead

4.6. An example of memetic isomorphism.
The producer of this image borrowed heavily from the Mas Selamat image (see figure 2.2), including the color of the font and the wording. Original creator unknown; image found in an online forum at http://www.kaskus.us/showthread.php?t=2287880 (accessed 16 December 2009).

for the organization; this rumor effectively painted him as a hypocrite and thus, by proxy, the organization as hypocritical.

In addition to textual and graphic mash-ups, popular video-sharing websites, where online participants can appropriate images and alter them in short video clips, were marshaled by prosumers eager to cast Noordin as gay. A spike in views occurred after the raid of 16 September 2009 in which the terrorist was killed, and another spike came following the press conference and announcement by Mun'im concerning the findings from the autopsy. These spikes show that the Indonesian online community was following these events as they occurred and was aware of (and participating in) the transmediation of the Noordin story.

The first YouTube video concerning the accusations appeared the same day as the announcement (30 September), entitled "Noordin m Top Pahlawan Malingsia Malaysia Youtubers" (Noordin m. Top Hero of Malingsia [thief + Malaysia] Malaysia Youtubers).[57] This video combines footage from Jakarta's MetroTV newscast covering the police autopsy press conference and material from an earlier video by NusantaraWarrior that feminized Noordin.[58] The post-announcement footage features a shot of the police station, with police and Mun'im Idris walking toward the camera, then cuts to a shot of Noordin's corpse. The reporter refers to the condition as "kelainan seks" (sexual abnormality/anomaly) as a result of "seks menyimpang" (deviant sex) and states that a spokesman for Noordin's family denied the allegations. Next, Mun'im is shown in a scrum of reporters, refusing to answer specific questions because he is on police property and inviting reporters to talk to him at the Universitas Indonesia campus where he is based. The video ends with images of Noordin's face transposed onto women's bodies, the same images NusantaraWarrior used following Noordin's death. The background music is "Bongkar," by Indonesian pop star Iwan Fals. The term *bongkar* means upside down or out of place, and in the song it has connotations of a disturbed social order in an era of repression (Iwan Fals was a prominent social critic of Suharto's New Order). If NusantaraWarrior's first video is a clear critique of Noordin, this second amplifies both the intensity of the creator's denigration of Noordin and attaches government veracity to an implied explanation for Noordin's feminization. Other YouTube videos followed (see table 4.1).

The second, fourth, and fifth postings under the search terms "Dubur Noordin Top" (Anus Noordin Top) are simply rebroadcasts of the news.[59] The third video, created by Gombress, is the first to incorporate an anti-Malaysian slant.[60] It begins with a crude joke about the diameter of Noordin's anus, then segues to the MetroTV broadcast. Following that is the headline, "Club Pondan Noordin M. Top Malaysiana" (Malaysian Transvestite Club Noordin M. Top), and a montage of video clips, including a broadcast of a Malaysian news report about a raid on a Malaysian gay club, Mahmoud

Table 4.1. YouTube videos under Search Terms "Dubur Noordin Top"

Rank	*Title*	*Creator*	*Date posted*	*No. of views*	*No. of comments*	*Theme*	*Rating (stars)*
1	Noordin Top melakukan seks menyimpang?	Wongbusan	9/30/09	1709	16	Metro TV broadcast	5
2	Noordin top diduga Acap melakukan seks menyimpang	Malaysian-Conscience	10/2/09	581	20	Metro TV broadcast	5
3	Moordin M Top Liwat Pondan Sodomi Malaysian Hero Tews	Gombress	10/1/09	384	20	Humor, target Malaysians, song "Bongkar" (Iwan Fals), Metro TV broadcast, images from Malaysian news and programming	*
4	Noordin M top Pahlawan Malingsia Malaysia youtubers	Nusantara Warrior	9/3/09	298	23	Humor, rebroadcast of #3, then images of Top as a woman	*
5	Noordin "Dubur" M Top	Preman-Berjubah	10/3/09	121	0	Metro TV broadcast	*

*Ratings disabled

Ahmadinejad's speech at Columbia University in which he denied that there were homosexuals in Iran, and a flamboyant Malaysian television show host, interspersed with footage of a Western woman laughing hysterically, again with background music of Iwan Fals's "Bongkar."

Almost all of the videos by Gombress and NusantaraWarrior feature Indonesian nationalist and anti-Malaysia themes, as do those of many of their YouTube "friends." Curiously, both Gombress and NusantaraWarrior state in their profiles that they currently live in Malaysia, the former as a dentist, the latter as a student at Universitas Teknologi Malaysia, the same university that Noordin attended. Comments posted for these videos (and others related to Noordin) reflect the animosity between some Indonesians and Malaysians, often spiral downward into cursing and name-calling, and reveal the degree to which rumors of this kind can spread beyond national borders by invoking geopolitical tensions. Indonesian and Malaysian respondents to NusantaraWarrior's "Pahlawan Malingsia" video traded these barbs, among others: "See, don't you know, all malingshits are homosexuals!"; "You know all Malaysians are homos! They're all asslickers!"; "How, without capital or resources can the indon slaves condemn M'sia? It is a reflection of their idiocy!"[61]

In the days following the announcement, there appeared several more YouTube videos addressing the accusations against Noordin. These videos, and the comment threads that follow them, became proxies for users to flame Malaysia and Malaysians with insults and for Malaysians to return these insults. They refer to recent feuds between Malaysia and Indonesia, such as the dispute over the Ambalat Islands and the Indonesian perception that Malaysia is appropriating Indonesian culture to promote tourism. These tensions have deep roots, dating at the very least to Malaysia's decolonization in the early 1960s and Indonesia's policy of *Konfrontasi* amid accusations that Malaysia was a postcolonial puppet state.[62] Thus, despite the geographic proximity of the two states, as well as their ethnic, linguistic, religious, and cultural similarities, some residents of both countries continue to stoke nationalist ideologies and mistrust of the other.

About five weeks later, the rumor spurred a spoof that stayed close to the original news stories but substituted a fictional character, Jomblo Juhari ("Jomblo" means without a girlfriend or boyfriend), and the blogger translated the original story into English. Mimicking line-for-line the original news story in parts, the parody also injected crude jokes: "It appears that besides not having a girlfriend, Jomblo Juhari also liked to be shot from behind."[63] The goal is clear: Noordin is similar to Jomblo the simpleton, and his activities are reprehensible.

Netizens ruminated on the posthumous accusations in online forums, blogs, and websites, reflecting the two main threads associated with the transmediation of the story: criticism of terrorists and Noordin himself, and attacks on Malaysia. The criticisms of Noordin and terrorism use words and images to feminize Noordin and terrorists, thereby invoking homophobic ideologies in support of nationalist sentiments; the criticisms of Malaysia use Noordin as a symbol or representative of Malaysian identity. By linking homosexuality to femininity and femininity to Malaysian identity in this way, these netizens were also engaged in a misogynist articulation of Malaysian nationality. This conflation demonstrates that whisper campaigns may have unintended or unforeseen consequences. Our perception is that the rumor's primary purpose was to defuse extremist rhetoric and the valorization of Noordin among the population as a devout Muslim and a martyr. Fueling nationalist rivalry, however, also benefits the state, as any pent-up citizen ire becomes focused on an outside rival rather than domestically, a tactic the government has used in the past to divert attention from the central government during crises. Hence, unlike the response to the Mas Selamat case, these mash-ups did not question the dominant perspective offered by the state and mainstream media. Instead, they served to perpetuate the image of Noordin as a hypocrite at the ideological expense of both JI and Malaysia.

The latent conflict between Malaysia and Indonesia became the predominant theme over time in the transmediation of this rumor. And again it perpetuated a stereotype: *Noordin Top is gay; therefore, all Malaysians are gay.* "Noordin Top Appears to be Homosexual (a Reflection of the [religious] Hypocrisy of Malingsia Society)," screamed another Topix.com report. The term "Malingsia" combines the word for thief (*maling*) with Malaysia, but this textual mash-up has brought to the fore another derogatory Indonesian term for Malaysia: "Magaysia."[64] With the rumor of Noordin's anatomy in circulation, latent nationalist fervor linked with a heteronormative national identity. Conspiracy rumors posited that Noordin was sent to Indonesia to perpetrate acts of terror to destabilize the country.[65] The whisper campaign, then, results in a double strategic communication victory for the Indonesian government: a famous terrorist leader is discredited and prevented from achieving martyrdom because his story is recast as that of a *munafiq*; at the same time, anti-Malaysian nationalist fervor increases, promoting a greater sense of Indonesian identity represented by the Indonesian state and, by extension, the government.

The rumors concerning Noordin fit seamlessly into a preexisting narrative of Malaysia as a home to deviants who are jealous of Indonesia—especially its varied cultures—and who wish to do it harm. The rumors also allowed Indonesians to use humor and parody with homophobic and misogynist ideologies. The transmediated examples concerning the case of Noordin are often done in humorous ways as a means to belittle a terrorist suspected of collusion in the deaths of many Indonesians and foreigners.

Robert Hariman has noted that parody reveals the "actors behind the masks." Parodic techniques, he argues, using Bakhtin's theory noted in chapter 1, unite in "carnivalesque spectatorship," whereby "institutional forms are revealed to be masks, power and status are shown to be acts, and the key to success is not transcendental backing but rather some combination of backstage maneuver and audience gullibility."[66] Chuck Tryon notes the decline in importance for traditional media and argues that online parody can challenge authority and shape political discourse.[67] Unlike the case of Mas Selamat mash-ups in Singapore, the humor used by online prosumers in this case accepts the official government position (as did the mainstream media in Indonesia, and without refutation by a spokesman for the gay rights organization GAYa Nusantara) but takes it one step further into the realm of ridicule.

Rumors that Ridicule

Rumors and accusations of deviant sexuality have been made toward prominent persons in the Malay Muslim world in the past. During the East Asian economic crisis of 1997–1998, demonstrators in Indonesia and Malaysia took to the streets, demanding political and economic reform and an end to corruption. In Indonesia, they succeeded in ousting a long-serving dictator, Suharto. In Malaysia, Deputy Prime Minister Anwar Ibrahim became a symbol for the reform movement, in opposition to Prime Minister Mahathir Mohammad, his former patron. In April 1998 the government accused Anwar of sodomy, which led to his dismissal and subsequent imprisonment until 2004. It was also rumored that Anwar was gay and had multiple adulterous relationships, and there were clear political motives for positioning him as deviant. His arrest helped deflect the progress of the reform movement in Malaysia, and the movement produced few long-lasting effects, unlike in Indonesia, where democratization has continued to progress. The Anwar case is interesting in that it was the accusation of homosexuality that was meant to turn a politician into a criminal (the act of sodomy is a crime in Malaysia, whereas in Indonesia it is not) rather than, as in Noordin's case, a damaging slur intended to sully the reputation of someone guilty other crimes.

Similarly, Habib Rizieq of the Jakarta-based FPI, a quasi-legal group engaged in extortion and protest nominally on behalf of Islam, was rumored to be in possession of pornography following his arrest after an FPI demonstration at Jakarta's National Monument turned violent. Though not charged with a pornography-related offense, he was imprisoned for the violence. The charge of possessing pornography, however, helped his critics to portray him as a hypocrite in the same way the rumor about Noordin portrayed him as a hypocrite.

The goal of the state's whisper campaign certainly fulfilled its intended effects. Among those who received and then rebroadcast the announcement that Noordin was gay or bisexual, and among those who then viewed these transmediated images, Noordin's reputation was tainted, and he (and his family and associates) were posthumously humiliated. Humiliation is a powerful weapon in the war against Islamist terrorism. As quoted in the epigraph to this chapter, terrorist Osama bin Laden feared humiliation more than death.[68]

In the contemporary information environment, rumor mash-ups amplify messages and lead to potential influence even when they are engaged in ridicule. Terrorist expert J. Michael Waller cites both historical and recent examples of ridicule, the latter including the film *Team America: World Police* and its targets, Kim Jong Il and Muslim terrorists, and a version of captured footage of Abu Musab al-Zarqawi, the founder and leader of AQI discussed in chapter 3. *Team America* appeals to sophomoric, scatological, and, we would argue, racist humor. One shot, for example, has the North Korean leader introduced under title graphics "F.A.G" and then saying "hello" in a stereotypical Asian accent. The video of al-Zarqawi portrays someone who wants to promote an image of a capable and fearsome terrorist. Yet the unedited video released by U.S. forces shows him to be incompetent, incapable of fixing a jam in a machine gun he was trying to fire, and a hypocrite wearing American-made tennis shoes. Likewise, one of his followers burns his hand after grabbing the searing hot barrel of the recently fired machine gun. In the case of the Zarqawi video, we see evidence of a state-sponsored whisper campaign designed to undermine an Islamist terrorist and his organization in ways that speak to Muslims in general. In the case of *Team America*, we see associations with homosexuality as a means of ridicule for a leader accused of terrorism (and, for an American audience, thereby suggesting the power of homophobia as a rhetorical meme).

Sometimes Islamist extremists inadvertently facilitate gendered rumors that they are hoping to quell. When Iran's President Mahmoud Ahmadinejad spoke at Columbia University in September 2007, he denied that there were homosexuals in Iran, even though the Islamic Republic regularly condemns gays to capital punishment and subsidizes a high number of gender reassignment surgeries.[69] That week, the late-night comedy show *Saturday Night Live* featured a digital short with comedian Andy Samberg serenading an Ahmadinejad impersonator (Fred Armisen). The video referenced the Columbia speech and showed the two in various romantic scenes in New York. The video went viral, with more than a million views on YouTube. Although the video was a parody, it reinforced the ridiculous nature of the Iranian president's speech.

Like these examples, the rumor about Noordin gained traction through the transmediation of narrative tropes that lend themselves to ridicule. The repetition of rumors associated with Noordin led to the reproduction of a colorful visual meme involving Noordin's phenotypes and physiognomy. A frequently circulated example emphasized his full lips marked by lipstick and distorted sexual organs. The frequency of repetition on various media such as YouTube, Facebook, and blogs heightened public awareness of this rumor beyond the more mainstream news media representations. As Chip Heath and others found, rumors go through a stage of emotional selection. More extreme versions of the rumor are far more likely to spread, as we have shown by the quick circulation of explicit graphical illustrations of the rumor across media.[70] This extension of extreme and emotionally charged rumor texts into cyber and mediated spaces shows how terrorist-related rumors mirror other rumors and stories as they spread and proliferate. Nils Bubandt proposed that "the intermodality of the rumor, its ability to piggyback on and intersect with other media, printed and electronic, legitimate and illegitimate, . . . gives it reach and impact."[71] This shape-shifting mobility also signals the need for more research on the perceived successes and failures of state-sponsored whisper campaigns, of which there is very little.

Conclusion

In light of growing concerns over Islamist extremism and insurgencies, study of the creation and transmediation of rumors regarding terrorists provides a way to analyze extant social anxieties and fears that fuel outcomes associated with counterterrorism, counterinsurgencies, and national identities. In the case of Indonesia, rumors have historically been employed in national politics.[72] With respect to the Noordin campaign, they achieved a powerful format by co-conscripting official and unofficial narratives across multiple media platforms. A whisper campaign, in short, ended up facilitating a rumor that drew upon master narratives that speak to Indonesians specifically and Muslims more generally, and one that served the interest of the state. Seen in this light, the study of rumor has implications for counterterrorism strategies and lay tactics of resistance in response to extremist stories.

For counterterrorism concerns, the spread of rumors regarding Noordin seems to have achieved a chilling effect on his legacy. It is striking to note that, unlike other terrorist leaders who have garnered posthumous acclaim, Noordin seems to have receded in discourse after the release of the rumor. His image was not enhanced with symbols normally associated with martyrdom in the Muslim tradition (such as the appearance of green birds that are posited to hold the souls of martyrs at funerals). Recent scholarship on celebrity studies points to the aggregation of fans to mourn for their heroes and idols collectively on mediated platforms, which then further inflames their passion and resurrects the fame of deceased celebrities.[73] In Noordin's case, online discourse appeared not to have any such vivifying effects. For example, the English-language ". . . There Lies a Beautiful Meadow" blog regularly posts about the deaths and funerals of Southeast Asian jihadis, noting the symbols of martyrdom seen at their funerals. The blog posted laudatory comments about Noordin after his death; but even though it covered the funerals of fighters killed with Noordin, it is strangely silent about his funeral. On the contrary, most online content furthered a narrative discourse that positioned his legacy as deviant and hypocritical.[74]

It is striking to note the congruence between the rumor and its spread within the cultural crucible of Indonesia specifically and the region more generally. In many ways, the attempt to malign Noordin posthumously by spreading the rumor that he was gay or bisexual can be interpreted as an effective covert communication attack on the terrorist. First, it feminizes a cold-blooded killer and, in the minds of some Indonesians, makes him mentally ill. Second, it portrays a supposedly pious Muslim as a sinner. Terrorists claim to be acting on behalf of some idealized conceptualization of a true Islam, and those who refuse to act or support them are portrayed as less pious. Third, it facilitates a narrative that would be difficult, if not impossible, for defenders of Noordin to dispel without access to the corpse or scientific debate. The conclusion seems forgone. In this way, the state's whisper campaign can be said to have been a powerful intercession into the terrorist's own narrative of success: piety and reestablishment of fundamental Islamic tenets.

Rumor propagation to discredit Noordin as an Islamic martyr appeared to gain traction on multiple media sites, evoking cultural taboos and moral anxieties surrounding homosexuality. As James Scott notes: "As a rumor travels it is altered in a fashion that brings it more closely into line with the hopes, fears and worldview of those who hear it and retell it. . . . The rumor, it appears, is not only an opportunity for anonymous, protected communication, but also serves as a vehicle for anxieties and aspirations that may not be openly acknowledged by its propagators."[75] On this basis, one must expect rumors to take quite divergent forms depending on the class, strata, region, or occupation in which they circulate and on what counterterrorism purposes they serve. In the context of Islam, it appeared that the accusation against Noordin degraded his Muslim credentials among followers and those open to his message. Hence, we witnessed how the accusation silenced Noordin's followers and invited ridicule via political parodies by netizens. Ridicule is a potent emotional means for terrorists to belittle fellow Muslims who are not willing to join their cause and is also as a potential weapon of the state's strategic communication efforts designed to weaken the appeal of extremists' messages among contested populations.

We close with two critical caveats. First, it is impossible to know whether Mun'im Idris, Nanan Sukarna, or anyone else was aware that the diagnosis of sodomy was based on discredited science. As the example of Egypt shows, some states continue to base their juridical claims of homosexual behavior on Tardieu's methods. We were unable to ascertain whether Mun'im or the Indonesian police spread this misinformation knowing it was false or not. Nor do we have any evidence that Noordin's anus was indeed funnel-shaped. That said, the underlying motive behind the accusation seems clear: to discredit Noordin among his supporters and would-be supporters by casting him in a homophobic narrative of deviance, perversion, and hypocrisy. This is a narrative that would and clearly did resonate with many Indonesians. Second, there is a connection between this case and other cases in Southeast Asia where rumors served key political purposes. This connection is evident not only in the example of Anwar Ibrahim's political career but also, and more importantly, in the subtle stirring of nationalist fervor spawned by the Noordin Top rumor. An increase in nationalism benefits the incumbent government by shifting blame for any administrative failure away from the government itself and on to Malaysia. In addition, the government appears to be the defender of Indonesian national identity by defusing the triple threat of Noordin Top—terrorist, sexual deviant, and Malaysian. We think this is compelling evidence of a whisper campaign.

If this whisper campaign is eventually deemed to be a success by other states fighting Islamist extremists, we may see it used again. We may also see the emergence of a rumor mosaic across the region if similar kinds of damning rumors are spread about other extremists and supporters of terror, for example, branding them as deviants and thus marshaling the hypocrite master narrative that is powerful among Muslims. In this case, the Noordin story appears to have been a successful instance of rumor employed as an information warfare countermeasure, primarily because of the nature of the origin of the Noordin rumor as well as its titillating nature, which allowed it to become a meme, gain traction, and spread across Indonesia and the region.

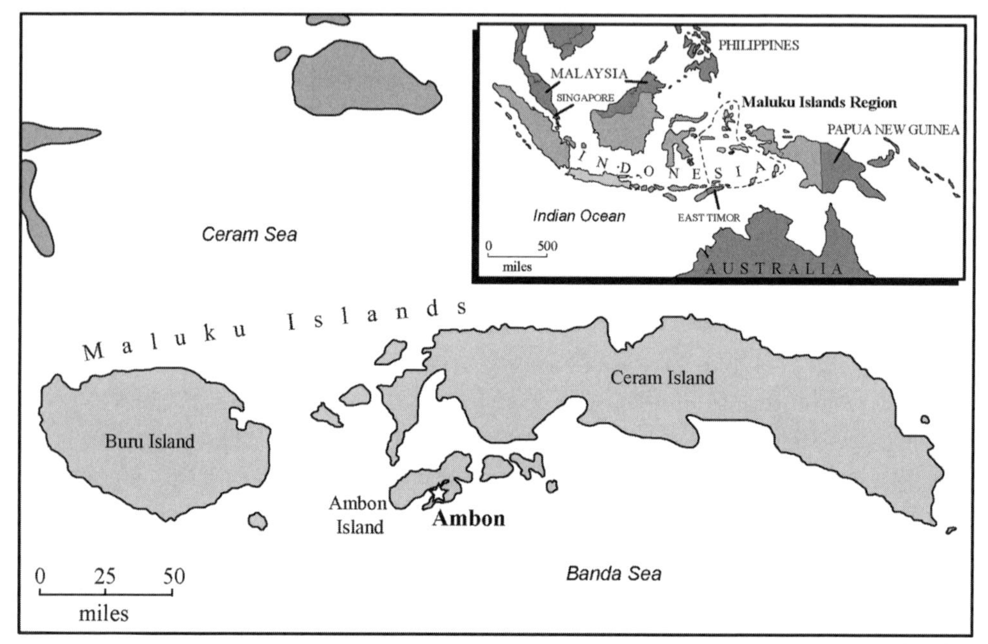
PHILIPPINES
MALAYSIA
SINGAPORE
Maluku Islands Region
PAPUA NEW GUINEA
INDONESIA
Indian Ocean
EAST TIMOR
0 500
miles
AUSTRALIA
Ceram Sea
Maluku Islands
Ceram Island
Buru Island
Ambon Island
Ambon
0 25 50
miles
Banda Sea

Becky Eden

5

Coercion and Consent

Narrative Countermeasures in the Battle for "Hearts and Minds"

Every empire, however, tells itself and the world that it is unlike all other empires, that its mission is not to plunder and control but to educate and liberate.

—Edward W. Said, "Blind Imperial Arrogance"

Commanders must recognize and continuously address that this "The American way is best" bias is unhelpful.

—U.S. Army/Marine Corps Counterinsurgency Field Manual

The preceding three case studies examined rumors and their function in narrative landscapes. In the case of Mas Selamat, a family of rumors about his escape sparked an online critique of government policy and efficacy. The different rumors intersected with pop culture iconography (movie posters, for example) and contributed to narratives positioning Mas Selamat as an outlaw hero rather than a terrorist threat. In the case of the Stack House facility in Iraq, a mosaic of rumors about the denizens and activities inside the compound smoothly integrated into a dominant narrative of the U.S. forces as Crusaders, eroding public support for both the U.S. troops and their Iraqi SWAT partners. The bovine poisoning rumor also fit into this narrative system, negating any goodwill that could have been generated by the veterinary outreach program, which itself was an attempt to effect change in a narrative landscape. And in Indonesia, government officials planted the rumors of Noordin Top's anatomical deformity and its supposed link to homosexuality.

This introduction of salacious rumor into a heteronormative society via a state-sponsored whisper campaign altered the narrative trajectory of Noordin Top, who did not receive an apotheosis as a martyr, and of Jemaah Islamiyah, painting one of its leaders as a hypocrite.

We have treated rumors as an observable phenomenon, with specific characteristics, and made the case that they are a serious phenomenon requiring attention in the context of strategic communication. Our discussions have analyzed how these rumors function as components of narrative systems, how they achieved narrative coherence and fidelity, and how they worked against the interests of governments and organizations. In this final chapter, we turn our attention to what can be done by a government or organization that faces a rumor threat. How can strategic communication teams defuse these narrative IEDs? Specifically, we discuss a range of narrative countermeasures by drawing upon a recent example of strategic communication witnessed by co-author Daniel Bernardi, who was part of a U.S. Navy team that faced a rumor threat in Ambon, Indonesia, and was able to leverage the research underway to write this book in his efforts to mitigate the rumor mill there.

In June 2010 a U.S. Navy advance echelon team (ADVON) of five officers, including Bernardi, and one civilian accountant was sent to Ambon to prepare for the arrival of the hospital ship USNS *Mercy* (T-AH 19), one of the Navy's two dedicated hospital ships (figure 5.1).[1] The *Mercy* was the flagship of the annual Pacific Partnership mission, a disaster relief and training exercise that "is designed to strengthen alliances, improve U.S. and partner capacity to deliver humanitarian assistance and disaster relief and improve security cooperation among partner nations."[2] In addition to U.S. Navy and Army medical personnel, members from non-governmental agencies (NGOs) were onboard.[3] The 2010 mission also included partner and host-nation navies from Australia, Canada, Indonesia, Japan, New Zealand, Singapore, and the United Kingdom. The hospital ship had already visited Vietnam, Cambodia, and the North Maluku region of Indonesia when it arrived in Ambon on 26 July 2010.

Planning for the Pacific Partnership visits to host-nation ports had been underway for six months prior to the *Mercy*'s departure for Southeast Asia. These planning efforts were supplemented by ADVON teams dispatched to ports such as Ambon prior to the ship's arrival. The U.S. Navy ADVON team facilitating the *Mercy* visit to Ambon was charged with working "with and

5.1. USNS *Mercy* at anchor off North Maluku Province, Indonesia, 19 July 2010. State Department photo by Tom Weinz.

through" the government of Indonesia and the Indonesian Navy, which meant that it coordinated all activities primarily through Indonesian naval officers. This arrangement was designed to build command-level interoperability between the U.S. Navy, the Indonesian military, and other regional partners to emphasize the cooperative arrangement between the countries, countering the common global perception of the United States as paternalistic or, worse yet, the "playground bully."[4] The entire team had just over four weeks to finalize arrangements with local government and medical officials, hire contractors, identify local areas that would benefit from medical and engineering projects, ensure that force protection protocols were achievable, and set up media engagements.

The media were a critical element, as both the U.S. Navy and its Indonesian partners wanted the Pacific Partnership visit to be noticed by as many Indonesians as possible. The ADVON team began scheduling press conferences with local and national media outlets, one-on-one interviews between host-nation press and U.S. Navy medical professionals, and opportunities for Indonesian media personnel to accompany joint medical events across the

Ambon region. It also scheduled three public appearances for the U.S. Pacific Fleet band, which traveled onboard the *Mercy*, as well as several community relations events at local orphanages and schools. The media products and opportunities highlighted an interlocking system of stories around the *Mercy* visit, emphasizing mutual cooperation and interoperability, goodwill, and cross-cultural exchange. All of these efforts were intended to ensure that residents of Ambon, and Indonesians more broadly, understood and supported the Pacific Partnership mission, the U.S. Navy, and, of course, the Indonesian government and its military.

It might be tempting to conclude that the Pacific Partnership mission was simply a platform for U.S. propaganda. Clearly, a key dimension of the mission centered on what the U.S. Navy classifies as public affairs and what the business community calls public relations—building goodwill in the populace through events and communication efforts. Unlike the propaganda tactics discussed in chapters 3 and 4, however, the Pacific Partnership's media engagements and community relation events were far from one-sided or covertly articulated. The ADVON team and senior leadership on the *Mercy* openly discussed the Pacific Partnership mission with the Indonesian press, rather than trying to persuade people through propaganda or the use of strong-arm tactics to further the U.S. political agenda.[5] As we discuss later, neither the U.S. Navy nor the Indonesian military attempted to control the Indonesian press. They did not spread disinformation, but instead provided journalists maximum access to staff personnel and information sources. The local media were free to report on the mission according to their journalistic standards and practices, and Pacific Partnership operators consistently produced press releases, images, and video of medical events for use by the local press. The press also accompanied U.S. and Indonesian military and NGO teams on a number of activities, using their own cameras and reporters to document what they saw without censorship from the U.S. or Indonesian militaries. In short, while the U.S. ADVON team and its Indonesian counterparts worked to frame the Pacific Partnership narrative in a positive light, the information they distributed, the means by which they engaged the media, and the access provided to the media all suggest a program more akin to a public relations campaign than state-sponsored propaganda.

While official U.S. Navy sources emphasized the strengthening of alliances and interoperational capabilities, it is clear to us that the Pacific Partnership activities simultaneously projected a significant strategic communication component, one that can craft a favorable image of the U.S. Navy with host-nation populations. In fact, the multinational mission evolved from Operation Unified Endeavor, the U.S. government's response to the devastating 2004 Boxing Day tsunami that killed an estimated 165,708 Indonesians.[6] For the U.S. military, Operation Unified Endeavor presented a positive story about American generosity to Muslims across the world at a time when unfavorable stories about the United States dominated international media. The U.S. response to the tsunami significantly slowed the tide of anti-American sentiment in Indonesia, the world's largest Muslim nation, which until that point had been increasing steadily.[7] First deployed in 2006, the Pacific Partnership was designed to further strengthen America's image in Indonesia and the Southeast Asian region while also ensuring interoperability for future disaster relief and humanitarian missions. In this light, we see the Pacific Partnership as very similar to the civil affairs and information operations mission discussed in chapter 3, wherein Multi-National Force–Iraq (MNF-I) planned to aid rural farmers by deploying civil affairs teams assisted by military veterinarians. The mission's objective (inoculation of cattle to improve the stability of the country's agricultural economy) had an evident strategic communication goal: provide a disincentive to support insurgents and an incentive to support MNF-I.

The Navy ADVON team immediately discovered that although the Indonesian military actively supported the *Mercy*'s mission and its associated medical and engineering projects, there was considerable apprehension about allowing the ship's U.S. Army veterinary officers and NGOs to conduct veterinary service events and capability demonstrations. One Indonesian naval officer, referencing the supposed poisoning operation in Iraq, explicitly asked the team what the veterinarians were "planning to do to the animals?"[8] Local medical professionals were also apprehensive. Several asked why the officers wanted to work on animals when there were so many young and elderly people in need of medical assistance.[9] In particular, concern coalesced around what the American veterinarians might do to the swine and, to a slightly lesser extent, the cattle. These reactions belied a classic dread rumor of local fears of a negative outcome to a coming event. Local journalists also seemed skeptical, and some expressed doubts about the efficacy of the operation. Members of the ADVON team were well aware that MNF-I's 2005 bovine inoculation campaign in Iraq turned into a bovine poisoning story that supported the growing and increasingly violent insurgency. They did not want to see a repeat of this situation in Indonesia in 2010.

In fact, both the Indonesian Navy and the Indonesian press were aware of the 2005 Iraq bovine poisoning story, which suggested that the rumor could end up undermining the Pacific Partnership mission and, more critically, U.S. relations with another Muslim country. More problematically, such a rumor could also undermine the Indonesian government. The government openly celebrated the *Mercy*'s visit; in fact, a presidential tour was scheduled and advertised.[10] Moreover, the Indonesian government was publicizing the hospital ship's participation in Sail Banda, a government-managed event designed to promote the tourist elements of the islands that make up the Maluku region in an effort to dampen the memory of the religious conflict that broke out in Ambon between Christians and Muslims in 1999 and to get people to stop polluting. The history of that conflict also loomed large in the minds of members of the ADVON team and their Indonesian counterparts.

The relatively recent sectarian violence, along with the region's religious demographics, made for a more volatile narrative landscape warranting special attention from the Indonesian government and its U.S. Navy partners. Unlike throughout most of Indonesia, the population of the entire Maluku region (including the North Maluku and Maluku provinces) is more than 40 percent Christian and Catholic,[11] and the Christian population in Ambon is even larger.[12] Although Muslims and Christians in the area have historically lived together in peace, the 1999 conflict resulted in 3,000 dead and 275,000 refugees (see figure 5.2).[13] Sail Banda was one effort among many by the Indonesian government to recast the image of the area as a safe and prosperous tourist destination. In fact, at the invitations of both the government and the U.S. Navy, the Indonesian press produced stories on the *Mercy*'s visit while the ship was in the North Maluku region, prior to its arrival in the even more sensitive region of Ambon. There was, in short, a great deal on the line for strategic communication stakeholders in both the U.S. Navy and the Indonesia government. Pacific Partnership 2010 was on everybody's radar.

The resurfacing of Iraq's bovine poisoning story in Indonesia raises several fundamental questions for the study of strategic communication, narrative landscapes, and hegemonic struggles. First, how did a rumor that upended a counterinsurgency operation in Iraq in 2005 show up alive and well in Indonesia in 2010? How did so many different sectors of the Ambon community—military, civilian medical professionals, and journalists—hear about

5.2. An Indonesian soldier evacuates refugees from Ambon during the 1999 religious riots.
Courtesy of the Ministry of Defense of the Republic of Indonesia.

the rumor and find it plausible? Might this rumor end up extending an Islamist master narrative seen in Iraq and beyond that strengthens cultural archetypes and casts the United States as a nefarious colonizer and the Indonesian government as Islamic hypocrites? Finally, what threat did the rumor pose, and, more important for the U.S. Navy and its host-nation partners, how might it be thwarted? Or, in military jargon, what non-lethal countermeasures might be used to defuse the rumor and its associated mosaic so that it would not do to Pacific Partnership 2010 what it did to MNF-I's civil affairs/information operation in 2005?

We raise these questions not to celebrate the military's use of non-lethal countermeasures but rather to share insights regarding the application of strategic communication principles to address real-world problems associated with rumor spread.[14] In this final chapter we consider these questions in the context of the theory of rumors as narrative IEDs outlined in chapter 1. We explain how and why the Iraq war's bovine poisoning rumor posed a threat to the Pacific Partnership mission specifically and to the image of

Americans in the eyes of Indonesians more generally. Next, we consider the cultural, historical, and sociopolitical context that facilitates rumor threats of this magnitude. Here we return to Antonio Gramsci's theory of hegemony, specifically his notion of "coercion and consent," as a model that can effectively describe and explain the relationship between rumors, narrative landscapes, and political conflict over governance. Finally, the last section of this chapter looks at the countermeasures the Navy ADVON team employed to deal with the bovine poisoning rumor, showing how strategic communicators are not helpless in the war of narratives shaping the relationship among governments, insurgents, counterinsurgent forces, and contested populations.

Ambon's Narrative Landscape

The history of the Maluku region, including a recent period of violence that fostered distrust between the Ambonese and the central government and between Christians and Muslims, plays a central role in the formation of a narrative landscape fertile for rumor spread. Ambon was a critical region in the pre- and early colonial periods. The North Maluku region was home to two important sultanates, Ternate and Tidore, that negotiated trade with the Spanish, Portuguese, British, and Dutch explorers of the region. The southern part of the Maluku region is also home to Banda Island, the original source of nutmeg and mace. As the Dutch consolidated their control in the late seventeenth century, they committed near total genocide of the Bandanese population in order to create a monopoly on the spice trade. Ambon, more centrally located, became the principle trading city for the spices coming from the region.

Although much of the population in the northern part of the Maluku region, including Ternate and Tidore, had converted to Islam by the time the Dutch consolidated their rule, in the central and southern regions many animists converted to Christianity under Dutch influence. As a result of the high rates of conversion, Christians from the region—who all became known as "Ambonese" to the Dutch despite their differing places of origin—became soldiers for the Dutch East Indies military (Koninklijk Nederlands-Indisch Leger, KNIL) in disproportionate numbers, as they were viewed as more trustworthy than those from other regions. Ambonese Christians received more pay and special benefits, including education for their children, while Ambonese Muslims and other Muslims serving in the KNIL did not, which stoked resentment. These Ambonese were also sent to fight in rebellious regions in the Dutch East Indies, such as Aceh in northern Sumatra, and local Muslims viewed them with disdain. In Ambon, Christian villages came to rely on the income from salaries and benefits of soldiers. Even during the revolution that led to Indonesian independence (1945–1949), many—but not all—Ambonese soldiers fought with the Dutch against the Indonesian Republicans in Java, which caused further resentment. In Ambon during the revolution, the pro-Dutch Ambonese were numerically a minority, but they exerted disproportionate influence because they were frequently armed, and villagers were afraid to oppose them and show loyalty to the Republican side. Many were also afraid of losing the influx of cash associated with KNIL pensions.

When the Republicans emerged victorious in the revolution, the pro-Dutch Ambonese attempted to opt out of joining Indonesia, setting up an alternative government, the Republik Maluku Selatan (the Republic of South Maluku or RMS). Pro-Indonesia Ambonese in Ambon were persecuted despite being numerically superior, but the Indonesian government was able to quell the rebellion quickly, and the RMS government fled the region. Although the RMS leadership and sympathizers in exile in Holland maintained their goal of a sovereign homeland in Maluku and committed acts of terror in Holland, including bombings and kidnappings in the 1970s, to draw attention to their cause, the vast majority of Ambonese—Christian and Muslim—accepted Indonesian sovereignty (RMS leaders have recently made statements signaling that they are willing to give up their claim). Separatism, sectarian and political violence, and economic disparity are longstanding and prominent features in the narrative landscape of Ambon and the Maluku region.

Because of their education and wealth, Ambonese exercised disproportionate power in the emergent Indonesian state. Ambonese Christians played a significant role in the early state-building process in Indonesia. They formed a political party, Parkindo (Partai Kristen Indonesia, or Indonesian Christian Party), to advance their goals (and the goals of Christians more broadly) and were successful in their drive to create a more secular state for Indonesia, including the elimination of the "Jakarta Charter" from the constitution, which would have mandated Sharia law. Christian Ambonese emerged as leaders in Ambon for the same reasons, but perhaps also in part as a concession by the Indonesian government in return for support. This pattern was maintained through the Soekarno era (1949–1965) and into

Suharto's New Order (1965–1998), but wider access to education meant that Ambonese Muslims were able to catch up to Ambonese Christians in this respect. In the early Suharto period, however, Ambonese Christians remained in positions of importance.

Beginning in the 1990s, Suharto began to favor Ambonese Muslims as part of his promotion of Islam elsewhere, and continuing Muslim immigration to the region shifted the population balance toward Muslims. Suharto appointed a Muslim governor, Akib Latuconsina, and rumors circulated that he was pursuing an Islamization policy in the civil service, appointing only Muslims.[15] As Jacques Bertrand points out, uncertainty helped fuel the violence: "Local competition for resources and positions, the polarization of religious identity, fears over future opportunities, and threats to each community provided fertile ground for conflict. Rapid democratic transition increased the uncertainty of outcomes in these struggles that had already created high tensions between Christians and Muslims well before Suharto's resignation."[16] Gerry van Klinken notes how the uncertainty spiraled downward, spurring more violence.[17] As we have explained earlier, rumors thrive in environments of uncertainty and serve to fill narrative gaps created by distrust or lack of access to credible sources of information.

As van Klinken shows, the social order in Ambon began to unravel in the chaotic transition to democracy that began in 1998 with the abdication of Suharto. In the context of a newly opened political system, Ambonese Muslims began to assert their right to occupy positions of influence, and Ambonese Christians attempted to defend the status quo. The spark that set off the violence in 1999 was a minor matter—an argument between a Muslim passenger and a Christian bus driver—but the stage had been set for conflict, and rumors operated to fuel these conflicts.

Initially, the conflict was somewhat limited between Ambonese Christians and Muslims. Each side, however, stoked fears by claiming that the other was attempting to eradicate it. Muslims accused Christians of another Crusade, of trying to dominate Muslims, and of attempting to separate from Indonesia—just after predominantly Catholic East Timor had done so—and hence sounded a call to jihad. Christians accused Muslims of attempting to wipe them out and mobilized forces to attack Muslims. In debates in Jakarta between Ambonese elites and intellectuals, the Muslim side, with its view of Christian separatists, won out (despite the lack of a serious threat of separatism).[18] Islamist media outlets were instrumental in garnering widespread sympathy, as well as recruits for Laskar Jihad and other paramilitary groups.[19] As Patricia Spyer notes, they created "the insistent, repetitive narrative of victimization."[20]

Christians also used rumors to perpetuate their narrative of Islamization, which resonated among Christian communities elsewhere in Indonesia and had consequential effects. Rumors of agents provocateur, frequently invoked in other conflicts in Indonesia, further inflamed the violence.[21] As the violence spiraled out of control, local police officers and military personnel began choosing sides according to their religious beliefs and participating in the violence. Soon Muslims in other regions, especially Java, began to train forces to send to Ambon. Evidence shows that the main Muslim group involved, Laskar Jihad, was founded by Jaffar Umar Thalib with the encouragement of Islamists within the Indonesian army. Laskar Jihad was officially condemned by Indonesian President Abdurachman Wahid and banned from traveling to the region, but its military collaborators aided the transport of fighters and weapons to Ambon.[22] Christians and Muslims staked out territory, and co-religionists left behind were murdered. Rumors, especially those about attacks that supposedly took place in mosques or churches, fueled the violence, and internally displaced persons fleeing to other regions spread more stories.[23]

Mainstream Indonesian news sources raised the specter of Ambonese separatism, even though the violence had nothing to do with the long-defeated RMS. This rumor was supported by the fact that the Indonesian government had never rescinded Ambon's status as a "red" area, that is, one in which the military is on constant high alert, despite no threat of separatism since the early 1950s.[24] In Ambon, the military and police presence is much greater than in most other places in Indonesia and comparable to West Papua, where a low-intensity separatist rebellion simmers. Rumors abound as to why the region has remained labeled a troubled area, including one explanation that the high-alert status elevates military service in the region and thus offers an avenue for military promotions. This rumor of artificial tension to benefit the military institution further complicated the narrative landscape faced by the Pacific Partnership team.

In the aftermath of the violence, rumors have continued to spread about threats and separatism in the region, and other violent groups owe their origins in some way to the Ambonese conflict. For example, a separatist group named Front Kedaulatan Maluku (Malukan Sovereignty Front, FKM) emerged in the Maluku region. Although interviews conducted in 2006 by author Chris Lundry with FKM members, sympathizers, and others in Ambon suggest that the group does not pose a serious challenge to Indonesian sovereignty and receives little sympathy from Ambonese,[25] the Indonesian state continues to use it as an example of the threat of separatism from the region.

Laskar Jihad, organized to fight the Christians in Ambon, eventually disbanded after falling under increased pressure from the Indonesian government following the 2002 Bali bombings. Its leader, Jaffar Umar Thalib, was arrested for inciting violence, but not before Laskar Jihad engaged in violent acts against Christians in Sulawesi and established a presence in West Papua and Aceh. Rumors about the group portray it as continuing its activities in West Papua, receiving funding and support from the Indonesian military, and sending members to Afghanistan to train.[26] As in Ambon, the separatists in West Papua are portrayed as Christian, although the real picture is much more complicated, with both Muslim separatists and Christian loyalists involved. Former members of Laskar Jihad have been linked to Islamist groups such as the Islamic Defenders Front, a handful of members have been linked to Jemaah Islamiyah, and there are suspected ties to al Qaeda.[27]

When the *Mercy* went to Ambon in 2010, it was operating in a region that had been wracked by sectarian violence only a few years prior and still showed the consequences of a very long and complicated history that intertwines religion, socioeconomics, and postcolonial politics. The tension and insecurity of the violence remains to some extent in Ambon, where rapid political change—as in other regions of Indonesia—continues to foster an environment of uncertainty. It is in this kind of environment that rumors thrive by filling narrative gaps. In the case of the *Mercy*'s 2010 trip to the region, countermeasures proved effective at quelling rumors before they could disrupt the carefully crafted narrative situating the *Mercy*'s visit as a peaceful partnership between the U.S. and Indonesian governments.

The Threat of Mercy

The survival and spread of the bovine poisoning rumor points to several key dimensions of rumor theory discussed in chapter 1. First, rumors circulate in narrative systems that draw upon cultural, historical, and political traditions and ideologies. Additionally, rumors fill critical gaps in the flow of information; they are a substitute for news. Rumors are also a barometer of the moods, frustrations, and fears of the people—including contested populations that sit between government and insurgent interests. As Major Stephanie Kelley wrote of Iraq, "Rumors both express and form public opinion. They are unlikely to take hold unless they are perceived as plausible, and the more a specific rumor is heard the more currency it gains, shifting the orientation of public thinking and ultimately steering opinion."[28] Finally, otherwise distinct rumors flow freely across narrative landscapes replete with conflicting, fractious, and volatile ideologies. Rumors are, in short, a kind of micro-story, one that can be explosive, if not random, hence our driving metaphor of narrative IEDs.

To describe, explain, and understand the significance of narrative IEDs, one must first look closely at the cultural context in which they emerge, spread, and mutate. This includes the values and beliefs of contested populations, their historical and narrative traditions, and the current state of their society. In chapter 2, we looked at the highly regulated city-state of Singapore, which nonetheless has an active and creative online subculture of political critics. In chapter 3, we analyzed the relationship between an active counterinsurgency and an active insurgent rumor mill in an ongoing conflict zone. And in chapter 4, we focused on a whisper campaign designed to shore up support of the democratizing Indonesian government as it worked to prevent increasingly violent domestic terrorist activity from developing into an insurgency. In this chapter we return to Iraq's bovine poisoning rumor through its porcine sibling in Indonesia.

It is important first to emphasize how cultural factors serve as significant influences on emerging rumors. In the Ambon case, for example, many Indonesians see veterinary services as distinct from medical services for people. Animal life is generally not deemed to be as valuable as human life, nor are animals treated anthropomorphically. This is not to say that the health needs of animals are not valued by Indonesians, but from their perspective a reasonable question is: *Why would you want to include veterinary events as part of a disaster relief exercise and interoperability training program in a country that was hit especially hard by a tsunami in 2004?* Furthermore, a large percentage of citizens in Ambon live in poverty and have little or no access to quality dental and medical care. Hence it is quite rational to expect the *Mercy* teams to focus first on healing people rather than attending to the veterinary needs of animals. By addressing the medical needs of animals, the *Mercy* mission also opened itself to a range of questions that implied suspicious intentions. *If you're not here to focus on the vast medical needs of the people, why are you here?* The Pacific Partnership ADVON team had to grapple with this cultural challenge by explaining the value of veterinary services as a critical dimension of comprehensive disaster response and relief preparations. Disaster and humanitarian relief efforts, such as tsunami and earthquake response, focus not only on saving lives immediately in danger, but also work to ensure that lives are not put in subsequent danger because of the breakdown of infrastructure, whether transportation (roads washed out, bridges damaged), communication, or power and food supply. Disease and injury to livestock following natural disasters can have a significant and deleterious effect on local populations long after the immediate suffering has been controlled. Thus, thorough disaster response exercises must include all phases of a relief effort.

Historical factors are also germane, as the U.S. Navy ADVON team faced mounting suspicions about their intentions and capability to provide care for the local population. The concerns about the intent of the operations expressed by host-nation military and government officials stemmed in part from a visit by the *Mercy* in 2006, when it transported several Indonesians from one island to another without first informing the Indonesian government.[29] Like all U.S. Navy ships, the *Mercy* was on a prearranged schedule; instead of missing events or arriving late to its next port, the decision was made to transport patients by helicopter after they completed post-operative care. In fact, the patients were all flown back to their original points of embarkation. Yet this operation appeared unofficial, even clandestine, in the minds of the local populace. Information gaps gave rise to rumors, which emerged as a story among Indonesian military and government officials that U.S. Navy doctors onboard the *Mercy* were performing malevolent medical experiments on patients who were deliberately kept from the sight of Indonesian officials. In preparing for the 2010 *Mercy* visit, the U.S. Navy ADVON team had to manage a recent history mired in geopolitical tensions spurred by rumors.

In addition to these cultural and historical factors, and considerably more alarming to some members of the ADVON team, were the implications behind the question raised by the Indonesian military: *What do you intend to do to these animals?* Many of the Indonesians encountered by the team were aware of the bovine inoculation campaign fiasco in Iraq some five years earlier and, not knowing all of the facts, did not want to subject their rural farmers to a nefarious U.S. plot to poison or experiment on their animals.

Indeed, the rumor in effect extended the narrative that cast the United States as being at war with Islam, which raised the suspicions of the Indonesian military, especially in the context of Ambon, where the memory of sectarian violence between Christians and Muslims remained vivid and where both sides were viewed as importing outsiders to help with the fight. *Were the Americans modern Crusaders bent on colonizing Muslim lands like the Maluku region for their natural resources?* Thus, a rumor that upended a carefully crafted information and outreach campaign in a Muslim country in 2005 traveled thousands of miles and spanned several years to surround preparations for a disaster relief exercise in another Muslim country in 2010. In the process, this rumor threatened an important geopolitical relationship already fraught with stress.

The narrative threat posed by the rumor was exacerbated by the fact that several large red crosses, the symbol of Christian faith, are painted on the *Mercy* (see figure 5.1). In the United States and the West in general, the red crosses signify the *Mercy* as a hospital ship as opposed to a combatant platform. The symbols and ship name are intended to portray anything but a threat. But to people unfamiliar with this tradition, yet aware of the history of crusading and colonizing Christian nations, crosses are also signs of war. *Might the Christians of the United States be coming here to help the Christians of Ambon achieve independence or at least local political dominance?* Although the Red Cross and its sister organization the Red Crescent are both well known and not controversial throughout Indonesia, the special history and demographics of the Ambon region make for a slightly different narrative landscape. Given the 1999–2001 religious conflict in Ambon, Iraq's bovine rumor, activated by the *Mercy*'s arrival, could easily incite local fears, spurring greater tension between Christians and Muslims. When assessing the narrative landscape, then, the strategic communicators needed to be cognizant of the possibility that an extremist group could take advantage of any rumor that cast the U.S. Navy as a colonizing or crusading force. The likelihood of this scenario was, admittedly, relatively low because the Indonesian Navy ship KRI *Dr. Soeharso*, which also has a small red cross painted on each side, sailed with the *Mercy* for some of the Pacific Partnership visits. Nevertheless, we think it important to consider all possibilities of a narrative landscape when considering strategic communication plans.

Ambon is not unlike rural Iraq: a region of tenuous cooperation among different groups—in the case of Iraq, Sunni, Shi'a, and Kurds; in the case of

Ambon, Christians, Muslims, and Buddhists, as well as native Ambonese and immigrants—marked by a recent history of episodic violence among those groups. Gramsci, the neo-Marxist theorist and communist provocateur, called this kind of social order a "moving equilibrium" of social alliances. In the case of Ambon, the moving equilibrium includes, as noted above, Christians and Muslims, but also impoverished people and a government interested in development, national authorities and local religious and political leaders, and a host of foreign cultures beamed to them through radio, television, and Web-based media. And as in Iraq, this unstable equilibrium facilitates the spread of rumors. As Nicholas DiFonzo reminds us: "Rumors tend to arise in situations that are ambiguous and/or pose a threat or potential threat—situations in which meanings are uncertain, questions are unsettled, information is missing, and/or lines of communication are absent."[30] The ADVON team had to grapple with cultural, historical, symbolic, and sociopolitical factors if it was to avoid the consequences of the Iraq bovine poisoning rumor.

Coercion and Consent

Rumors, as we have shown throughout this book, pose a critical threat to both hegemonic and counter-hegemonic forces in the battle to sway contested populations to one side or the other. In Singapore, the escape of an Islamist terrorist resulted in rumors that, once mashed-up with pop culture references online, critiqued the restrictive Singaporean government and in the process undermined its narrative of security and competence. In the United States, rumors of Iraqi WMDs spread by the Bush administration facilitated support for a preemptive invasion of the Arab nation; in Iraq, other rumors, including the Stack House family of rumors, aided and abetted an increasingly violent insurgency targeting MNF-I and host-nation forces. And in Indonesia, a whisper campaign undermined an Islamist terrorist and his organization by leveraging heteronormative societal norms to cast both as hypocritical. Critical to the U.S. Navy ADVON team, the emergence of the bovine poisoning rumor in Indonesia threatened, at least in part, to turn the Indonesian population's attention from disaster relief planning and humanitarian outreach back to anti-Americanism.

For Gramsci, consent characterizes an unstable socialization process whereby the governed both passively and actively agree to their alienation from the means of economic production. In some cases, a set of misdirecting ideologies naturalizes consent among the so-called masses. This is what Marx originally called "false consciousness"—a kind of ideological control that the proletariat does not know it is under (hence, in Marxist theory, the need for revolution, dictatorship over the proletariat, and eventually socialism). In other cases, the governed consciously agree to their exploitation because resistance would subject them to violence or further economic deprivation. In Ambon, most Christians acquiesce to the Indonesian central government because they either see acceptance as in their best interest or conclude that to do otherwise would cause undue hardship on their families.

As cultural phenomena traversing a narrative landscape, rumors participate in this hegemonic struggle. Galit Hasan-Rokem notes: "Rumors are thus intricately interwoven with images of control and power. We may view them as manipulative machinations of power, taking advantage of products of popular culture, or instead we may consider them as subversive operations undermining power structures, drawing their energy from the vitality of popular or rather folk culture."[31] Like their explosive cousins, narrative IEDs often miss their target or fail to go off. Others, however, hit their target, gain traction among contested populations by forming into mosaics that draw upon master narratives, and spread from city to city and region to region. They are easily constructed from the available fragments within a narrative landscape, facilitating their spread and their use by everyday citizens. These rumor threats make Gramsci's moving sociopolitical equilibrium that much more unstable and volatile, especially when contested populations feel alienated from economic, religious, and cultural self-determination. Arguably, this set of circumstances coalesced in Iraq in 2005, a situation that both the U.S. Navy and the Indonesian government hoped to avoid in Ambon in 2010.

Although the social, economic, and cultural factors spawning the violent Islamist extremism that confronts the West and a range of nations in the Middle East, Africa, and Asia are clearly distinct from those that informed the struggles of the Bolshevik Revolution in the early years of the twentieth century, Gramsci's model is insightful for its emphasis on the intimate relationship between ideology, culture, and political power. Indeed, the Italian theorist's work illuminates the perpetuation of rumors during hegemonic struggles. For Gramsci, political society—essentially, the police, military, legal system, and so on—dominates the people it is charged with representing through coercive tactics; they use, in other words, force and violence to maintain power, authority, and social order. This is seen in the Singaporean case discussed in chapter 2, where government leaders restricted freedom of assembly and expression through the legal and police systems. It is perhaps more clearly seen in the Iraq case discussed in chapter 3, where both U.S. and host-nation armies waged war with an equally violent insurgency of foreign fighters, Ba'ath party loyalists, Shi'a militia, and disenfranchised Sunnis. The same can be said of Indonesia, where the legal apparatus, military, and police have consistently used repressive laws and physical force as a means of maintaining power, be it against Catholics in Timor-Leste or against moderate Muslims and Christians in Ambon, where the government fears that the people of the region might follow Timor-Leste's lead and seek independence.[32]

Coercion is also a tactic employed by Islamist extremists, and violent groups more generally, both in their attempts to spread fear among contested populations and in their efforts to thwart the operations of the host-nation and counterinsurgency forces. In Singapore, Mas Selamat was linked to a host of terrorist activities in the region and imprisoned (but not charged) for plotting to attack Singapore's international airport and other targets in 2002 by crashing planes into them. In Iraq, insurgents routinely engage in terrorist acts, from planting IEDs on major highways to suicide bombings in urban markets to rapes, kidnappings, and extortion throughout Baghdad. Finally, in Indonesia Noordin Top and his group Jemaah Islamiyah have been linked to the 2002 Bali bombing, the 2003 Marriott Hotel bombing, the 2004 Australian embassy bombing, the 2005 Bali bombings, and the 2009 Marriott and Ritz-Carlton bombings, among others. These coercive acts have killed scores of Muslims and Christians alike.

Yet Gramsci also talked about the cultural dimensions of authority and repressive power. For the Italian theorist, civil society—family, church, media, social organizations, and so on—wages an ideological struggle for the consent of the people to be ruled. Gramsci focused on the reproduction of class stratification in the context of both feudalism and capitalism. Yet his theory of hegemony turns Marxist historical materialism upside-down in that it stresses the critical importance of culture and ideology, or Marx's superstructure, in both maintaining and dividing the people's relationship to the economic mode of production. For this reason, Gramsci's model is seen as less reductive than traditional Marxist approaches, where all meaning is linked downward to the economic base, and more expansive, where civil society comprises a range of economic and cultural elements. Seen in this light, Gramsci's theory has implications for struggles beyond those involving capitalism and largely economic forces. It offers us a way to understand the ideological dimensions of other forms of social stratification, political struggles, and the exercise of power, including racial, ethnic, religious, and sectarian, to win the consent of contested populations to be governed by one side or the other.

These social relations and their attendant narratives form the apex of insurgencies pitting Islamist extremism against more moderate and frequently democratic forces. To this end, the *U.S. Army/Marine Corps Counterinsurgency Field Manual*, a radical revision of the U.S. military's small war doctrine assembled by General David Petraeus in the wake of the Iraqi insurgency, is instructive:

> All governments rule through a combination of consent and coercion. Governments described as "legitimate" rule primarily with the consent of the governed; those described as "illegitimate" tend to rely mainly or entirely on coercion. Citizens of the latter obey the state for fear of the consequences of doing otherwise, rather than because they voluntarily accept its rule. A government that derives its powers from the governed tends to be accepted by its citizens as legitimate. It still uses coercion—for example, against criminals—but most of its citizens voluntarily accept its governance.[33]

Written after the insurgent surge in Iraq, when it was clear to the United States and its few remaining coalition partners that the war had turned into an occupation that was losing the support of the Iraqi people, the new field manual employs critical theory and cultural studies to instruct U.S. forces on how to manage the searing paradoxes that define small warfare today. The list is of paradoxes is worth paraphrasing:

- Sometimes, the more you protect your force, the less secure you may be.
- Sometimes, the more force is used, the less effective it is.
- The more successful the counterinsurgency is, the less force can be used and the more risk must be accepted.
- Sometimes doing nothing is the best reaction.
- Some of the best weapons for counterinsurgents do not shoot.
- The host nation doing something tolerably is normally better than us doing it well.

- If a tactic works this week, it might not work next week; if it works in this province, it might not work in the next.
- Tactical success guarantees nothing.
- Many important decisions are not made by generals.[34]

As we have done in this book, the *Counterinsurgency Field Manual* goes on to identify narrative and ideology as both the weapon of insurgence and the appropriate countermeasure for counterinsurgency and host-nation forces: "The most important cultural form for counterinsurgents to understand is the narrative. . . . Commanders should pay particular attention to cultural narratives of the [host-nation] population pertaining to outlaws, revolutionary heroes, and historical resistance figures. Insurgents may use these narratives to mobilize the population."[35]

Past paradigms of political/military control involved a simple binary: militaries occupied land, civilians in the occupation zone complied with military authority, and as soon as a military controlled a significant portion of the population and industrial centers and defeated an opposing military, the action was complete. In today's environment, however, the situation is very different. Militaries control less and less actual ground area by physical occupation, and unseen, irregular insurgent forces pose a substantial threat to military forces and civilian populations. These insurgent forces are effective because they receive either overt or covert support from the civilian population. They blend in, they live among the local population, and they move about without raising alarm. Thus, the key to control and governance shifts from occupying land to persuading the local populations to cooperate and consent to governance. From a Gramscian perspective, the achievement of this cooperation and consent requires coercion. In the past, this was achieved by force, a method still practiced by extremist insurgent forces when they bomb mosques and cafés and threaten local communities. Military forces working on behalf of allied and host-nation governments practice forcible coercion against these insurgents but must treat local populations differently.

What the *Counterinsurgency Field Manual* tells us, and a clear implication of Gramsci's theory of hegemony, is that counterinsurgency operations, as well as those practices designed to thwart a nascent insurgency as seen in Singapore and Indonesia, must emphasize information operations (consent) over force (coercion) and, in so doing, focus on understanding the culture in which they are operating, the narrative terrain they must navigate, and the ideologies most apt to sway a contested population. The first step in this process is to be rigorously self-reflexive about one's own values, narrative traditions, and ideologies. Again, the *Field Manual* is worth quoting in full: "American ideas of what is 'normal' or 'rational' are not universal. To the contrary, members of other societies often have different notions of rationality, appropriate behavior, level of religious devotion, and norms concerning gender. Thus, what may appear abnormal or strange to an external observer may appear as self-evidently normal to a group member. For this reason, counterinsurgents—especially commanders, planners, and small-unit leaders—should strive to avoid imposing their ideas of normalcy on a foreign cultural problem."[36] Winning hearts and minds, as the U.S. military likes to phrase it, means recognizing the power of narratives—and, as we have demonstrated throughout this book, rumors—to alienate and mobilize contested populations. Narratives, and especially the narrative IEDs of rumors, can be seen as a form of "soft" coercion: rather than traditional coercion (threat to life), soft coercion implies violence and threats (such as livestock poisoning) and negative impacts on quality of life, which can mobilize the opposition to consent. Albeit in a much less consequential and dangerous way than encountered by troops in Iraq or Afghanistan, this impact of rumors on the narrative landscape was the challenge faced by the U.S. Navy ADVON team as it grappled with the emergence of a porcine poisoning rumor in Ambon.

Narrative Countermeasures

U.S. military commanders unfamiliar with the *Counterinsurgency Field Manual* might easily dismiss as simple falsehoods rumors such as those encountered by the ADVON team in Indonesia. The notion that the *Mercy*-based veterinary officers and representatives of the NGOs would perform experiments on animals as part of a disaster relief mission is, from a U.S. perspective, ridiculous; it offends our sense of self, rooted in a series of narratives supporting American exceptionalism and generosity. Perhaps also ridiculous from the U.S. perspective is the notion of separating veterinary services from medical services in the context of disaster relief and humanitarian assistance missions. Unvaccinated livestock, the core of rural food supplies, both spread and succumb to diseases, especially in the wake of a natural disaster. Yet, when it comes to understanding and defusing narrative IEDs, the American perspective is not what is at issue and can be a distraction to defusing their impact. Instead, strategic communicators must focus on the perspective of the local people, their civic and cultural leadership, and their government organizations if outreach programs are to mitigate the threats posed by narrative IEDs.

In developing appropriate countermeasures, the *Counterinsurgency Field Manual* also instructs readers to "Learn the insurgents' messages or narratives. Develop counter-messages and counter-narratives to attack the insurgents' ideology. Understanding the local culture is required to do this."[37] In other words, be attentive to the cultural and historical traditions that speak to contested populations and serve as the source of the counter-narratives that can be deployed to attack the insurgents' communications. To be sure, the insurgents are engaged in such tactics. To drive a wedge between MNF-I, the nascent Iraqi government, and contested populations such as rural farmers, the bovine poisoning rumor positioned the United States as a pillaging force. The United States became Crusaders, and the insurgents became archetypical heroes fighting for Islamist principles. The *Mercy* ADVON team was aware that the rumor and its associated mosaic worked to the strategic communication advantage of al Qaeda in Iraq and other Iraqi insurgent groups and did not want to see it become effective in Indonesia. And although the lessons learned from Iraq provided them with an opportunity to avoid the mistakes made by their colleagues in 2005, Indonesia in 2010 was a much different country than Iraq in 2005. In Iraq, MNF-I needed to use the local culture and its narratives against the insurgents as the insurgents had done to MNF-I. In Indonesia, however, there were no insurgents; rather, the ADVON team needed to solicit cooperation and consent from a skeptical population. The principle of understanding and being sensitive to local culture remained a central tenet of the communication plan, but applying rumor theory generated three additional elements: (1) because rumors rush in to fill narrative gaps (particularly true in cases of anxiety or dread rumors), gaps in the narrative landscape had to be minimized and filled when identified; (2) local master narratives had to be identified to ensure that mission actions did not unwittingly contribute to an existing negative paradigm; and (3) messages had to be crafted that maintained narrative fidelity with the prevailing local narrative landscape.

Drawing upon the *Counterinsurgency Field Manual,* their knowledge of the bovine poisoning rumor in the Iraq war, and the preliminary research for this book, the ADVON team responded quickly to the threat posed by the Ambon porcine poisoning rumor. Recognizing that rumors fill information gaps, the team explained to Indonesian military, medical, and media professionals the value of including veterinary exercises in the mission's disaster relief training. By inoculating the pigs and cattle of rural farmers in Ambon, the operation endeavored to ensure that the region would have a more stable—and distinctly local—food supply. This emphasis established a narrative of assistance and support, leading to self-sufficiency. The U.S. personnel also debunked the Iraqi bovine poisoning rumor, pointing out that insurgents advanced it with the result that the Iraqi food supply diminished and made the Iraq people more dependent on foreign imports. In short, they offered Indonesian decision-makers in the military, medical, and media communities a clear rationale, consistent within the narrative frame of cooperation and mutual support, for the value of veterinary service to the Pacific Partnership mission.

Disseminating facts is, of course, only an initial countermeasure and one part of the narrative gap-filling process. As DiFonzo also notes, "The truth or falsity of the statement is perhaps of secondary importance."[38] Critical to counter-narrative communication strategy is an effort to get ahead of the story by disseminating as fast and as widely as possible a framing narrative. In the case of the Pacific Partnership, that narrative portrayed the USNS *Mercy* working with the Indonesian government to provide medical relief to the people of Ambon as they trained for future disaster relief missions. Hence, quick response to a negative story such as a dread rumor is important; but equally important is the need to advance a narrative that is unconnected to the negative story but nonetheless works to undermine it by shoring up gaps in the narrative landscape. Dread rumors, as has been noted by Robert Knapp, Gordon Allport and Leo Postman, and DiFonzo, arise in information vacuums. Providing a framing narrative fills the narrative landscape, mitigating the build-up of anxiety and more dread rumors.

In fact, the ADVON team released two press releases before any events took place, one a week before the *Mercy* docked in Ambon harbor, and one the day the ship arrived. Distributed in English and Indonesian, each made clear the purpose of the ship's visit: "Pacific Partnership 2010 is the fifth in a series of annual U.S. Pacific Fleet endeavors conducted in Indonesia as a disaster relief exercise aimed at strengthening regional partnerships and increasing interoperability with host nations, partner nations, and international humanitarian and relief organizations."[39] This was the team's initial step to "get ahead of the narrative" and thus to frame the Pacific Partnership.

The ADVON team also arranged for two large-scale press conferences, one before the *Mercy* arrived and another a few days after it dropped anchor. National print, broadcast, and Internet media representatives from Jakarta attended. Some of these media outlets had been critical of the U.S. Navy and America more generally. For example, one reporter attending the first press conference at the Swiss Bell Hotel in Ambon asked, "How can you support the Israeli government when it kills innocent Christians defending Muslims?" Other reporters avoided international politics in favor of asking questions that emphasized local interests, such as Sail Banda. More than twenty national, regional, and local print and television reporters attended the second press conference onboard the *Mercy*. They were transported to the anchored ship via a small boat for a meeting with the Pacific Partnership Commodore, Captain Lisa M. Franchetti, USN, and her senior staff, followed by a tour of the ship's medical facilities and lunch with the crew.

The commodore responded fully and openly to all of the questions posed by the journalists, yet repeatedly returned to Pacific Partnership messages stressing disaster relief, interoperability training, and geopolitical partnership. The reporters witnessed a surgical procedure performed on an elderly Indonesian man, visited with Indonesian patients undergoing post-operative recovery, including a mother who had recently given birth, and talked with and interviewed sailors from all decks. Over the next few days, national, regional, and local news outlets saturated the public discourse with positive stories about the *Mercy*'s mission, facilities, and crew. These stories converged into a narrative system conveying the mission's themes of goodwill, assistance, and partnership.

Several stories emphasized the fact that a woman, Commodore Franchetti, commanded the Pacific Partnership mission. During the press conference, several female reporters asked questions about how the commodore balanced her role as a mother with her duties as the mission commander. In fact, more questions of this nature were posed than questions of a political nature, although some reporters did ask questions that attempted to connect the Pacific Partnership mission with the wars in Iraq and Afghanistan. Yet it was interesting to observe that the latter were literally drowned out by questions that focused on the commodore. In a country where women do not serve in great numbers in the military or police force, and most are not in traditional positions of authority, the image of Commodore Franchetti commanding a Navy operation while also talking of her young daughter proved to be a persuasive frame and compelling human interest story. The story also proved to be an effective part of the overall Pacific Partnership narrative that combated the potential for rumors to derail the benefits of the visit. The emphasis on Commodore Franchetti as exercise commander, career naval officer, and mother added an empathetic story to the narrative landscape. As a result, fewer gaps were available for rumors to take root. Also, the potential for the humanitarian and relief components of the mission, if improperly cast, to provide an anti-American narrative of paternalism was tempered by the attention in the press to Commodore Franchetti and her personal stories of cooperation and partnership in balancing her career and family.

Another story used by the ADVON team to frame the Pacific Partnership narrative centered on performances of the U.S. Pacific Fleet Band, a group of uniformed U.S. Navy sailors. The team arranged for the rock ensemble section of the band to give three free performances, two at night in downtown Ambon and one during the day in a crowded neighborhood market (see figure 5.3). Each of the evening performances drew an estimated seven thousand Indonesians, as several city blocks were roped off to automobile traffic so the crowds could enjoy the band's diverse range of songs, from Michael Jackson to the Black Eyed Peas. The afternoon performance drew several thousand people from adjoining poor neighborhoods and schools. Representatives of the press were invited to join the band onstage at each event, resulting in images of cheering crowds in local newspapers and on websites. Radio interviews with band members were broadcast on rock and pop radio stations and were deemed positive by Pacific Partnership leadership in that they cast the U.S. Navy—and by extension Americans—as creative, open, and generous. These performances and the associated stories were about building goodwill and thereby building consent. Western music, and American pop culture, is very popular in Indonesia, and the concerts contributed to a positive associations concerning the U.S. Navy, the partnership between the U.S. and Indonesian governments, and the Pacific Partnership mission.

The ADVON team was successful in getting ahead of the story, of putting out a narrative of cooperation, gender equality, and American creativity by providing access to the commodore, her staff, and the Navy band. None of these tactics, however, addressed the specific threat posed by the bovine

5.3. Members of the U.S. Pacific Fleet Band perform in front of thousands of Indonesians, 1 August 2010.
U.S. Navy photo by Mass Communication Specialist 2nd Class Eddie Harrison.

poisoning rumor—at least not with respect to using credible local officials and media outlets. "Rumors depend upon plausibility and upon credibility," Gary Alan Fine and Irgan Khawaja argue, "but from where do these concepts derive? The answer is from experience as socialized through institutions, organization, and relations."[40]

To ensure that the Indonesian people understood the value of veterinary services and to diffuse the potential of the porcine poisoning rumor to disrupt the Pacific Partnership mission, two Indonesian reporters were invited to accompany the first veterinary operation. The reporters—one from a national television outlet and one from a regional newspaper—trekked up a mountain in a Maluku rainforest, witnessed the work of the military and NGO veterinary professionals, were given unfettered access to them for interviews and follow-up questions, and were allowed to take pictures and video of the entire event (figure 5.4). The stories they wrote, like those from Commodore Franchetti's press conference and the Navy band performances, were deemed by Pacific Partnership leadership to be positive—that is, "fair, accurate, and on message." The news reports stressed, among other things, that the veterinary team included NGOs and Indonesian veterinary officials and

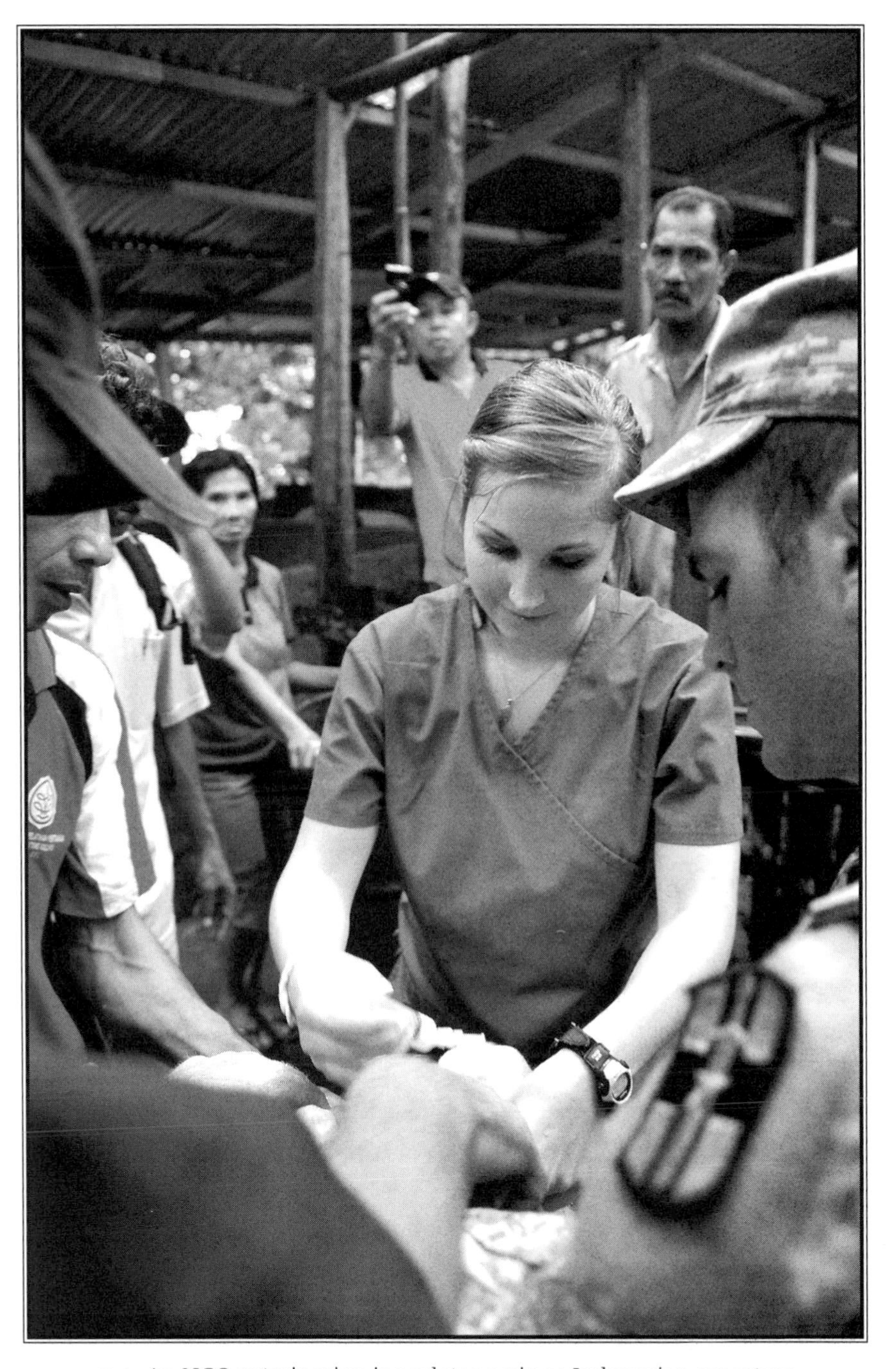

5.4. An NGO veterinarian inoculates a pig as Indonesian reporters look on in Ambon, Indonesia, 29 July 2010.
U.S. Navy photo by Mass Communication Specialist 2nd Class Jon Husman.

that the farmers appreciated the services. Several additional veterinary outreach and service missions were conducted by the *Mercy* team. No further questions were posed to the ADVON team from the Indonesian military, local medical professionals, or reporters who either implicitly or explicitly linked Pacific Partnership veterinary services with the bovine poisoning rumor from the Iraq war.

From our perspective in studying rumors and rumor countermeasures, the fact that the Navy leadership viewed the press coverage of the veterinary mission as successful matters only insofar as it indicated the degree to which the rumor IEDs were defused and the potential for additional rumor IEDs was minimized. The Pacific Partnership team seeded the narrative landscape with stories of cooperation, assistance, and cultural outreach through local media, that is, outlets with more credibility among the people than U.S. media sources. Partnering with local media ensured that stories that were components of the Pacific Partnership narrative system were rendered with fidelity to the local narrative landscape. At the same time, the lingering presence of the Iraq bovine poisoning rumor, memories of the helicopter transfers during the 2006 *Mercy* visit, and the handful of questions pressing U.S. officials on policy in the Middle East indicated the potential for some anti-American sentiment. Here, the deployment by the local press of an ad hoc counter-narrative of its own creation—Pacific Partnership is led by a woman and mother, and Pacific Partnership is part of the Indonesian Sail Banda exercise—effectively side-stepped the potential for charges of paternalism and American unilateralism. In such a landscape, wherein anxieties are reduced and information gaps are minimized, rumors struggle to take hold.

Primarily, the counter-rumor strategy deployed by this U.S. Navy team was one of information saturation, preventing the conditions for rumor spread. One of the key factors that make a narrative landscape fertile soil for rumors is an information gap. Our experience and analysis also confirms this state of affairs, with examples in Singapore, where the government's delay in reporting Mas Selamat's escape spawned conspiracy rumors; in Indonesia, where frequent misreporting of Noordin Top's death primed the pump of the Indonesian rumor mill; and in Iraq, where a lack of information explaining the devastation faced by citizens every day meant that the available information, no matter how implausible to outside observers, became the currency of the day. In Ambon, the combination of education about the value of veterinary services with the alternative stories of Commodore Franchetti and the Pacific Fleet Band filled the narrative landscape.

In Iraq, the bovine poisoning rumor aided the insurgent cause and lent itself to a master narrative that painted the U.S. as colonizers. In the unstable sociopolitical equilibrium that defines Ambon in particular and Indonesia more generally, a similar rumor might have just as easily disrupted a civil affairs and information operation that the U.S. and Indonesian governments valued. In the end, the ADVON team identified and diffused the rumor IED by offering alternative stories that formed a persuasive narrative to displace the colonizer archetype and the attendant story forms associated with it. Furthermore, the operation showed respect for the host culture and transparency via interactive communication by allowing host-nation media full access to command leadership, ship facilities, community relations, and veterinary operations. More public relations and marketing than propaganda, these public affairs strategies are arguably as effective as the whisper campaign techniques used in the American build-up to the invasion of Iraq and the Indonesian "Noordin Top is gay" rumor mill. They are also credible given that they engage sources and media platforms already trusted by local populations. Unlike some other cases in the past, the Pacific Partnership media engagements rested on what it regarded as accurate information distributed transparently and thus without control through host-nation media.

Conclusion

> *And ye shall hear of wars and rumors of wars, see that ye be not troubled, for all these things must come to pass, but the end is not yet. . . . For nation shall rise against nation and kingdom against kingdom . . . then shall they deliver you up to be afflicted and shall put you to death . . . but he that shall endure unto the end, he shall be saved.*
>
> —Matthew 24:6–13

> *Just before the Hour, there will be days in which knowledge will disappear and ignorance will appear, and there will be much killing.*
>
> —*Sahih Muslim*, Book 34, Number 6454

The above Bible verse and hadith are often quoted to signal end times and the accompanying rise in rumors and acts of terror as the world approaches its last days. Although we do not claim to know the chronemics of apocalypticism, it is interesting to note how eschatological writings feature prominently in many world religions, including those engaged in the contemporary struggle against terrorism, such as Islam, Christianity, and Judaism. It is also interesting to note the integral role that rumors are projected to play in religiously inspired belief systems, which intensifies their social significance and effects.

In this concluding chapter, we discussed narrative countermeasures and provided concrete examples from a recent program that highlighted how communication and the media may be used effectively to engage and shape contested populations. We noted how anxieties in Ambon about foreign veterinary activities did not explode into a strategic communication debacle for the Pacific Partnership, in part because the *Mercy* ADVON team got ahead of the rumor mill and provided enough information into the narrative landscape to thwart the spread of an Indonesian version of the poisoning rumor that proved so debilitating in Iraq. Defusing this rumor by information saturation would seem to confirm Tamotsu Shibutani's theory that rumors are a type of news, drowned out by other news and information. But, as we explained in chapter 1, and as our case studies throughout the book confirm, addressing rumors as a component of narrative systems provides a more thorough and complete understanding of the phenomenon of rumors. The presence of the livestock poisoning rumor in Ambon was clearly born of lack of information and local cultural knowledge. But what spawned the latent suspicions? What narrative system existed that predisposed the local population to be wary of the visiting Americans? Into a region with a recent history of Christian-Muslim violence sailed a ship with a large red cross painted on the side. In the 2006 exercise, local citizens were ferried out to a U.S. Navy ship by helicopter with no explanation of when or where they would return. Understood as operating within this narrative system, the poisoning rumor started to make more sense.

Our conceptualization of rumors as narrative IEDs points to the ecology of social and technical relationships that are implicated in strategic communication programs. Most theorists address the psychological aspects of rumors, but this focus ignores other critical meso- and macro-level elements, particularly how rumors interface with the cultural beliefs and local conditions in which they circulate. A narrow focus on rumors as psychological tools also obscures their power as social and cultural forces to affect actions, intentions, and the strategies of governments and organizations that face them and, in some cases, deploy them.

Although rumors are often dismissed as mere hearsay or comprehended as tangential information, we argue that rumors count as significant aspects of strategic communication and, accordingly, should be analyzed alongside other stories that constitute the narrative landscape. In chapter 1, we explained that a narrative is both a social object and a mental process and that a narrative is a system of subcomponents, one of which is rumors. Audiences take in data and organize them according to existing templates, templates that are provided by the combination of personal experience and surrounding culture. This mode of reception explains why the concept of narrative landscape, which is the complex array of prevailing narratives in a cultural arena, is crucial to understanding the potency of rumors. People hear and understand rumors within the templates provided by the narrative landscape in which they live. Rumors that advance familiar narrative systems, such as the variety of stories that position the Arab communities as victims to Crusader invaders, become more persuasive than others. As such, rumors should not be taken lightly or excluded from civic memory or operational databases as "mere" rumors, implausible or ridiculous. As we have shown in our case studies, rumors are the reality of the citizens who believe them. Citizens believe rumors when they integrate with prevailing narrative systems that structure belief and ideology. In this way, whether rumors constitute "truth" is still of import, but determining the truthful elements is of subordinate concern for authorities and organizations who first need to understand the proverbial hearts and minds of contested populations before planning and managing costly activities to engage them.

The conceptualization of rumors as narrative IEDs thus enjoins us to recognize them in processes of consent and coercion in counter-hegemonic and hegemonic struggles for strategic influence. These processes can operate anywhere but are currently especially volatile at points of friction between the West (Western Europe and the United States, which have dominated global development since the colonial era and are perceived to be predominantly Judeo-Christian) and developing nations with a Muslim majority. Processes of coercion and consent ensure that rumors are perpetuated among populations who comply with authorities out of volition or force. They also underscore the dynamic growth and spread of rumors as embedded in cultural systems and narrative landscapes, as well as the fact that an increasing number of them are mediated by old and new communication technologies, including web-based media. Rumors gain narrative traction when they cohere with existing master narratives, archetypes, and story forms and are spread via communication networks, including face-to-face interpersonal and varied types of new and social media. Thus, just as energetic and material diplomatic efforts are made to bridge cultures, attention should similarly be cast on monitoring rumors, their creation, spread, and vulnerabilities, in order to enhance international understanding and neutralize criticism and censure.

More than simply stories (believable or not), rumors are in fact *narrative IEDs*. They can have explosive and deleterious effects on the strategic communication plans of governments, police forces, military operations, NGOs, and other organizations. Our book has focused on rumors associated in some way with Islamist extremism and the struggle to earn the consent of the population to be governed. Rumors are particularly potent in this domain, as they can more easily arise than be defused; they tend to favor those with local knowledge, such as the insurgents in Iraq, rather than the outsider, such as the U.S. forces. Yet, we propose that recognizing rumors for their narratological foundations and operation offers a methodology for dealing with them. Filling narrative gaps eases anxiety within a population, making the narrative landscape less fertile for rumor growth and spread. Framing government programs, actions, and events in a manner consonant with prevailing narratives makes them more palatable and less vulnerable to rumors.

GLOSSARY

Archetype: A model of a person, event, or setting upon which other persons, events, and settings are patterned and which tends to symbolize or express fundamental aspects of the human condition. Archetypes can be transcultural and long-lived, commonly understood by otherwise distinct cultures across time. Rumors link to archetypes that allow people to identify immediately with a character.

Coercion and Consent: Two of the hegemonic processes by which states, communities, and agents (including insurgents and counterinsurgents) struggle for dominance. These two processes figure prominently in agents' access to the "hearts and minds" of the people they hope to govern.

Contested Population: A local, civilian population that resides politically/ideologically between insurgent forces and established government forces or between government initiatives and outward dissent. One side or the other (insurgent or government) must win the support of this population in order to govern effectively.

Mash-up: A piece of cultural content marked by a recombination of graphics, image, and text from various sources to create a derivative work. This hybrid form of representation injects new meaning into the connotations of the original works and is oftentimes created without permission from the original artists.

Master Narrative: A story system that circulates across historical and cultural boundaries, resolving archetypal conflicts through established literary and historical forms. Because they are deeply embedded within a culture and are repeated in a plethora of texts and contexts, master narratives are particularly powerful systems that shape opinion, perspective, and ideology.

Metonym: Rhetorical figure of speech in which something is not called by its own name but, rather, by the name of something intimately associated with it.

Narrative: A system of interrelated stories that share common elements and a rhetorical desire to resolve a conflict by structuring audience expectations and interpretations.

Narrative Cohesion: The consistency of internal logic to an individual story. This term is borrowed and adapted from rhetorician Walter Fisher, who uses "narrative probability" to describe "what constitutes a coherent story." Encounters among bodies of stories that conform to different paradigms of internal logic necessitates further articulation of the forms of narrative cohesion.

Narrative Fidelity: Another term borrowed from Walter Fisher to describe the extent to which "the stories that [people] experience ring true with the stories they know to be true in their lives." Given the various dimensions of "truth," narrative fidelity refers to the compatibility of stories within a narrative system, that is, the consistency and complementarity of a story with prevailing narrative systems. As a subclass of stories, rumors can exhibit narrative fidelity. When they do, their likelihood of acceptance and further dissemination increases.

Narrative IED: A metaphor describing rumors. Rumors operate on narratological levels (that is, they are stories, they get told in certain ways, they link with other stories) and, much like an improvised explosive device, can be made quickly, jury rigged from available parts, concealed or planted unobtrusively. They can have devastating and/or unexpected effects and are thus a type of weapon available both to the strong and to the weak (the insurgent, the rebel, the dissident, and the non-military actor).

Narrative Landscape: Another metaphor to describe the complex array of narratives prevalent within a specific social, economic, political, and mediated environment. As each narrative is a system of stories (and potentially numerous subnarratives), the narrative landscape is the domain within which rumors arise, circulate, and compete for prominence.

Origin Conundrum: A situation wherein the source of a rumor cannot be easily identified, which is the case for most rumors. Counterintuitively, ambiguity of source (along with ambiguity of veracity) is a key component in rumor plausibility, because ambiguity facilitates malleability and coherence in narrative systems.

Propaganda: A systematic form of purposeful persuasion that attempts to influence the emotions, attitudes, opinions, and actions of specified target audiences for ideological, political, or commercial purposes. Propaganda generally functions through the controlled transmission of one-sided messages (which may or may not be factual) via mass media and other communication channels.

Prosumption: A portmanteau of "production" and "consumption," referring to the hybrid practices of individuals who act as both producers and consumers of media. The combination of digital culture and widespread digital tools enables interactive responses and appropriation of media content (see also "mash-up"). Prosumption disrupts the traditional segregation of media producers (a small cadre of businesses and government organizations) and media consumers (the majority of citizens).

Resistance: An act or instance of opposition to an aspect of governance that meets with disagreement and disapproval by a population or individual. Resistance can be a formal, organized group or the more informal actions of individuals or loosely affiliated groups pursuing grassroots tactics against dominant powers and strategies. Resistance may be executed by feats of arms or by communication of ideas.

Rumor: A shorthand term for speculation, half-truths, and misinformation in the form of stories or story elements that, to some contested populations, appear to be rational. We classify rumor as a special type of story owing to form, class, function, and operation within narrative systems.

Rumor Antecedent: The action or statement that gives rise to a rumor. Not all rumors have clearly identified antecedents.

Rumor Context: The social, cultural, politico-legal crucible for the creation and propagation of rumors.

Rumor Countermeasure: A technique used to defuse the strategic communication potency of an existing rumor. Rumor countermeasures can include statements of fact and assertions of truth, but must do so with cognizance of the intersection of the rumor and the prevailing narrative landscape. Rumors themselves can be effective countermeasures to combat terrorist or insurgent propaganda, especially when the countermeasures meet the goals of "narrative cohesion" and "narrative fidelity."

Rumor Family: A number of rumors that share a common subject or focus and can be traced to a common antecedent.

Rumor Meme: An online instance of a rumor that experiences viral dissemination via transmediation. Memes are compelling ideas, catchphrases, graphics, or stories that are disseminated, generating virus-like imitations and reproductions through remixes and mash-ups. Memes need not be exact in their reproduction in order to reinforce beliefs and incorporate successive transmission as part of the transmediation activity.

Rumor Mill: The circulation of rumors via multiple communication platforms among discrete populations, in our cases, contested populations or populations that rest between insurgent and counterinsurgent interests.

Rumor Mosaic: A number of complementary rumors that collectively and collaboratively reinforce a prevailing narrative (or narratives). Some rumor mosaics may implicitly or explicitly draw upon master narratives as a means of powerfully appealing to local interests.

Rumor-mongering: The intentional spread of rumors. This spread of rumors can be nefarious or with specific intent to cause difficulty for another person or group, or it can be undertaken by individuals capriciously or to satisfy a psychological need to mimic an authoritative source.

Rumor Reserves: Dormant rumors, that is, rumors that are no longer in circulation but nonetheless rest in the memories of specific populations and can be put back into circulation under the right circumstances (sociopolitical unrest, unexplained events that recall the events narrated in otherwise dormant rumors, and so on).

Rumor Theory: A body of scholarship that seeks to explain the nature and function of rumors. To date, the majority of rumor theory incorporates psychological and sociological approaches, as well as some treatment from folklorist perspectives. We argue that the narrative implications of rumors must be examined for fuller understanding of rumors, particularly in regard to strategic communication.

Rumor Threat: A rumor or rumor mosaic with the potential to affect a strategic communication, civil affairs, public outreach, or community relations effort negatively. Rumor threats are most apparent and potent when the rumors fill an information vacuum by integrating with, invoking, and creating narratives that resonate (describe, explain, and rationalize a phenomenon, often by relying on master narratives) with a local population.

Story: A particular sequence of events, or actions, involving characters in specific settings, recounted for rhetorical purposes. Every story must have the following dimensions: time (sequence of events and actions); space (settings), representations (characters); and rhetoric (communication of an idea).

Story Form: Recognizable patterns of story that are easily comprehended because of their familiarity. They allow people to comprehend easily new stories as they enter the narrative system. The patterns consist of consistent relationships among characters, events/actions, and settings.

Strategic Communication: The production, transmission, and exchange of messages for the purpose of creating meaning (communication) in the service of a specific macro-level goal (strategic). Government strategic communication efforts seek to inform, and sometimes persuade, their citizens. Counterinsurgency strategic communication efforts also seek to inform and persuade, but in a more specific context around protecting the citizenry and instilling faith in governmental stability.

Text: A discernible set of symbols that communicate a message (including a rumor). The symbols can be in the form of writing, speech, pictures, song, motion pictures, performance, and theater, among others. Islamist extremist texts include sermons, speeches, videos, blog posts, posters, Taliban "night letters," and so on. Texts constitute a unit of analysis.

Thought Contagion: The process by which memes, including rumors, evolve and spread in society to influence the narrative landscape.

Transmediation: Appropriation, reconfiguration, and retransmission of messages across different media platforms. Each change of medium involves both alteration of form and, sometimes subtly, meaning.

NOTES

Introduction

1 Gary Alan Fine and Bill Ellis, *The Global Grapevine: Why Rumors of Terrorism, Immigration, and Trade Matter* (New York: Oxford University Press, 2010), 4.

2 Walter R. Fisher, *Human Communication as Narration: Toward a Philosophy of Reason, Value, and Action* (Columbia: University of South Carolina Press, 1989).

Chapter 1: Rumor Theory

1 As chapter 2 discusses at length, online circulation of imagery was a significant part of the rumor and critique process in the case of Mas Selamat. See http://xmercenaries.com/four9er/wp-content/uploads/2008/03/masescapealcatrazqq1.jpg.

2 We define Islamist extremists as individuals and groups that, through a combination of ideological coercion and physical violence, seek to impose their will against any state or civilian target that does not share the group's interpretation of Islam.

3 Allport and Postman identified rumors in the service of propaganda during World War II as "whispering campaigns." The label remains in use by scholars and military personnel alike. See Gordon W. Allport and Leo Postman, *The Psychology of Rumor* (New York: Henry Holt and Company, 1947).

4 Tamotsu Shibutani, *Improvised News: A Sociological Study of Rumor* (New York: Bobbs-Merrill Company, 1966), 62 (authors' emphasis). The Indonesian term for rumor is "*berita angin*," or "news on the wind."

5 Jayson Hardin, "The Rumor Bomb: Theorising the Convergence of New and Old Trends in Mediated US Politics," *Southern Review: Communication, Politics & Culture* 39, no. 1 (2006): 84–110.

6 James Poniewozik, "The Myth of Fact," *Time*, 23 August 2010, 62. According to a CNN-Opinion Research poll conducted in 2010, 27 percent of Americans believe President Obama was probably or definitely not born in this country.

7 See, for example: Nicholas DiFonzo and Prashant Bordia, *Rumor Psychology: Social and Organizational Approaches* (Washington, DC: American Psychological Association, 2007); Gary Alan Fine and Irfan Khawaja, "Celebrating Arabs and Grateful Terrorists: Rumor and the Politics of Plausibility," in *Rumor Mills: The Social Impact of Rumor and Legend*, ed. Gary Alan Fine et al. (New Brunswick: Aldine Transaction, 2005), 189–206; and Jean-Noël Kapferer, *Rumors: Uses, Interpretations, and Images*, trans. Bruce Fink (New Brunswick: Transaction Publishers, 1990).

8 Prashant Bordia and Nicholas DiFonzo, "Problem Solving in Social Interactions on the Internet: Rumor as Social Cognition," *Social Psychology* 67, no. 1 (2004): 33–49.

9 David Coady, "Rumor Has It," *International Journal of Applied Philosophy* 20, no. 1 (2006): 41–55.

10 See, for example: Allport and Postman, *Psychology of Rumor*; DiFonzo and Bordia, *Rumor Psychology*; Kapferer, *Rumors*; Patrick B. Mullen, "Modern Legend and Rumor Theory," *Journal of the Folklore Institute* 9, no. 2/3 (1972): 95–109; and Timothy R. Tangherlini, "'It Happened Not Too Far from Here . . .': A Survey of Legend Theory and Characterization," *Western Folklore* 49, no. 4 (1990): 371–90.

11 See Mullen, "Modern Legend," 96–98; DiFonzo and Bordia, *Rumor Psychology*, 26.

12 Tangherlini, "It Happened," 375.

13 DiFonzo and Bordia, *Rumor Psychology*, 26.

14 Mullen, "Modern Legend," 108.

15 Edward Branigan, *Narrative Comprehension and Film* (New York: Routledge, 1992), xi, 18.

16 Bordwell, like many film scholars, uses the terms "spectator" and "viewer" instead of "reader" to signify the difference between his approach and psychoanalysis, semiotics, and literary models of film analysis. In this book we use "reader" for its broader usage in the field of narratology.

17 David Bordwell, *Narration in the Fiction Film* (Madison: University of Wisconsin Press, 1985). At times Bordwell's approach can seem rigid and, ironically given his emphasis on history, reductive in its overly generalized view of the film spectator. It ignores, for instance, narrative ideologies and reader emotions and unconscious processes. Nonetheless, it provides a useful platform for discussing the relationship between the constructed nature of film and the constructing processes of readers.

18 Mikhail Bakhtin, *Speech Genres and Other Late Essays*, trans. Vern W. McGee (Austin: University of Texas Press, 1986), 91.

19 For Muslims, the biblical revelations referenced in the Qur'an were subsequently lost or corrupted over the centuries, necessitating the revelation of the Qur'an.

20 Stuart Hall, "Encoding/Decoding," in *Culture, Media, Language: Working Papers in Cultural Studies 1972–79*, ed. Stuart Hall et al. (London: Hutchinson, 2008), 128–38.

21 Ibid., 138.

22 The term "crusade" and its connotations suggest the cultural variation that complicates the encoding/decoding process: "crusade" in a Western/Christian context generally connotes a righteous war; "crusade" in an Arab or Islamic context generally connotes "invasion" or "oppression." Thus, for the average Iraqi, hearing Bush's "crusade" as "invasion" would be a consistent, dominant decoding of the statement, but not the encoding Bush intended.

23 "Zarqawi' Shows Face in New Video," BBC News, 25 April 2006 (http://news.bbc.co.uk/2/hi/middle_east/4944250.stm).

24 Translation by Jeffry Halverson, July 2010.

25 For Gramsci's original writings, see Antonio Gramsci, *Selections from the Prison Notebooks*, ed. and trans. Quintin Hoare and Geoffrey Nowell Smith (New York: International Publishers, 1971). For an analysis of Gramsci's work, see Dante L.

Germino, *Antonio Gramsci: Architect of a New Politics* (Baton Rouge: Louisiana University Press, 1990).

26 Muhammad Yaqub Kulayni, *Kitab al-Kafi*, hadith 616, ch. 37; retrieved from http://www.al-shia.org/html/eng/books/hadith/al-kafi/part4/part4-ch37.htm.

27 Ibid.

28 Jeffry Halverson, Steven R. Corman, and H. L. Goodall Jr., *Master Narratives of Islamist Extremism* (New York: Palgrave Macmillan, forthcoming 2011), chap. 14.

29 On 2 May 2011 Osama bin Laden was killed by U.S. forces at a residential compound in Abbottabad, Pakistan. Immediately, rumors began circulating on extremist websites discrediting media accounts of the raid. Unfortunately, these events occurred after this manuscript went to press, preventing a more thorough analysis in these pages.

30 There are a number of other Islamic archetypes used by Islamist extremists, as well as story forms and key historical narratives, or "master narratives," not listed here. These are discussed in a book by our colleagues at Arizona State: Halverson, Corman, and Goodall, *Master Narratives of Islamist Extremism* (New York: Palgrave, 2011). Our work on archetypes, story forms, and master narratives borrows from this book.

31 See Gilles Kepel, *Muslim Extremism in Egypt: The Prophet and Pharaoh,* trans. Jon Rothschild (Berkeley: University of California Press, 2003).

32 Our term "story form" is a concatenation of ideas drawing from literary and cultural theorists as wide-ranging as Walter Fisher, Kenneth Burke, Vladimir Propp, and Claude Levi-Strauss. The closest existing term to our "story form" is H. Porter Abbott's "masterplot," but we feel his attention to "master" connotes too stringent an application, and his choice of plot is too focused on actions. See H. Porter Abbott, *The Cambridge Introduction to Narrative* (Cambridge: Cambridge University Press, 2008), 47.

33 Kenneth Cragg, *The Event of the Qur'an: Islam in Its Scripture* (Oxford: Oneworld, 1994), 112.

34 "If US Could Create Avatar, It Could Fake 9/11 Attacks: Mahathir," *Jakarta Globe,* 21 January 2010. Available from http://www.thejakartaglobe.com/home/if-us-could-create-avatar-it-could-fake-911-attacks-mahathir/354031.

35 See Halverson et al., *Master Narratives,* for a thorough study of master narratives in the context of Islamist extremism.

36 Here we are attempting to avoid what we see as the false dichotomy established in debates between Structuralists, who look for universal structures, and Post-Structuralists, who critique as reductive all "meta-narratives" that claim to be universal. Narratives are built on structures such as cause and effect, but those structures—though long-lived in cases of narratives that survive through the ages such as master narratives—are not significant across all of time and all cultures. Narrative structures—their elements and cause-and-effect principles—are always already historical with respect to both storytelling and story comprehension. So too, then, are master narratives, story forms, and archetypes.

37 Hall, "Encoding/Decoding," 137.

38 For a history of the Crusades from the Islamic perspective, see Carole Hillenbrand, *The Crusades: Islamic Perspectives* (Edinburgh: Edinburgh University Press, 1999).

39 Halverson et al., *Master Narratives.*

40 See Robert F. Worth, "950 Die in Stampede on Baghdad Bridge," *New York Times,* 1 September 2005. Referenced also in DiFonzo and Bordia, *Rumor Psychology,* 35.

41 See, for example: Ralph L. Rosnow, John H. Yost, and James L. Esposito, "Belief in Rumor and Likelihood of Rumor Transmission," *Language and Communication* 6, no. 3 (1986): 189–94; Allport and Postman, *Psychology of Rumor.*

42 United States, Department of the Army, *The U.S. Army/Marine Corps Counterinsurgency Field Manual,* U.S. Army Field Manual no. 3-24; Marine Corps Warfighting Publication no. 3-33.5 (Chicago: University of Chicago Press, 2007), 25. The manual was put together in the wake of the Iraqi insurgency,

Chapter 2: Rumor Transmediation

1 "Out with the Whole Truth and Nothing but the Truth," blog entry, 2 March 2008. Retrieved from http://wherebearsroamfree.blogspot.com/2008/03/out-with-whole-truth-and-nothing-but.html.

2 Amnesty International, "Singapore: The Death Penalty—The Hidden Toll of Executions," January 2004. Available online: http://www.amnesty.org/en/library/asset/ASA36/001/2004/en/74c4cb33-d64e-11dd-ab95-a13b602c0642/asa36 0012004en.pdf.

3 Raman Iyer, "Family Learns of Indian Inmate's Death only through Cellmate," Top News, 6 July 2008, http://www.topnews.in/law/family-learns-indian-inmates-death-only-cellmate.

4 Singaporean governance is described as paternal or "soft" authoritarianism to differentiate it from the "hard" authoritarianism associated with, for example, Latin American or African dictatorships. It is culturally based on Confucian values that emphasize respect for authority and conformity, but is not particularly violent or coercive as long as citizens toe the line. Singapore is a one-party state; although elections are held, there is relatively weak competition from small opposition parties, which often face persecution.

5 For more on prosumers and terrorist narratives in Singapore, see Pauline Hope Cheong and Chris Lundry, "Prosumption, Transmediation, and Resistance: Terrorism and Man-hunting in Southeast Asia," *American Behavioral Scientist,* in press. Parts of this chapter are based on their early research.

6 Although the blogs and forums that were examined in this study are unaffiliated with the government, some bloggers surmised that agents of the government had responded to some of the blogs and forums in an attempt to reduce criticism of and promote sympathy for the government. One such poster, Nicholas Lazarus, used the same wording and argument in responses to several blogs. An example of criticisms outing him can be found on the Geraldgiam.sg blog, where one anonymous respondent wrote: "Nicholas Lazarus is not a foreigner. He is a member of Young PAP [YPAP]. He had left the same comments [copy & paste] on blog posts [related to Mas Selamat's escape] listed in the *Singapore Daily.* Google his name and other kinds of twisted logic by him can be found too." Gerald Giam, "Mas Selamat's Prison Break: Some Questions for the Home Affairs Minister," 28 February 2008, http://geraldgiam.sg/2008/02/mas-selamats-prison-break-some-questions-for-home-affairs-minister/. Lazarus did not respond to these criticisms.

7 Jay David Bolter and Richard Grusin, *Remediation: Understanding New Media* (Cambridge, MA: MIT Press, 2000).

8 Gabriel Weimann and Conrad Winn, *The Theater of Terror: Mass Media and International Terrorism* (New York: Longman, 1993); Eytan Gilboa, "The CNN Effect: The Search for a Communications Theory of International Relations," *Political Communication* 22, no. 1 (2005): 27–44.

9 Gabriel Weimann, *Terror on the Internet: The New Arena, the New Challenges* (Washington, DC: United States Institute of Peace Press, 2006).

10 Jerrold M. Post, Keven G. Ruby, and Eric D. Shaw, "From Car Bombs to Logic Bombs: The Growing Threat from Information Terrorism," *Terrorism and Political Violence* 12, no. 2 (2000): 97–122.

11 Timothy L. Thomas, "Cyber Mobilization: The Neglected Aspect of Information Operations and Counterinsurgency Doctrine," in *Countering Terrorism and Insurgency in the 21st Century: International Perspectives,* ed. James J. F. Forest, 3 vols. (Westport, CT: Praeger Security International, 2007), 1:369.

12 See David Betz, "The Virtual Dimension of Contemporary Insurgency and Counter-Insurgency," *Small Wars & Insurgencies* 19, no. 4 (2008): 510–40; Aidan Kirby and Vera Zakem, "Jihad.com 2.0: The New Social Media and the Changing Dynamics of Mass Persuasion," in *Influence Warfare: How Terrorists and Governments Fight to Shape Perceptions in a War of Ideas*, ed. James J. F. Forest (Westport, CT: Praeger Security International, 2009), 27–48.

13 Steve R. Corman, Angela Tretheway, and Bud Goodall, "A 21st Century Model for Communication in the Global War of Ideas: From Simplistic Influence to Pragmatic Complexity," Consortium for Strategic Communication Publications, 2007; retrieved from http://comops.org/article/114.pdf.

14 Gabriel Weimann, "The Psychology of Mass-Mediated Terrorism," *American Behavioral Scientist* 52, no. 1 (2008): 69–86; Philip A. Karber, "Urban Terrorism: Baseline Data and a Conceptual Framework," *Social Science Quarterly* 52, no. 3 (1971): 521–33.

15 Jeffrey C. Alexander, "From the Depths of Despair: Performance, Counterperformance, and 'September 11,'" *Sociological Theory* 22, no. 1 (2004): 88.

16 Anat Shoshani and Michelle Slone, "The Drama of Media Coverage of Terrorism: Emotional and Attitudinal Impact on the Audience," *Studies in Conflict & Terrorism* 31, no. 7 (2008): 627–40.

17 Kenneth Payne, "Winning the Battle of Ideas: Propaganda, Ideology, and Terror," *Studies in Conflict & Terrorism* 32, no. 2 (2009): 109–28.

18 Betz, "Virtual Dimension," 510–40.

19 Jan Fernback, "Legends on the Net: An Examination of Computer-mediated Communication as a Locus of Oral Culture," *New Media & Society* 5, no. 1 (2003): 29–45.

20 Sonia Livingstone, "New Media, New Audiences?" *New Media & Society* 1, no. 1 (1999): 59–66.

21 Henry Jenkins, *Convergence Culture: Where Old and New Media Collide* (New York: New York University Press, 2006), 3.

22 Marjorie D. Kibby, "Email Forwardables: Folklore in the Age of the Internet," *New Media & Society* 7, no. 6 (2005): 770–90; Russell Frank, "When the Going Gets Tough, the Tough Go Photoshopping: September 11 and the Newslore of

Vengeance and Victimization," *New Media & Society* 6, no. 5 (2004): 633–58; Lawrence Lessig, *Remix: Making Art and Commerce Thrive in the Hybrid Economy* (New York: Penguin Press, 2008).

23 Cass R. Sunstein, *On Rumors: How Falsehoods Spread, Why We Believe Them, What Can Be Done* (New York: Farrar, Straus and Giroux, 2009).

24 James Scott, *Weapons of the Weak: Everyday Forms of Peasant Resistance* (New Haven: Yale University Press, 1985).

25 Infocomm Development Authority of Singapore, "Singapore Infocomm Statistics at a Glance," http://www.ida.gov.sg/Publications/20070822125451.aspx#usage Hse1.

26 Indrajit Banerjee and Benjamin Yeo, "Internet and Democracy in Singapore: A Critical Appraisal," in *Rhetoric and Reality: The Internet Challenge for Democracy in Asia*, ed. Indrajit Banerjee (Singapore: Eastern Universities Press, 2003), 259–87.

27 K. C. Ho, Zaheer Baber, and Habibul Khondker, "'Sites' of Resistance: Alternative Websites and State-Society Relations," *British Journal of Sociology* 53, no. 1 (2002): 127–48.

28 Lars Willnat and Annette J. Aw, "Political Communication in Asia: Challenges and Opportunities," in *Handbook of Political Communication Research*, ed. L. L. Kaid (Mahwah, NJ: Lawrence Erlbaum, 2004), 479–503.

29 Robert K. Yin, *Case Study Research: Design and Methods*, 2nd ed. (Thousand Oaks, CA: Sage, 1994).

30 International Crisis Group, "Indonesia Backgrounder: How the Jemaah Islamiyah Terrorist Network Operates," Asia Report no. 43, 11 December 2002. Available from http://www.crisisgroup.org/en/regions/asia/south-east-asia/indonesia/043-indonesia-backgrounder-how-the-jemaah-islamiyah-terrorist-network-operates.aspx.

31 I. Saad, "Mas Selamat's Relatives Aided Escape." Retrieved from http://www.channelnewsasia.com/stories/singaporelocalnews/view/1094848/1/.html.

32 In reports of the International Crisis Group, among the most frequently cited sources regarding terrorism in Southeast Asia, Mas Selamat is mentioned only twice prior to 2008.

33 "Relatives of Suspected Terrorist Jailed for Hiding Fugitive," Singapore News Alternative, 22 November 2010, http://singaporenewsalternative.-blogspot.com/2010/11/family-members-of-mas-selamat-jailed.html.

34 B. Nadarajan, "The Face that Launched 5.5 Million Cell Phone Alerts."Retrieved 2 March 2008 from http://www.straitstimes.com/Free/Story/ STIStory_212374.html.

35 C. Oon, "Minister Praises Citizens, but Stresses Need to Build Strong Network of Trust," *Straits Times*, 12 March 2008.

36 S. A. Chia and C. L. Goh, "JI Man Mas Selamat's Escape; Guards Were Negligent Says MM," *Straits Times*, 5 April 2008. Retrieved from http://sgblogs.com/entry/very-poor-service-straits-times/197123.

37 The Bulletin of Singapore Bloggers published its unofficial poll regarding the escape. Only 40 percent of respondents linked the escape to the "incompetence of officers." In other categories, 30 percent thought it was an inside job, 17 percent thought it was black magic, 9 percent thought it was because "Mas Selamat was too smart"; and 4 percent answered other. http://tomorrow.sg/archives/2008/03/03/your_take_-_the_main_reason_why_.html.

38 Gopalan Nair, "Was Mas Selamat Assisted in His Escape? And by Who?" blog post, 28 September 2008, http://singaporedissident.blogspot.com/2008/02/was-mas-selamat-kastari-assited-in-his.html.

39 On 4 March, Nair hailed Mas Selamat as a hero who had escaped the tyranny of Singapore's Internal Security Act. Nair is a former Singaporean who was persecuted for his outspoken opposition to the government as well as for running for office as a candidate of the Workers Party (Singapore functions as a one-party state led by the People's Action Party). He fled to the United States, where he was granted asylum, and he gave up his Singaporean citizenship in 2004. Although it is not difficult to understand why Nair is critical of the government, his rallying behind Mas Selamat was curious, given the accusations against the JI member. In a personal communication to the authors, Nair emphasized that he was not a Muslim and did not support terrorism; rather, he argued that Mas Selamat had not undergone a fair trial and therefore was being detained illegitimately. Nair also claimed that Mas Selamat had merely spoken or thought his ideas, but had not acted on them and therefore was not guilty of any crimes.

40 Cherian George, "The Other Casualty of the Great Escape: Mainstream Media Credibility," Journalism.SG website, 2 March 2008, http://journalism.sg/2008/03/02/the-other-casualty-of-the-great-escape-mainstream-media-credibility/.

41 Raymond Bonner, "Terror Suspect Escapes in Singapore," *New York Times*, 27 February 2008. Online: http://www.nytimes.com/2008/02/27/world/asia/27iht-terror.3.10483062.html.

42 See, for example, http://xmercenaries.com/four9er/wp-content/uploads/2008/03/catchmeifyoucan2002moviez1.jpg; http://www.exampaper.com.sg/study-break/crouching-terrorist-leaping-maiden.

43 http://www.talkingcock.com/html/sections.php?op=viewarticle&artid=89. The name "Pac-Mat" also reflects Singaporean slang. "Pak"—as Pac in the game's title is pronounced—means "sir" or "father" in Malay, or to hit or strike in Singlish. "Mat" is a Singaporean Malay term for a ruffian.

44 "Pac-Mat upgraded!" Retrieved from http://www.talkingcock.com/html/article.php?sid=2517.

45 Pierre Bourdieu and Jean-Claude Passeron, *Reproduction in Education, Society, and Culture*, trans. Richard Nice (1970; reprint, London: Sage Publications, 1990).

46 http://www.mrbrown.com/blog/2008/04/mas-selanats-es.html.

47 http://singaporedissident.blogspot.com/2008/02/was-mas-selamat-kastari-assited-in-his.html.

48 Tzvetan Todorov, *The Fantastic: A Structural Approach to a Literary Genre*, trans. Richard Howard (Cleveland: Case Western Reserve University Press, 1973).

49 http://www.youtube.com/comment_servlet?all_comments=1&v=5wjFryHFaFM.

50 Dennis McQuail, "On the Mediatization of War," *International Communication Gazette* 68, no. 2 (2006): 107–18.

51 Greg Dalziel, "Rumors and Collective Sense-Making about Security Incidents," paper presented at the International Communication Association Conference, Singapore, 25 June 2010.

52 Joseph McCarthy and Danah Boyd, "Digital Backchannels in Shared Physical Spaces: Experiences at an Academic Conference," *Proceedings of the SIGCHI Conference on Human Factors in Computing Systems (CHI '05) Extended Abstracts* (New York: ACM Press, 2005).

53 M. Hydar, "Lipstick Jungle: Why we might have helped Mas Selamat escape." Retrieved from http://theonlinecitizen.com/2010/11/lipstick-jungle-why-we-might-have-helped-mas-selamat-escape/.

54 Retrieved from http://www.mrbrown.com/blog/2010/11/grissom-bauer-and-dunham-weigh-in-on-mas-selamats-case.html.

55. Henry Jenkins, "Slash Me, Mash Me, Spread Me . . . Confessions of an Aca/Fan," April 24 2007, http://www.henryjenkins.org/2007/04/slash_me_mash_me_but_please_sp.html.

56 http://blog.simplyjean.com/2008/02/29/toilet-break-4-mas-limping-terrorist-selamat/.

57 Abu Bakr, "Another Akhi Escaped," blog post, 29 February 2010, http://abubakr1400.blogspot.com/search?q=%22mas+selamat%22.

58 "Penulis blog, Philip Chua menulis: 'Singapura telah melakukan kesalahan bodoh dan kini menjadi bahan ketawa internasional.' Beliau menambahkan, tidak ada tahanan yang melarikan diri dari pusat tahanan 'teroris' di Barat atau Guantanamo, lebih-lebih lagi melibatkan seorang ketua rangkaian 'teroris' yang aktif di sebuah negara tetangga." Fadly, "Kecerobohan Singapura jadi Bahan Ledekan," *Ar Rahmah*, http://arrahmah.com/-index.php/news/read/1635/kecerobohan-singapura-jadi-bahan-ledekan#ixzz0yz231qTj.

59 Steven M. Marks, Thomas M. Meer, and Matthew T. Nilson, "Manhunting: A Process to Find Persons of National Interest," in Forest, ed., *Countering Terrorism and Insurgency*, 1:208–34.

Chapter 3: Rumor Mosaics

1 In late 2009, Multi-National Force–Iraq was renamed United States Force–Iraq.

2 This rumor first came to our attention in conversations with journalists embedded with U.S. forces in Iraq and was confirmed by information operations officers stationed in the country.

3 Iraq's "Triangle of Death" is an area of extreme Sunni insurgent violence, between Baghdad and Al-Hillah, bordered by the Euphrates River to the west.

4 These rumors were collected in three ways: interviews with American military and press personnel upon return from patrols and information-gathering activities in Iraq; interviews with Iraqi military personnel familiar with the area; and face-to-face conversations with Iraqi citizens conducted by co-author Daniel Bernardi. A U.S. Navy Reservist, Bernardi served as the public affairs officer for Special Operations Taskforce–Central from June 2009 to February 2010.

5 Stephanie Kelley, "Rumors in Iraq: A Guide to Winning Hears and Minds," *Strategic Insights* 4, no. 2 (February 2005). For details of Kelley's larger study, see "Rumors in Iraq: A Guide to Winning Hearts and Minds" (M.A. thesis, Naval Postgraduate School, 2004); available at http://www.au.af.mil/au/awc/awcgate/nps/kelley_sep04.pdf.

6 Kelley, "Rumors in Iraq" (2004), 27.

7 The United States cast its threat in the context of international law following UN Security Council Resolution 1441, which followed numerous other Security Council resolutions demanding that Hussein give inspectors from the UN and the International Atomic Energy Administration (IAEA) "immediate, unconditional and active cooperation."

8 See Hans Blix, *Disarming Iraq* (New York: Pantheon Books, 2004).

9 Yet the rumor of Hussein's WMD stockpile remains active, as various political factions supporting the war suggest that it was moved to Syria or Iran prior to the invasion.

10 Condoleezza Rice, quoted in "Top Bush Officials Push Case against Saddam," CNN, http://articles.cnn.com/2002/sep/08.

11 "President Bush Outlines Iraqi Threat," Cincinnati Museum Center, Cincinnati, Ohio, 7 October 2002, http://georgewbush-whitehouse.archives.gov/news/releases/2002/10/-20021007-8.html.

12 Quoted in James Bamford, *A Pretext for War: 9/11, Iraq and the Abuse of America's Intelligence Agencies* (New York: Doubleday, 2004), 325.

13 Several journalists have researched and written about the ways in which the Bush administration used the media to spread the story that Hussein's WMD program posed an imminent threat to the United States. Many of their sources lead to individuals with a vested interest in seizing power in Iraq, including Ahmed Chalabi and other Iraqi defectors who needed U.S. support to topple the dictator. See especially Michael Isikoff and David Corn, *Hubris: The Inside Story of Spin, Scandal, and the Selling of the Iraq War* (New York: Three Rivers Press, 2007), Thomas E. Ricks, *Fiasco: The American Military Adventure in Iraq* (New York: Penguin, 2007), and Seymour M. Hersh, *Chain of Command: The Road from 9/11 to Abu Ghraib* (New York: HarperCollins, 2004).

14 *Meet the Press* transcript for 14 September 2003, http://www.msnbc.msn.com/id/-3080244/.

15 The National Commission on Terrorist Attacks upon the United States (9-11 Commission) and the Senate Select Committee on Intelligence both concluded that there was no evidence of ties between Hussein and al Qaeda. This finding is also supported by declassified Defense Department reports. Although these reports came out after the war, they revealed that there was considerable disagreement inside the governments of the United States and United Kingdom about Iraq's purported WMD program and its links to al Qaeda.

16 The term is Andrew Gilligan's, from his 29 May 2003 report on the BBC, http://news.bbc.co.uk/2/hi/uk_news/politics/3090681.stm.

17 For an account of the mismanagement of the occupation, particularly during the Coalition Provisional Authority period managed by Paul Bremer, see Rajiv Chandrasekaran, *Imperial Life in the Emerald City: Inside Iraq's Green Zone* (New York: Knopf, 2006).

18 This point is stressed throughout the literature on rumors. As Nicholas DiFonzo summarizes: "This is the famous law of rumor: Rumors abound in proportion to the ambiguity or uncertainty inherent in a situation, and the importance of the topic." DiFonzo, *The Watercooler Effect: A Psychologist Explores the Extraordinary Power of Rumors* (New York: Avery, 2008), 35.

19 For an insightful study of how U.S. strategic communication during the Iraq war amounted to information fratricide, see Christopher Paul et al., "Challenges to Shaping Civilian Attitudes and Behaviors in a Theater of Operations," in *Influence Warfare: How Terrorists and Governments Fight to Shape Perceptions in a War of Ideas*, ed. James J. F. Forest (Westport, CT: Praeger Security International, 2009), 173–94.

20 Sebastian Gorka and David Kilcullen, "Who's Winning the Battle for Narrative? Al-Qaida versus the United States and Its Allies," in Forest, ed., *Influence Warfare,* 233.

21 Simon Cottee makes a similar point: "wherever the causes of terrorism may ultimately lie, the act of killing, maiming and terrorizing innocent people is enabled by a framework of justifying and mitigating narratives." See Cottee, "Mind Slaughter: The Neutralizations of Jihadi Salafism," *Studies in Conflict & Terrorism* 33, no. 4 (2010): 331.

22 The fatwa, a legal opinion or ruling, was also signed by Ayman al-Zawahiri, Abu-Yasir Rifa'i Ahmad Taha, Shaykh Mir Hamzah, Fazlur Rahman. It can be found in its entirety at http://www.fas.org/irp/world/para/docs/980223-fatwa.htm.

23 In some cases a rumor might predict an event (a bank cannot cover its deposits), leading to actions that bring about the event (a run on the bank). For a broad overview of this and other arguments about the social psychology of rumors, see DiFonzo, *Watercooler Effect.*

24 Or as Robert H. Knapp suggests: "No rumor will travel far unless there is already a disposition among those who hear it to lend it credence. But once rumors are current, they have a way of carrying the public with them. Somehow, the more a rumor is told, the greater is its plausibility." See Knapp, "A Psychology of Rumor," *Public Opinion Quarterly* 8, no. 1 (1944): 47; also David Coady, "Rumor Has It," *International Journal of Applied Philosophy* 20, no. 1 (2006).

25 Coady, "Rumor Has It," 45. For the reference to the biological metaphor, see Tamotsu Shibutani, *Improvised News: A Sociological Study of Rumor* (Indianapolis: Bobbs-Merrill Company, 1966).

26 "Maximum disclosure, minimum delay" is taught at the U.S. military's school for public affairs, the Defense Information School (DINFOS). See http://www.dinfos.osd.mil/.

27 See, for example, Seymour Chatman, *Story and Discourse: Narrative Structure in Fiction and Film* (Ithaca: Cornell University Press, 1978), and Gérard Genette, *Narrative Discourse: An Essay in Method,* trans. Jane E. Lewin (Ithaca: Cornell University Press, 1980).

28 Jeffry Halverson, Steven R. Corman, and H. L. Goodall Jr., *Master Narratives of Islamist Extremism* (New York: Palgrave Macmillan, forthcoming 2011).

29 United States, Department of the Army, *The U.S. Army/Marine Corps Counterinsurgency Field Manual,* U.S. Army Field Manual no. 3-24; Marine Corps Warfighting Publication no. 3-33.5 (Chicago: University of Chicago Press, 2007), 14.

30 Which is not to suggest that lies are a legitimate or effective countermeasure.

31 Jean-Noël Kapferer, *Rumors: Uses, Interpretations, and Images,* trans. Bruce Fink (New Brunswick: Transaction Publishers, 1990), 229–31.

32 Hans-Joachim Neubauer, *The Rumor: A Cultural History* (London: Free Association Books, 1999), 133–39.

33 Following U.S. and Iraqi military guidelines provided to embedded journalists, we do not publish the names of the Hillah SWAT constables below the rank of colonel to ensure that they cannot be identified and targeted by insurgents.

34 The common subject of the Stack House rumor family is the combination of the facility, its users, and its use. The single rumor antecedent is the U.S. occupation of the site, beginning in 2004. Thus, this family differs from the Mas Selamat

family in that the antecedent is an ongoing phenomenon rather than a single event in the past.

35 The U.S. commander of Stack House as well as senior members in charge of Hillah SWAT reported this belief to us.

36 The decrease in lethal attacks on Iraqi and U.S. forces in the region can also be linked to the U.S. surge and to the increasing capabilities of Hillah SWAT.

37 Transcript of an audio tape, attributed to Osama bin Laden and broadcast on Al-Jazeera in November 2002, available via BBC News: http://news.bbc.co.uk/2/hi/middle_east/2455845.stm. During the Gulf War, Powell was Chairman of the Joint Chiefs of Staff and Cheney was Secretary of Defense under President George H. W. Bush.

38 See Halverson, Corman, and Goodall, *Master Narratives,* chap. 9, for a thorough discussion of Hulagu Khan and the Tatar master narrative.

39 Abu Musab al-Zarqawi, letter to Osama bin Laden, 2004. Available online through Global Security: http://www.globalsecurity.org/wmd/library/news/iraq/2004/02/040212-al-zarqawi.

Chapter 4: Whisper Campaigns

1 Subsequently we use Noordin, consistent with Malay usage. This chapter also draws partly on Chris Lundry and Pauline Hope Cheong, "Rumors and Strategic Communication: The Gendered Construction and Transmediation of a Terrorist Life Story," in *Matters of Communication: Political, Cultural, and Technological Challenges,* ed. Timothy Kuhn (New York: Hampton Press, 2011), 145–166.

2 Televisindo, "Detik Detik Penyerbuan Noordin M Top (8 Agustus 2009)," YouTube video, 8 August 2009; available from http://www.youtube.com/watch?v=rtXp_-mo6A3o. Also iksan85, "Detik Detik Penyergapan Noordin M Top," YouTube video, 8 August 2009; available from http://www.youtube.com/watch?v=sshwFfaJiQM.

3 Televisindo, "Detik Detik."

4 Knapp, "A Psychology of Rumor," 28.

5 Although the intentions of the Indonesian authorities cannot be independently verified, we advance a significant amount of evidence that suggests their aim was to taint Noordin's Islamic identity and discredit his terrorist achievements.

6 International Crisis Group, "Terrorism in Indonesia: Noordin's Networks," Asia Report no. 114, 5 May 2006: 1. Available from http://www.crisisgroup.org/en/regions/asia/south-east-asia/indonesia/114-terrorism-in-indonesia-noordins-networks.aspx.

7 The United States was wary of releasing Hambali to Indonesian authorities, given the relatively light sentence imposed on Abu Bakar Basyir.

8 International Crisis Group, "Terrorism in Indonesia."

9 Ibid.

10 Chris Lundry, "Possible New JI/AQ Offshoot Claims Jakarta Bombings (Updated)," *COMOPS Journal,* 30 July 2009. Available from http://comops.org/journal/-2009/07/29/possible-new-jiaq-offshoot-claims-jakarta-bombings/.

11 Nufrika Osman, "Terrorist Noordin M Top Was Sodomized: Indonesian Forensic Expert," *Jakarta Globe,* 30 September 2009.

12 Bayu Hermawan, "Polri: Dubur Noordin Tak Diutak-Utik," *Inilah,* 1 October 2009. Available from: http://www.inilah.com/berita/2009/09/30/161702/polri-dubur-

noordin-tak-diutak-atik/. This story and all subsequent translations of Indonesian text are by Lundry. *Visum et repertum* ("seen and discovered") refers to the forensic report and the assumption of confidentiality about the results.

13 A collection of essays that explore the topic of homosexuality and Islam across a wide variety of regions and cultures is *Gay Travels in the Muslim World,* ed. Michael Luongo (New York: Harrington Park Press, 2007).

14 "Bashir Wants to Preach in Australia," *Jihad Watch,* 30 August 2006. Available from http://www.jihadwatch.org/2006/08/bashir-wants-to-preach-in-australia.html.

15 Mathias Hariyadi, "Java, Conference of Gays and Lesbians Blocked by Islamic Extremists," AsiaNews.It, 27 March 2010. Available from http://www.asianews.it/news-en/Java,-Conference-of-gays-and-lesbians-blocked-by-Islamic-extremists-18002.html.

16 In 2003 U.S. Senator Rick Santorum (R., PA) created a media uproar by professing that sodomy is "antithetical to a healthy, stable, traditional family." Associated Press, "Excerpt from Santorum Interview," *USA Today,* 23 April 2003. Available from http://www.usatoday.com/news/washington/2003-04-23-santorum-excerpt_x.htm.

17 Sugeng Wibowo, "Ahli Forensik UI: Ada Kelainan di Tubuh Noordin M Top," *Surya,* 30 September 2009. Available from http://www.surya.co.id/2009/09/30/ahli-forensik-ui-ada-kelainan-di-tubuh-noordin-m-top.html.

18 Sipri Seko, "Ahli Forensik: Dubur Noordin Rusak," *Kupang Pos,* 30 September 2009. Available from http://www.pos-kupang.com/getrss/viewrss.php?id=36333.

19 "Nanan: Soal Dubur Noordin Seharusnya Dirahasiakan," *Kompas,* 30 September 2009. Available from http://nasional.kompas.com/read/xml/2009/09/30/17405148%20/nana.

20 William A. Peniston, *Pederasts and Others: Urban Culture and Sexual Identity in Nineteenth-Century Paris* (New York: Harrington Park Press, 2004), 53. George Rousseau describes Tardieu's debt to Paolo Zacchia (1584–1659), an authority on legal medicine. See Rousseau, "Policing the Anus: Stuprum and Sodomy According to Paolo Zacchia's Forensic Medicine," in *The Sciences of Homosexuality in Early Modern Europe,* ed. Kenneth Borris and George Rousseau (New York: Routledge, 2008), 75, 84.

21 Quoted in Peniston, *Pederasts and Others,* 54. Prior to the nineteenth century, convictions of sodomy relied on confessions, often obtained through torture, over physical examinations. See Mary Elizabeth Perry, "The 'Nefarious Sin' in Early Modern Seville," in *The Pursuit of Sodomy: Male Homosexuality in Renaissance and Enlightenment Europe,* ed. Kent Gerard and Gert Hekma (New York: Harrington Park Press, 1989).

22 Quoted in Peniston, *Pederasts and Others,* 54. These descriptions seem ridiculous today, but Tardieu's reputation gave them credibility at the time.

23 Vernon A. Rosario notes that the criminality of sodomites was not a matter of their physical activities but arose from their "travesties of class and gender." Effeminate affectations were associated with the aristocracy, and homosexuals of low birth who adopted these affectations were seen as threatening the social order. Blackmail was another concern. See Rosario, *The Erotic Imagination: French Histories of Perversion* (New York: Oxford University Press, 1997), 75–77; Victoria Thompson, "Creating Boundaries: Homosexuality and the Changing Social Order

in France, 1830–1870," in *Homosexuality in Modern France*, ed. Jeffrey Merrick and Bryant T. Ragan Jr. (New York: Oxford University Press, 1996). These claims are repeated in the context of the late colonial Dutch East Indies. According to Tom Boellstorff, "sex between men seems to have become seen as threatening the racial hierarchy upon which colonial authority rested . . . the product of global connection and a threat to social order." See Boellstorff, *The Gay Archipelago: Sexuality and Nation in Indonesia* (Princeton: Princeton University Press, 2005), 54.

24 Ironically, sodomy was also linked to Islam during the period in which Tardieu was writing. Among Europeans, there were widespread perceptions of Muslims as homosexuals and of homosexuals deviating from an imagined "national character." There is, in other words, a historical connection between homosexuality, criminality, and nationality that intimately links Islam to homosexuality and homosexuality to moral deviance, impurity, and national otherness—conditions that are in turn condemned in the extremist Islamic ideology to which Noordin subscribed. See Human Rights Watch, *In a Time of Torture: Egypt's Crackdown on Homosexual Conduct* (New York: Human Rights Watch, 2004), 111.

25 Peniston, *Pederasts and Others*, 57.

26 Kelsey wrote in his 1883 medical text, *Diseases of the Rectum and Anus* (New York: William Wood and Company, 1893), "there is no reason for believing that the frequent introduction of the male organ should cause its [the anus's] paralysis any more than the equally frequent passage of fæces. However it may be in warmer climates, I know that it would not do in America to infer the practice of unnatural vice from a relaxed and funnel-shaped anus, as seems to be the case in France" (13). See, however, Samuel Goodwin Gant, *Diseases of the Rectum and Anus* (Philadelphia: F. A. Davis Company, 1906), 303.

27 Peniston, *Pederasts and Others*, 58–59.

28 Human Rights Watch, *In a Time of Torture*, 111.

29 Scott Long, "When Doctors Torture: The Anus and the State in Egypt and Beyond," *Health and Human Rights* 7, no. 2 (2004): 127.

30 Human Rights Watch, *In a Time of Torture*, 109.

31 Ibid.

32 For more on the ideological nature of the eugenics movement, see Stephen Jay Gould, *The Mismeasure of Man* (New York: W. W. Norton, 1996).

33 Anna Soumalainen et al., "Congenital Funnel Anus in Children: Associated Anomalies, Surgical Management and Outcome," *Pediatric Surgery International* 23, no. 12 (2007): 1167–70.

34 Qur'an 7:80–81. Translation by Jeffry R. Halverson.

35 Qur'an 26:165–66. Translation by Jeffry R. Halverson.

36 As Boellstorff notes, however, transvestites are viewed differently than homosexuals who do not cross-dress, because for some Indonesians the former are expressing an internal/external consistency, whereas the external appearance of the latter is not aligned with internal orientation. Boellstorff, *Gay Archipelago*, 177.

37 Ibid., 169.

38 Benedict Anderson, *The Spectre of Comparisons: Nationalism, Southeast Asia, and the World* (New York: Verso, 1998), 112. Saskia Wieringa notes that similar assertions—that a deviant practice was introduced by "the West"—emerged as lesbians gained recognition in the 1980s. Wieringa, "Communism and Women's Same-Sex Practises in Post-Suharto Indonesia," *Culture, Health & Sexuality* 2, no. 4 (2000): 441–57.

39 Boellstorff, *Gay Archipelago,* 52–54.

40 Dédé Oetomo, "Is There a Place for Us Across the Golden Bridge?" Center for Minority, Gender and Human Rights, 2009. Available from http://centerforminoritygender-andhumanrights.org/archives/author/doetomo/.

41 The events of 1 October 1965 (erroneously referred to as the 30th of September Movement in Indonesia) remain contested to this day. Its results, however, are widely agreed upon: the killings of hundreds of thousands of Indonesians who were suspected communists, ethnic Chinese, and others. The event was portrayed by Major General Suharto, who assumed power shortly after the event, as a coup d'état attempt by the Communist Party, but analysis shows this claim to be at a minimum an exaggeration (if not an outright falsity). See John Roosa, *Pretext for Mass Murder: The September 30th Movement and Suharto's Coup d'État in Indonesia* (Madison: University of Wisconsin Press, 2008), and others.

42 Wieringa, "Communism and Women's Same-Sex Practises," 452; Roosa, *Pretext for Mass Murder,* 40, 198.

43 Boellstorff, *Gay Archipelago,* 55–57.

44 Ibid., 225–27. Gays in some other Southeast Asian countries are even less assertive than those in Indonesia and face legal persecution. In Singapore, Malaysia, Vietnam, and Burma, for example, homosexuality is a crime.

45 Dédé Oetomo, "Gay Men in the Reformasi Era," *Inside Indonesia* 66 (April–June 2001). Available from http://www.insideindonesia.org/edition-66/gay-men-in-the-reformasi-era.

46 "FPI Depok Serang Acara Kontes Waria," GAYa Nusantara, 1 May 2010. Available from http://www.gayanusantara.or.id/.

47 "Indonesia's Top Muslim Body Seeks Ban on Gay Film Festival," *Jakarta Globe,* 1 October 2010. Available from http://www.fridae.com/newsfeatures/2010/10/01/10347.indonesia-s-top-muslim-body-seeks-ban-on-gay-film-festival.

48 Richard Stephen Howard, "Falling into the Gay World: Manhood, Marriage and Family in Indonesia" (Ph.D. diss., University of Illinois, Urbana-Champaign, 1996), 156 and *passim.*

49 Tom Boellstorff, *A Coincidence of Desires: Anthropology, Queer Studies, Indonesia* (Durham: Duke University Press, 2007), 170.

50 Both the United States and the Soviet Union are rumored to have hatched plans to blackmail Soekarno by making sex films, the former using an actor to portray Soekarno, the latter by baiting him with an attractive female spy. The Soviets are rumored to have given up when they realized that it would not be particularly damaging to Soekarno's reputation. See Joseph Burkholder Smith, *Portrait of a Cold Warrior* (New York: G. P. Putnam's Sons, 1976), 238–40, 248, and Roger Boar and Nigel Blundell, *The World's Greatest Spies and Spymasters* (London: Octopus Books, 1984), 129n.

51 Andrew Lam, "Expect More Islamist Terror in Indonesia," *New American Media,* 2 July 2008. Available from http://blogs.newamericamedia.org/nam-round-table/1291/expect-more-islamist-terror-in-indonesia.

52 Although Internet penetration in the country is still low (around 12.5 percent), Indonesia's huge population means that there are around 30 million Internet

users, making it thirteenth in online presence of all countries. Moreover, Internet usage in Indonesia is rapidly growing, around 49 percent annually. Furthermore, almost all new cell phones in Indonesia have Internet capability. Stephen Kaufman, "Indonesian Internet Penetration Expected to Skyrocket: Indonesia's Online Population Grows 49 Percent Annually," America.gov website, 24 March 2010. Available from http://www.america.gov/st/democracyhrenglish/2010/March/20100323153622esnamfuako.8532373.html.

53 Althaf, "Noordin M Top Rajai Yahoo Selama 2009," *Ar-Rahmah*, 12 December 2009. Available from http://www.arrahmah.com/index.php/news/read/6243/noordin-m-top-.

54 Gus Rachmat, "Kerusakan Dubur Noordin M Top Akibat Penetrasi Benda Tumpul" [Web log comment], 1 October 2009. Available from http://gusrachmat.wordpress.com/-2009/10/01/kerusakan-dubur-noordin-m-top-akibat-penetrasi-benda-tumpul/. As described above, the possibility that a homosexual man in Indonesia would marry and have children to maintain a public image is consistent with observed behaviors.

55 Nurul Ulfah, "Dubur Corong Pertanda Apa?" *Detik Health*, 2 October 2009. Available from http://us.health.detik.com/read/2009/10/02/180018/1214074/766/dubur-corong-pertanda-apa.

56 Memetic isomorphism is the process by which a rapidly spreading idea or image on the Internet retains its basic elements but is changed in order to fit a different circumstance. In this case, the Mas Selamat wanted poster that originated from the Singaporean site TalkingCock.com became a meme through its viral dissemination, and then Indonesian users adopted the poster's template (including wording and fonts) but substituted images of Noordin Top.

57 NusantaraWarrior, "Noordin m Top Pahlawan Malingsia Malaysia Youtubers," YouTube video, 30 September 2009. Available from http://www.youtube.com/watch?v=_VfcEcm-yrU.

58 That earlier video was posted on the day of Noordin's demise. NusantaraWarrior, "Noordin M Top Tewas Terkencing Kencing 17/09/2009" (Noordin M Top Killed While Pissing Himself in Fear 17/09/2009), YouTube video, 17 September 2009. Available from http://www.youtube.com/results?search_query-Noordin+M+Top+Tewas+Terkencing+Kencing+17%2F09%2F2009&search_type=&aq=f.

59 A variety of search terms were used to locate videos connected to this rumor, from the simple "Noordin" or "Nordin," to more specific, such as "Dubur Noordin Top."

60 Gombress, "Noordin M. Top Liwat Pondon Sodomi Malaysian Hero Tewas" (Noordin M. Top Sodomite Transvestite Sodomy Malaysian Hero Killed), YouTube video, 1 October 2009. Available from http://www.youtube.com/results?search_-query=Noordin+M.+Top+liwat+pondon+sodomi+Malaysian+hero+tewas&search_type=&aq=f. Some of these images were posted by Gombress in earlier videos criticizing Malaysians.

61 NusantaraWarrior, "Pahlawan Malaysia."

62 Recent spats between Malaysia and Indonesia include Malaysia's use of a Balinese dance, Tari Pendent, the song "Rasa Sayang," and batik—all claimed by Indonesians as Indonesian—to promote Malaysian tourism. Regarding the Ambalat Islands, the World Court awarded two disputed islands to Malaysia in 2002, rankling Indonesian nationalist sentiment.

63 Indonesia Page: All About Indonesia, "Jomblo Juhari," 11 October 2009. Available from http://indonesiapage.-blogspot.com/2009/11/jomblo-juhari.html.

64 Chris Lundry, "Getting to the Bottom of Explosive Rumors Concerning Noordin Top," *Comops Journal*, 1 October 2009. Available from http://comops.org/journal/wp-admin/post.php?-action=edit&post=1550.

65 Taufik Wijaya, "'Fakta' Bukan Jaringan Islamiyah (JI) Pimpinan Noordin M Top," *Detik News*,. 25 July 2009. Available from http://www.detiknews.com/comment/2009/07/25/-162611/1171439/10/fakta-bukan-jaringan-islamiyah—ji—pimpinan-noordin-m-top.

66 Robert Hariman, "Political Parody and Public Culture," *Quarterly Journal of Speech* 94, no. 3 (2008): 247–72.

67 Chuck Tryon, "Pop Politics: Online Parody Videos, Intertextuality, and Political Participation," *Popular Communication* 6, no. 4 (2008): 209–13.

68 Quoted in J. Michael Waller, *Fighting the War of Ideas Like a Real War: Messages to Defeat the Terrorists* (Washington, DC: Institute of World Politics Press, 2007).

69 Helen Cooper, "Ahmadinejad, at Columbia, Parries and Puzzles," *New York Times*, 25 September 2007. Available from http://www.nytimes.com/2007/09/25/-world/middleeast/25iran.html.

70 Chip Heath, Chris Bell, and Emily Sternberg, "Emotional Selection in Memes: The Case of Urban Legends," *Journal of Personality and Social Psychology* 81, no. 6 (2001): 1028–41.

71 Nils Bubandt, "Rumors, Pamphlets, and the Politics of Paranoia in Indonesia," *Journal of Asian Studies* 67, no. 3 (2008): 789–817.

72 Benedict R. O'G. Anderson, *Language and Power: Exploring Political Cultures in Indonesia* (Ithaca: Cornell University Press, 1990).

73 J. Sanderson and P. H. Cheong, "Tweeting Prayers and Communicating Grief over Michael Jackson Online," *Bulletin of Science, Technology & Society* 30, no. 5 (2010): 328–40.

74 A recent blog post by Indonesian Imbalo about making pilgrimages to gravesites included a visit to the grave of Noordin Top. In a conversation with Noordin's family, the blogger was apparently told of two green birds appearing during Noordin's burial. It is clear that the statement reflects his family's interest in providing some kind of positive legacy for Noordin as a martyr. Imbalo Namaku blog, "Kuburan dan wisata," 21 April 2010. Available from http://imbalo.wordpress.com/2010/04/21/kuburan-dan-wisata/.

75 James Scott, *Domination and the Arts of Resistance: Hidden Transcripts* (New Haven: Yale University Press, 1990), 145.

Chapter 5: Coercion and Consent

1 The team included an operations officer (OIC), medical officer, logistics officer, force protection Naval Criminal Investigative Services agent, a Navy civilian accountant, and a public affairs officer (PAO). One of the authors of this book, Daniel Bernardi, a U.S. Navy Reserve officer, served as the team's PAO. The team swelled to ten members, including a surgeon charged with identifying surgical cases and a liberty officer, as the ship approached the Ambon region.

2 U.S. Navy, "Pacific Partnership 2010," http://www.cpf.navy.mil/subsite/PP10/About.html. In addition to Indonesia, the Pacific Partnership 2010 mission

included USNS *Mercy* visits to Cambodia, Vietnam, and Timor-Leste. Palau and Papua New Guinea were visited by other ships participating in the Pacific Partnership mission. It is also important to note the distinction between a United States Ship (USS) and a United States Navy Ship (USNS): USS ships, such as all warships of the U.S. Navy, are commissioned by Congress and are owned by and represent the U.S. government; USNS ships, on the other hand, are wholly owned by the Navy and are support ships rather than warships and are noncombatant. USNS ships are captained by civilian ship's masters and staffed primarily by merchant marine sailors. They generally have only a small complement of Navy personnel on board to execute unique missions (flight operations, medical operations, secure communications, and operational planning). Use of a USNS ship, and a hospital ship especially, as the exercise flagship reduces the overt symbolic communication of aggression that frequently accompanies the presence of USS warships, particularly in regions that are ambivalent about or wary of U.S. intentions.

3 The complete list of participating NGOs included: East Meets West, Civic Force, International Relief Teams, LDS Charities, Nour International, Islamic Relief Society of North America, HOPE worldwide, HUMA, Operation Smile, Operacion Unies, Peace Winds America/Japan, Project Handclasp, Project HOPE, Surgical Eye Expeditions, Vets Without Borders, University of California San Diego Pre-Dental Society, and World Vets. Other participating organizations included: U.S. Embassy Country Teams, U.S. Agency for International Development (USAID), and U.S. Public Health Service.

4 The entire Pacific Partnership mission involved numerous countries in both the planning and the execution phase; the details of the Ambon ADVON team here analyzed are based on Bernardi's observations of U.S.-Indonesian planning and cooperation.

5 A too loose definition of "propaganda," we think, collapses the distinction between governments wanting to frame their respective narratives and those wanting to dictate it by any means necessary.

6 Debarati Guha-Sapir and Willem Gijsbert van Panhuis, "Health Impact of the 2004 Andaman Nicobar Earthquake and Tsunami in Indonesia," *Prehospital and Disaster Medicine* 24, no. 6 (2009): 494.

7 A report by Terror Free Tomorrow, based on polls conducted in the aftermath of the tsunami relief effort, showed that the number of Indonesians with favorable opinions of the United States increased and the number with unfavorable opinions decreased, both substantially. See Terror Free Tomorrow, "One Year Later: Humanitarian Relief Sustains Change in Muslim Public Opinion," 2006. Available from: http://www.terrorfreetomorrow.org/articlenav.php?id=82.

8 Daniel Bernardi personal diary of events, 19 July 2010. In order to ensure the confidentiality of the ADVON and Indonesian officers, we will not cite names.

9 Bernardi diary, 27 July 2009.

10 The presidential visit was canceled the day before the event was to take place.

11 The Indonesian government differentiates between Christian (Protestant) and Catholic in its statistical reporting.

12 According to the Ambon information website, updated in 2008, out of a population of 2,088,516 in the entire Maluku region, 59.02 percent are Muslim, 35.9 percent are Protestant, 5.18 percent are Catholic, and Buddhists, Hindus, and

others make up less than 1 percent. See http://www.websitesrcg.com/ambon/Malukupop.htm (accessed 28 October 2010).

13 International Crisis Group, "Indonesia: The Search for Peace in Maluku," Asia Report no. 31, 8 February 2002. Available at http://www.crisisgroup.org/en/regions/asia/south-east-asia/indonesia/031-indonesia-the-search-for-peace-in-maluku.aspx.

14 Preliminary research by co-authors Daniel Bernardi and Scott Ruston on the Iraq bovine poisoning rumor was presented at the Political and Social Impact of Rumors Conference hosted in February 2010 by the Centre for Excellence in National Security at the Rajaratnam School of International Studies, a division of Nanyang Technological University, Singapore. The results of this research, especially theorizing rumors as operant within narrative systems, informed Bernardi's media plans while serving as the ADVON public affairs officer in Ambon, Indonesia.

15 Jacques Bertrand, *Nationalism and Ethnic Conflict in Indonesia* (New York: Cambridge University Press, 2004), 118.

16 Ibid., 129.

17 Gerry van Klinken, "New Actors, New Identities: Post-Suharto Ethnic Violence in Indonesia," in *Violent Internal Conflicts in Asia Pacific: Histories, Political Economies and Policies*, ed. Dewi Fortuna Anwar et al. (Jakarta: Yayasan Obor Indonesia, 2005), 88.

18 Ibid., 88.

19 Noorhaidi Hasan, *Laskar Jihad: Islam, Militancy, and the Quest for Identity in Post-New Order Indonesia* (Ithaca: Cornell University Southeast Asia Publications, 2006), 108–9.

20 Patricia Spyer, "Fire Without Smoke and Other Phantoms of Ambon's Violence," *Indonesia* 74 (October 2002): 33.

21 Bertrand, *Nationalism and Ethnic Conflict,* 123.

22 Zachary Abuza, *Political Violence and Islam in Indonesia* (New York: Routledge, 2007), 68; Theodore Friend, *Indonesian Destinies* (Cambridge, MA: Belknap Press of Harvard University Press, 2003), 480–84; Damien Kingsbury, *Power Politics and the Indonesian Military* (New York: Routledge, 2003), 91–92, 180, 234–35; Robert Hefner, "Islam and Asian Security," in *Strategic Asia 2002–03: Asian Aftershocks,* ed. Richard J. Ellings and Aaron L. Friedberg (Seattle: National Bureau of Asian Research, 2002), 378.

23 Bertrand, *Nationalism and Ethnic Conflict,* 126; Gerry van Klinken, "The Maluku Wars: Bringing Society Back In," *Indonesia* 71 (April 2001): 13. See also Hasan, *Laskar Jihad*,104.

24 Chris Lundry, "Separatism and State Cohesion in Indonesia" (Ph.D. diss., Arizona State University, 2009), esp. 89–149.

25 Ibid., 125–27.

26 Angel Rabasa, "Radical Islamist Ideologies in Southeast Asia," in Hudson Institute, *Current Trends in Islamist Ideology,* vol. 1 (2005), http://www.currenttrends.org/research/detail/radical-islamist-ideologies-in-southeast-asia; Abuza, *Political Violence*, 68.

27 Greg Fealy, "Inside the Laskar Jihad," *Inside Indonesia,* 22 February 2010. Available at http://www.insideindonesia.org/stories/inside-the-laskar-jihad.

28 Stephanie Kelley, "Rumors in Iraq: A Guide to Winning Hearts and Minds," *Strategic Insights* 4, no. 2 (February 2005), 1.

29 In 2006 USNS *Mercy* conducted a five-month humanitarian mission and visited several Indonesian cities, specifically Banda Aceh (21–31 July), Takaran (11–17 August), and Flores (20–26 August).

30 Nicholas DiFonzo, *The Watercooler Effect: A Psychologist Explores the Extraordinary Power of Rumors* (New York: Avery, 2008), 42.

31 Galit Hasan-Rokem, "Rumors in Times of War and Cataclysm: A Historical Perspective," in *Rumor Mills: The Social Impact of Rumor and Legend*, ed. Gary Alan Fine et al. (New Brunswick: Aldine Transaction, 2005), 31.

32 Timor-Leste, known in the West as East Timor, was invaded by Indonesia in 1975 under the false pretense of stopping the spread of communism in the region. In the struggle for independence from 1975 to 1999, the Indonesian military killed tens of thousands of civilians and destroyed the small nation's infrastructure before independence was achieved in 2002. For detailed accounts of the crisis in East Timor, see: Carmel Budiardjo and Liem Soei Liong, *The War Against East Timor* (London: Zed Books, 1984); James Dunn, *The Timor Story* (Canberra: Parliament of Australia, Legislative Research Service, 1976); Jill Jolliffe, *East Timor: Nationalism and Colonialism* (St. Lucia: University of Queensland Press, 1978); Joseph Nevins, *A Not-So-Distant Horror: Mass Violence in East Timor* (Ithaca: Cornell University Press, 2005).

33 United States, Department of the Army, *The U.S. Army/Marine Corps Counterinsurgency Field Manual*, U.S. Army Field Manual no. 3-24; Marine Corps Warfighting Publication no. 3-33.5 (Chicago: University of Chicago Press, 2007), 37.

34 Ibid., 48–50.

35 Ibid., 93.

36 Ibid., 27.

37 Ibid., 162–63.

38 DiFonzo, *Watercooler Effect*, 97.

39 Pacific Partnership Public Affairs, "Pacific Partnership Joins Forces with Sail Banda," 19 July 2010. Available at http://www.navy.mil/search/display.asp?story_id=54745.

40 Gary Alan Fine and Irgan Khawaja, "Celebrating Arabs and Grateful Terrorists: Rumor and the Politics of Plausibility," in Gary Alan Fine et al., *Rumor Mills*, 203.

SELECTED BIBLIOGRAPHY

Abbott, H. Porter. *The Cambridge Introduction to Narrative*. Cambridge: Cambridge University Press, 2008.

Allport, Gordon W., and Leo Postman. *The Psychology of Rumor*. New York: Henry Holt and Company, 1947.

Anderson, Benedict R. O'G. *Language and Power: Exploring Political Cultures in Indonesia*. Ithaca: Cornell University Press, 1990.

Anwar, Dewi Fortuna, Hélène Bouvier, Glenn Smith, and Roger Tol, eds. *Violent Internal Conflicts in Asia Pacific: Histories, Political Economies and Policies*. Jakarta: Yayasan Obor Indonesia, 2005.

Bamford, James. *A Pretext for War: 9/11, Iraq, and the Abuse of America's Intelligence Agencies*. New York: Doubleday, 2004.

Bernardi, Daniel, and Scott W. Ruston. "The Triangle of Death: Strategic Communication, Counterinsurgency Ops, and the Rumor Mill." Paper presented at the Political and Social Impact of Rumours Conference, Centre of Excellence for National Security (CENS), S. Rajaratnam School of International Studies (RSIS), Nanyang Technological University (NTU), Singapore, 2010.

Bertrand, Jacques. *Nationalism and Ethnic Conflict in Indonesia*. New York: Cambridge University Press, 2004.

Blackmore, Susan. *The Meme Machine*. New York: Oxford University Press, 2000.

Boellstorff, Tom. *A Coincidence of Desires: Anthropology, Queer Studies, Indonesia*. Durham: Duke University Press, 2007.

———. *The Gay Archipelago: Sexuality and Nation in Indonesia*. Princeton: Princeton University Press, 2005.

Bolter, Jay David, and Richard Grusin. *Remediation: Understanding New Media*. Cambridge, MA: MIT Press, 2000.

Bordia, Prashant, and Nicholas DiFonzo. "Problem Solving in Social Interactions on the Internet: Rumor as Social Cognition." *Social Psychology Quarterly* 67, no. 1 (2004): 33–49.

Branigan, Edward. *Narrative Comprehension and Film*. New York: Routledge, 1992.

Bruns, Axel. *Blogs, Wikipedia, Second Life, and Beyond: From Production to Produsage*. New York: Peter Lang, 2008.

Bubandt, Nils. "Rumors, Pamphlets, and the Politics of Paranoia in Indonesia." *Journal of Asian Studies* 67, no. 3 (2008): 789–817.

Coady, David. "Rumour Has It." *International Journal of Applied Philosophy* 20, no. 1 (2006): 41–55.

DiFonzo, Nicholas. *The Watercooler Effect: A Psychologist Explores the Extraordinary Power of Rumors.* New York: Avery, 2008.

——, and Prashant Bordia. *Rumor Psychology: Social and Organizational Approaches.* Washington, DC: American Psychological Association, 2007.

Feldman, Allen. "Violence and Vision: The Prosthetics and Aesthetics of Terror." *Public Culture* 10, no. 1 (1997): 24–60.

Fine, Gary Alan, Véronique Campion-Vincent, and Chip Heath, eds. *Rumor Mills: The Social Impact of Rumor and Legend.* New Brunswick: Aldine Transaction, 2005.

Forest, James J. F., ed. *Countering Terrorism and Insurgency in the 21st Century: International Perspectives.* 3 vols. Westport, CT: Praeger Security International, 2007.

——, ed. *Influence Warfare: How Terrorists and Governments Fight to Shape Perceptions in a War of Ideas.* Westport, CT: Praeger Security International, 2009.

Germino, Dante L. *Antonio Gramsci: Architect of a New Politics.* Baton Rouge: Louisiana State University Press, 1990.

Gramsci, Antonio. *Selections from the Prison Notebooks.* Edited and translated by Quintin Hoare and Geoffrey Nowell Smith. New York: International Publishers, 1971.

Halverson, Jeffry, Steven R. Corman, and H. L. Goodall Jr. *Master Narratives of Islamist Extremism.* New York: Palgrave Macmillan, 2011.

Hardin, Jayson. "The Rumor Bomb: Theorising the Convergence of New and Old Trends in Mediated U.S. Politics," *Southern Review: Communication, Politics & Culture* 39, no. 1 (2006): 84–110.

Hariman, Robert. "Political Parody and Public Culture." *Quarterly Journal of Speech* 94 no. 3 (2008): 247–72.

Heath, Chip, Chris Bell, and Emily Sternberg. "Emotional Selection in Memes: The Case of Urban Legends." *Journal of Personality and Social Psychology* 81, no. 6 (2001): 1028–41.

Hersh, Seymour M. *Chain of Command: The Road from 9/11 to Abu Ghraib.* New York: HarperCollins, 2004.

Ho, K. C., Zaheer Baber, and Habibul Khondker. "'Sites' of Resistance: Alternative Websites and State-Society Relations." *British Journal of Sociology* 53, no. 1 (2002): 127–48.

Isikoff, Michael, and David Corn. *Hubris: The Inside Story of Spin, Scandal, and the Selling of the Iraq War.* New York: Three Rivers Press, 2007.

Jenkins, Henry. *Convergence Culture: Where Old and New Media Collide.* New York: New York University Press, 2006.

Kapferer, Jean-Noël. *Rumors: Uses, Interpretations, and Images.* Translated by Bruce Fink. New Brunswick: Transaction Publishers, 1990.

Kelley, Stephanie. "Rumors in Iraq: A Guide to Winning Hearts and Minds." M.A. thesis, Naval Postgraduate School, 2004.

Kingsbury, Damien. *Power Politics and the Indonesian Military.* New York: Routledge, 2003.

Lundry, Chris. "Separatism and State Cohesion in Indonesia." Ph.D. diss., Arizona State University, 2009.

——, and Pauline Hope Cheong. "The Gendered Construction and Transmediation of a Terrorist's Life Story." In *Matters of Communication: Political, Cultural, and Technological Challenges,* edited by Timothy Kuhn. New York: Hampton Press, 2011.

Mullen, Patrick B. "Modern Legend and Rumor Theory." *Journal of the Folklore Institute* 9, no. 2/3 (1972): 95–109.

Neubauer, Hans-Joachim. *The Rumour: A Cultural History*. Translated by Christian Braun. London: Free Association Books, 1999.

Nye, Joseph. *The Powers to Lead*. New York: Oxford University Press, 2007.

Post, Jerrold M., Keven G. Ruby and Eric D. Shaw. "From Car Bombs to Logic Bombs: The Growing Threat from Information Terrorism." *Terrorism and Political Violence* 12, no. 2 (2000): 97–122.

Ricks, Thomas E. *Fiasco: The American Military Adventure in Iraq*. New York: Penguin, 2007.

Scott, James C. *Domination and the Arts of Resistance: Hidden Transcripts*. New Haven: Yale University Press, 1990.

Shibutani, Tamotsu. *Improvised News: A Sociological Study of Rumor*. Indianapolis: Bobbs-Merrill Company, 1966.

Sunstein, Cass R. *On Rumors: How Falsehoods Spread, Why We Believe Them, What Can be Done*. New York: Farrar, Straus and Giroux, 2009.

Tangherlini, Timothy R. "'It Happened Not Too Far from Here . . . ': A Survey of Legend Theory and Characterization." *Western Folklore* 49, no. 4 (1990): 371–90.

Tryon, Chuck. "Pop Politics: Online Parody Videos, Intertextuality, and Political Participation." *Popular Communication* 6, no. 4 (2008): 209–13.

United States, Department of the Army. *The U.S. Army/Marine Corps Counterinsurgency Field Manual*. U.S. Army Field Manual no. 3-24; Marine Corps Warfighting Publication no. 3-33.5. Chicago: University of Chicago Press, 2007.

Waller, J. Michael. *Fighting the War of Ideas like a Real War: Messages to Defeat the Terrorists*. Washington, DC: Institute of World Politics Press, 2007.

Weimann, Gabriel. "The Psychology of Mass-Mediated Terrorism." *American Behavioral Scientist* 52, no. 1 (2008): 69–86.

———. *Terror on the Internet: The New Arena, the New Challenges*. Washington, DC: United States Institute of Peace Press, 2006.

———, and Conrad Winn. *The Theater of Terror: Mass Media and International Terrorism*. New York: Longman, 1993.

INDEX

The letter *f* refers to a figure, *t* to a table, and *n* to a note.

ABOUT THE AUTHORS

DANIEL LEONARD BERNARDI is professor and chair of the Cinema Department at San Francisco State University. He earned a Ph.D. in Film and Television Studies from the University of California, Los Angeles. His main academic interests are: narrative theory, cultural studies, and new media. Bernardi is also an officer in the Unites States Navy Reserves. He has served at sea on the USS *Coronado* (LPD 7), the USS *John C. Stennis* (CVN 74), the USS *Blue Ridge* (LCC 19), and the USS *Cleveland* (LPD 7), as well as at shore in Italy, Iraq, Indonesia, and several island countries in Oceania and at the Pentagon with the Chief of Navy Information. From May 2009 to February 2011 he was recalled to active duty in support of Operation Iraqi Freedom, where he worked with Special Operations Task Force–Central. He is the author of *Star Trek and History: Race-ing Toward a White Future*, several edited books, and numerous articles on film, television, and new media.

PAULINE HOPE CHEONG is an associate professor of communication at the Hugh Downs School of Human Communication at Arizona State University (www.paulinehopecheong.com). She is a co-principal investigator of a multidisciplinary project on extremist narratives and has received awards for her research on communication technologies and culture. She has published in numerous international journals and is lead co-editor of *Digital Religion, Social Media and Culture: Perspectives, Practices, Futures* as well as *New Media and Intercultural Communication: Identity, Community and Politics*.

CHRIS LUNDRY is an assistant research professor at the Consortium for Strategic Communication in the Hugh Downs School of Human Communication, Arizona State University, where he is the group's Southeast Asia expert. A political scientist by training, he explores intersections of identity and conflict, separatism, terrorism, human rights, and democracy. He has worked with several non-governmental organizations in Indonesia and East Timor, and monitored both the 1999 plebiscite in East Timor as a United Nations–accredited observer and the 2004 Indonesian presidential elections with the Carter Center.

SCOTT W. RUSTON is an assistant research professor with Arizona State University's Hugh Downs School of Human Communication, where he specializes in narrative theory and media studies. He combines his academic background with experience as a Naval Reserve Officer to bring awareness of narrative, cultural studies, and new media technologies to issues of strategic communication and plans/policy development. In addition, he is an expert on the art, education, and entertainment uses of mobile and interactive media and has published on narrative and mobile media technologies in journals such as *Storyworlds: A Journal of Narrative Studies* and *The International Journal of Technology and Human Interaction.*